Stalking the Feature Story

Stalking the Feature Story

By William Ruehlmann

Writer's Digest Books
Cincinnati, Ohio

Library of Congress Cataloging in Publication Data

Ruehlmann, William, 1946 -
Stalking the feature story.
Includes index.
1. Reporters and reporting.
I. Title.
PN4781.R84   070.4'3   77-17547
ISBN O-911654-51-8

Second printing, 1978

Writer's Digest Books
9933 Alliance Road
Cincinnati, Ohio 45242

"The practice of art can only be done successfully, and for the good of others, by human beings who bring with them a little intelligence, a little wit, a little honor — a seascapist must love an ocean before he can make its movement stand still."

—Jimmy Breslin

Acknowledgments

Special acknowledgment is given to the following authors and publications for generously granting their permission to reprint material in this book:

"A Page from a Reporter's 1930s Notebook," by Dorothy McCardle. Reprinted by permission of the *Washington Post*.

"Jinx Wins Out in 6th at Latonia," by William Ruehlmann. Reprinted by permission of the *Kentucky Post*.

"Normal Kids/Super Children" chart, from *At Wit's End,* by Erma Bombeck. Copyright Field Enterprises, Inc. Courtesy of Field Newspaper Syndicate.

"A Night in a Squad Car Out of 'Two-Four': Trouble Partners, Trouble in the Street," by Mary Breasted. Copyright 1976 by The New York Times Company. Reprinted by permission.

"Ambulance Duty Provides a Wide Range of Experiences," by J.Y. Smith. Reprinted by permission of the *Washington Post*.

"The Glass Bonfire," by William Ruehlmann. Reprinted by permission of the *News Record*.

"Midnight Hunt for a Killer," by William Ruehlmann. Reprinted by permission of the *Kentucky Post*.

"Three for the Emergency Room," by William Ruehlmann. Reprinted by permission of the *Kentucky Post*.

"When Hunters Become the Hunted," by Craig Waters. Reprinted from *New Times,* courtesy of Craig Waters.

"Grabbed a Coat and Got a Sock," by William Ruehlmann. Reprinted by permission of the *Kentucky Post*.

"This Cat Tale Ends Happily," by William Ruehlmann. Reprinted by permission of the *Kentucky Post*.

To Mom and Dad

Contents

To write well, first see well. Acquiring the camera eye. "Be one on whom nothing is lost." The difference between writer and reporter. A professional attitude toward "temporary art." Skepticism for received opinion — and one's own. Defining the feature.
"A Page from a Reporter's 1930s Notebook"
    by Dorothy McCardle
"Jinx Wins Out in 6th at Latonia" by William Ruehlmann

Abstraction. The language of Vaguespeak. Seeing the war through the single soldier. Detail. Don't ask the reader's emotion — earn it. Avoiding bias. Making the blue pencil superfluous.
"A Night in a Squad Car Out of 'Two-Four':
    Trouble Partners, Trouble in the Street" by Mary Breasted
"Ambulance Duty Provides a Wide Range of Experiences"
    by J.Y. Smith

Foreword

My introduction to Bill Ruehlmann was via a swatch of his copy in a Cincinnati magazine. The words made my brain dance. Good reporters can always excite an appreciative editor. Bill is a pristine phrase slinger. He collected his mighty armada of words and his storehouse of grammar in the collegiate grind. He emulated the stealthy eye of a jungle cat plus its greedy ear. His style, verve, and quest to grasp life remind me strongly of Lafcadio Hearn, the superb reporter-editor who stalked the byways of Cincinnati in the late-1800s, turning up marvelous human interest stories. With Hearn's magic touch, Bill detects and catalogs the full range of emotions that drive us all — he does actually *stalk* the feature story.

My high admiration for Bill's freelance efforts prompted me to dragoon him as a feature writer on the *Kentucky Post* staff. He was an instant sensation. He dived straight into the gizzard of every story. His copy throbbed with *real* life. He dug painstakingly, wrote fast, and often— and, of course, superbly.

Obviously, it is well to have tools of any trade— whether carpenter, artist or reporter— but they are of small use without knowing how they work. Bill Ruehlmann uses the writer's tools with great ease and skill. His stories make music in the mind. His imagery dances. His people-in-print may growl, whisper, declaim, scream, sob, love, lie, leap, sulk . . . but they are all vibrantly alive. His pen slits their veins and draws onto paper the life juice out of man and beast.

Some writers can grind it out but can't teach. Bill expertly does both. Without reservation I recommend this book of Bill's to anyone, old or new in the writing game. Chapter three by itself is worth the price of admission.

> — *Vance Trimble**
> *Editor*
> The Kentucky Post

*Winner, Pulitzer Prize for National Reporting.

Introduction

On my first working day as a reporter I stopped at a drugstore for some directions and returned to the car to find myself locked out. I was in a hurry— I'd tracked down a man in connection with a murder who had once been "The Paper Sack Bandit," and I needed to talk to him before deadline.

An old wino with a wooden leg was watching, and the dismay must have shown on my face because he came over to help. He scrounged a coat hanger, handed me a pint bottle in the manner of a man offering a butler his gloves, and went to work on the door. "Piece of cake," he told me. It was: In 30 seconds he had it open.

I thanked him, hopped in and took off— showering my sheaf of notes over several city streets. I had left them sitting on the roof.

So much for the hotshot scribe under pressure. But what a thrill it all was! Every day different, hobnobbing with corporation men and cops and coal miners, moving in and out of mansions and shacks with bones on the floor and no dog. I went up private elevators and down fire poles, rode in scout cars and rescue vans, watched airstrips from conning towers and rivers from pilot houses. My beat was Covington and Newport, story-rich Kentucky towns across the Ohio from Cincinnati. One got up in the morning with no notion of what lay ahead— maybe a stiff stuck down behind the floodwall or some $4,000 flimflam or a dog trained to smell out dealers. Whatever it was would be interesting, because I was a feature writer, and the endless drama of everyday life was lavish material to me. "Talk about your fiction!" Carl Sandburg once said. "Man, that first page today has human stuff on it that puts novels in the discard."

It does, it really does. And some of that stuff is dynamite. Years later I was on a story in South Boston during the busing troubles there. An ex-gang leader from Southie who had been through two wars and a difficult peace went with me to talk to the editorial page editor of a major newspaper about what we had on vigilante violence and a paramilitary outfit called the "Marshalls." When we finished she cleared her throat and proposed we do something light on a picnic at Carson Beach— the games the kids played, the music, like that. My associate, who had half a head full of steel and plastic surgery from a mob attempt on his life, sat and stared at her.

She assured us she knew Southie. She had a plumber from there whose name eluded her.

"That woman's living in another world," my friend told me.

So we printed in less influential pages, but we printed, and my education continued. A tougher editor once told me, "You'll earn an extra degree out there." Street men and women will; if the dynamite interests you, it's there.

And so of course is Carson Beach. *All* of it is worth knowing and writing about. That is the premise of this book. A book is not the best place to learn reporting, but it can be the staging area for your own personal reconnaissance of whatever region you happen to be in. This is to encourage you to infiltrate, remembering the two recurrent themes of these pages: 1) see for yourself, up close; and 2) write as carefully as you can.

Then shoot for speed. All the example stories in this volume were written under deadline pressure, as was what you're reading right now. My thanks to those fine reporters who gave so generously of their recent finished writing. Don't hold them responsible for the titles— those are the work of copyeditors of varying talent.

Thanks too to John Brady of *Writer's Digest,* who made suggestions that improved the manuscript, and to Paula Sandhage, who offered important editorial help and support. And all gratitude to Vance Trimble, Editor of the *Kentucky Post,* who introduced me to the wonders of a city room, and to Lynn Ruehlmann, who manages to share such strange enthusiasms.

—William Ruehlmann

1. Vision

To write well, first see well

The leafless trees beyond my window are laced with silver filigrees of ice this morning. The rough grate of a scraper on somebody's windshield cuts against the huff of a late-December wind, and the headstones to the graves in Winthrop cemetery across the street are sifted with snow like frosted figures on the smooth white surface of a wedding cake. It's a morning you want to walk in.

That is, if I describe it to you well enough. But I can't rely on my imagination to give you the crusty feel of crisp frozen ground underfoot or the razor-drag of chill air across a face. I must see these things, know them, before I can communicate them.

Writers are verbal creatures, but good ones don't talk off the top of their heads. If a writer's work is to be valid, he must observe vividly; he writes after the fact, not from inspiration. He writes of what he has seen — what he has seen *well*. His best material is what is directly before him, like my snowscape. I can see the solitary jogger moving through the graveyard, the steam of his breath trailing back from his tassel-cap like the little wings on Mercury's hat; I can see the alley cat angling toward the ash cans on the corner like an infiltrator, sneaking from bush to sugary bush belly low.

So don't make it up. The only individual smart as a writer is a reader, and the reader won't be fooled. If you're describing the sleek heft of a net full of cod coming in over the side of a fishing boat, you had better have been there, or the reader will be quick to call it hooey. Being there is the only way you are going to know a Cincinnati policeman is 16 pounds heavier on duty because of the equipment on his belt, and that there are 12 brass-colored bullets in the cartridge holder by his holster. You can get this kind of information second-hand, but that is like making love with rubber gloves on; the textures of a scene will elude you.

Here is pop culturist Tom Wolfe describing the "old babes" who stand before the slot machines in Las Vegas:

> There they are at six o'clock Sunday morning no less than at three o'clock Tuesday afternoon. Some of them pack their old hummocky shanks into Capri pants, but many of them just put on the old print dress, the same one day after day, and the old hob-heeled shoes, looking like they might be going out to buy eggs in Tupelo, Mississippi. They have a Dixie Cup full of nickels or dimes in the left hand and an Iron-Boy work glove on the right hand to keep the calluses from getting sore.

Can you doubt he has been there? The Dixie Cup full of change is an essential detail that could not have been invented — it's better than fiction. Or note war correspondent Michael Herr on an incident in Vietnam:

> After the Catholic chaplain was killed, the Protestant had to give communion. His name was Takesian, an Armenian from Boston, one of those hip, blunt clerics who loved to talk. . . . He was using sliced C-ration bread and canteen water to deliver the sacraments, and some of the Grunts were skeptical about receiving them from a Protestant. "Listen, you silly bastards," Takesian said. "You could all get your ass shot off any time now out there. Do you think God gives a damn *how* you've been blessed?"

Herr covered the war with a company of Marines, not from behind a desk. The result is this kind of eyewitness, immediate art.

The writer then is only as good as his perception. So how does one learn to observe well?

Acquiring the camera eye

Flies take off backwards. So in order to swat one, you must strike slightly behind him.

An interesting detail, and certainly one a writer would be able to pick up on. Other people see flies; a writer sees how they move.

Good observation depends on two things: concentration and analysis. As a writer, you are an observer by occupation; that means you're always on the job. Everything you see, hear, smell, taste and touch is potential material.

So you are not entitled to walk the streets abstractedly meditating upon First Causes. You must concentrate on what is going on around you as a matter of habit — and paying this kind of constant attention can be hard work. If you are a writer, however, you will warm to the game.

An example: On My way to work one day I stopped for ham and eggs at a Park Street cafe in Boston. I found myself a stool at the counter, ordered, and buried my nose in coffee and the morning paper. The young lady next to me was carrying on an animated conversation with the staff and the other customers: She addressed by name the chef at the grill, the woman serving doughnuts across the room, the boy at the orange juice machine and the large man seated at the other side of my stool.

When I accidentally knocked a fork to the floor, I was surprised to discover a slim white cane canted against the counter beside it. The girl was blind.

She had identified each individual simply by the sounds they made in the course of their morning work. She knew by the clatter of the cup rack, the sizzle of the stove top, the tap of a steel-toed shoe, where the workers were and who they were.

I noted to my further surprise that the fellow she was talking with at my other elbow had a seeing eye dog at his feet.

Now which of the three of us do you suppose was the truly blind one?

The perceptions of the unsighted lady and gentleman were in far better use than mine. I was on automatic pilot, plodding through the comatose waking-sleep of the workaday drone. I didn't know what was going on. I hadn't seen.

What's worth seeing on the way to work?

Simply everything. A world is waiting for those with the eyes to see it; the writer knows that the miraculous happens routinely, the extraordinary is commonplace. On my way to work I cross Boston Common, and on any given morning I might see the following: a 60-year-old unicyclist; a panhandler clutching a torn copy of *David Copperfield;* a folksinger with a child in a sack on her back; a stroller in a sandwich board proclaiming the perils of imminent nuclear attack; the governor of Massachusetts leaving the subway for the State House; a cluster of Hare-Krishnas chanting gravely over beating drums and bells. I will pass: a private detective agency; an anti-vivisectionist's league; the one-time home of Daniel Webster; a mountain-climbing club; a flop house the cramped upstairs room in which Henry Wadsworth Longfellow was married.

There's more. Across the Common, exclusive Beacon Hill is not at all the cobblestoned cranny of rectitude legend has it to be. Winos hang out here. Tourists get mugged, sometimes for keeps. Dogs literally dot the sidewalks with their peculiar donations. Making one's way to work can be less a stroll than serious broken-field running.

All of this is material. It's around you, too. You are no longer a pedestrian— you are a witness.

Walt Whitman was a magnificent witness. Here is his incisive description of what he observed at the moment the news of the attack on Fort Sumter reached New York City April 13, 1861:

> I had been to the opera in 14th Street that night, and after the performance was walking down Broadway toward twelve o'clock, on my way to Brooklyn, when I heard in the distance the loud cries of the newsboys, who came presently tearing and yelling up the street, rushing from side to side even more furiously than usual. I bought an extra and crossed to the Metropolitan Hotel (Niblo's) where the great lamps were still brightly blazing, and, with a crowd of others, who gathered impromptu, read the news, which was evidently authentic. For the benefit of some who had no papers, one of us read the telegram aloud, while all listened silently and attentively. No remark was made by any of the crowd, which had increased to 30 or 40, but all stood a minute or two, I remember, before they dispersed. I can almost see them there now, under the lamps at midnight again.

So can we; that is the kind of writing that can make a silence reverberate for over a hundred years. Notice the quality of Whitman's perception; for him the crucial material was auditory, not visual. The contrast between the screaming newsboys and the subdued citizenry is central to the scene. Whitman caught it and sent it forward in time to us, gaslit.

This skill in seizing the essence of a scene did not come to Whitman because he sprang from the womb a poet. He earned it, worked for it. "Wherever I go, indeed, winter or summer, city or country, alone at home or traveling, I must take notes," he wrote.

Whitman was still taking notes on the world he saw in his old age, long after he had finely honed his craft. That is a habit the novice would do well to imitate. Walk the park; set down your perceptions; go home and work them up, trying to make your journey in prose as real as the ambulatory one. Leave nothing out.

But with the conscious concentration that insists on mechanically recording everything, you must also acquire the analytical sense: Where is this item going, what does it mean? If you do not exert your intellect on what you see, your observation can reduce itself to cataloging reality instead of revealing it. Now that you have the data, what does it signify?

Looking out on a city square from the second-floor window of a library one hot July noon, I noticed the long double line of benches there were taken up by elderly people, some feeding the squirrels and birds, some reading, some just sitting. A sudden siren split the air. As the ambulance arrived, I saw that one old man had fallen forward on the sidewalk, where he lay quite still amid a litter of peanut shells and crumpled paper.

As the rescue squad rushed to him, scattering pigeons on either side, I saw a curious thing. All the way up and down either row of benches, the elderly sitting there were moving. Very slightly. Whether seated in close proximity to the fallen man or some distance from him, they were sliding subtly *away* in their seats — sometimes as little as a foot, sometimes a little more. None of them looked at him.

The meaning of this silent charade was perfectly clear. These people were disassociating themselves from death. By refusing to acknowledge the fallen man, they were ridding themselves of the disconcerting knowledge that it could have been any of them — indeed, still could be, and soon. A distressing thought for a stroke-inducing summer's day.

It was a very human moment. But the entire human quality would have gone out of it if I had not been moved to wonder what it meant. As a writer, the accompanying question in your mind to any interesting phenomenon is: Why? Why is that shoplifting suspect missing his shoes?

Why do churchgoers always fill the back pews first? Why is a worm floating in the bottom of an unopened bottle of tequila?

The answers can be interesting.

"Be one on whom nothing is lost"

These words were Henry James' advice to aspiring writers, and they remain excellent counsel. At a cocktail party, the writer is the one who spots the manta-ray pattern of a spilled drink on a Danish rya carpet; at basic training, the writer is the one who registers the precise cant of a Camel in a drill sergeant's mouth.

There is a famous photograph by Jenaro Olivares that shows the spontaneous revelry subsequent to a bullfight. A cheering crowd rises to its feet in the background; in the foreground, a matador is held aloft on the shoulders of exultant spectators. In one corner a police officer gestures outward in warning, his back to the procession.

A perceptive viewer will note that the bullfighter's face is twisted in pain, not triumph — the blood on his suit of lights suggests he has undergone a goring. But the writer will be the one who observes the boy at the bottom of the picture. The boy stands pressed close to the laughing man who carries the matador, and the boy is picking that man's pocket, right under the noses of the cops.

A writer on assignment opens his senses and monitors them. His body is an open wound, sensitive to everything. When John Steinbeck set about describing the experience of a battle, he conveyed sensations, not the movement of troops:

> While the correspondent is writing for you of advances and retreats, his skin will be raw from the woolen clothes he has not taken off for three days, and his feet will be hot and dirty and swollen from not having taken off his shoes for days. He will itch from last night's mosquito bites and from today's sand-fly bites. Perhaps he will have a little sand-fly fever, so that his head pulses and a red rim comes into his vision. His head may ache from the heat and his eyes burn with the dust. The knee that was sprained when he leaped ashore will grow stiff and painful. . . .

By carefully recounting the muffled "proom" of shellfire, the sour smell of the wall of a blown-up building and the disinfectant flavor of warm canteen water, Steinbeck effectively takes the reader into the trenches with him.

Like a spy on alien ground, a writer should be able to move freely amid the unfamiliar and return with a story. He or she does that by noticing things that others take for granted. The obsessive neatness of a bureaucrat's desk may reveal not efficiency but the fact that the man has nothing to do; a pretentious private library may contain books with uncut pages. Each room is furnished with a collection of clues to what goes on inside.

The difference between writer and reporter

A writer can remain within the warm locked room of his imagination; a reporter cannot. If feature writing is to be your bag, you're going to have to crawl out from under your hat and bother people.

Let's face it: Individuals with a literary turn of mind tend to be introverts. They are by nature reflective creatures rather than aggressive ones. That is why they are drawn to books and the printed word. A reporter is certainly entitled to remain an introvert, but not on company time. On the job he is a professional intruder with an infinite capacity for legwork. He is Archie Goodwin, not Nero Wolfe. He addresses all strangers with confidence and marches into every situation as if he belonged there.

If you remain merely a writer — that is, one more consistently at home in the library than on the street — you are not going to get the kinds of stories that matter in this business. You must take the native curiosity of the scholar out into the field and approach pauper and politico with equal persistence. There will be those who won't want to talk to you. You're going to have to go *through* them to get the story.

Steve Nevas of WGBH-TV had done a series of stories on a grand jury investigation in Boston. The series sorely displeased Mayor Kevin White, presumably because they cast a cold eye on the local administration. One day Nevas showed up at City Hall with a cameraman to attend an open press conference. He found the door barred by a mayor's minion who told him he wasn't welcome. Nevas stood up for his rights and kept on going, insisting he would have to be thrown out bodily. Meanwhile the cameraman ground away. The result was that Nevas came out with *two* stories: what happened at the press conference (in spite of the fact that White actually attempted to turn off the Channel Two mike) and the treatment the reporter had received at the door. Those two spots done for deadline told more about the way things were being run in Beantown than a dozen treatises on urban affairs.

When riots broke out in Harlem in 1968, Jimmy Breslin of the *New York Herald Tribune* attended. He was met with interest by a group of young persons headed up by a kid with a gold polo shirt and a shaved head:

"What you lookin' at, you big fat white bastard?" he said.

"Oh, come on, it's too hot for this nonsense," we told him.

"We're goin' to show you what's nonsense," he said. "We're goin' to stick some nonsense right into your fat white belly."

A fireman, rubber boots flopping on the melting tar street, walked over from an engine. He had an ax in his hand. A new ax. Big, with a light yellow wooden handle. The kid with the shaved head didn't even notice him. He just kept walking past the car and went back to the shop where the three waited for him.

"What the hell are you doing here?" the fireman said. "Don't you listen to the newspapers?"

Well, Breslin listens to nobody, which is why he is such a fine reporter.

But the risk factor is rarely so physical as Breslin's ghetto encounter. The constant risk is to one's ego. You risk embarrassment. You risk having people say no to you, some of them not very nice people. You risk getting yourself thrown out of places.

If your ego is more important to you than getting the story, you're probably better off becoming a poet. But there's no money in it.

A professional attitude toward temporary art

Ernest Hemingway, on and off a feature writer all his life, once wrote: "If you have made your living as a newspaperman, learning your trade, writing against deadlines, writing to make stuff timely rather than permanent, no one has any right to dig this stuff up and use it against the stuff you have written to write the best you can."

I can't agree. Indian sand painters were under no illusion that their work would last forever, but that did not keep them from doing it well. The pursuit of excellence is the hallmark of the pro; magazine and newspaper pieces may be quite out of date after the next issue, but that does not prevent you from doing everything you can to make them superb for the present moment.

In spite of Hemingway's stated impatience with his early journalism, the evidence of his work suggests that he always wrote as well as he could. How else to account for passages like the following, which appeared in the *Toronto Daily Star* January 27, 1923?

> The Fascist dictator had announced he would receive the press. Everybody came. We all crowded into the room. Mussolini sat at his desk reading a book. His face was contorted into the famous frown. He was registering Dictator. Being an ex-newspaper man himself he knew how many readers would be reached by the accounts the men in the room would write of the interview he was about to give. And he remained absorbed in his book. Mentally he was reading the lines of the two thousand papers served by the two hundred correspondents. "As we entered the room the Black Shirt Dictator did not look up from the book he was reading, so intense was his concentration, etc."
>
> I tip-toed over behind him to see what the book was he was reading with such avid interest. It was a French-English dictionary — held upside down.

Flawlessly observed and flawlessly written. Because of that, Hemingway's "stuff" *has* become permanent, medium to the contrary. His European dispatches are almost as widely anthologized as his short stories.

You cannot write with the conviction that your work will be one day reprinted to the extent that Hemingway's has, but you ought to write in such a fashion that if it is, you will have no apologies for it. Nothing is as destructive to a writer's self-esteem — and, ultimately, his ability — as shoddy craftsmanship. Make it well. Whether or not the thing lasts, the care you have taken will be the measure not only of your talent, but of your integrity.

Dashiell Hammett, creator of Sam Spade and the Continental Op, wrote only fiction, but his unsentimental admonition to the novice is a sound charge to scribes of every stamp:

> When you write you want fame, fortune and personal satisfaction. You want to write what you want to write and to feel it's good and to sell millions of copies of it and have everybody whose opinion you value think it's good, and you want this to go on for hundreds of years. You're not likely ever to get all these things, and you're not likely to give up writing or commit suicide if you don't, but that

is— and should be— your goal. Anything less is kind of piddling.

Deadlines won't allow for dawdling. But like the successful sprinter, you can run against the clock without getting clumsy.

A word on accuracy: Novelists can make up their material — you can't. If you report the Dean of Students at Orange U. wears pink shorts, they had better not be lavender. If the discoverer of a dead body in a riverbed says "The hide tightened right up on my head," those had better be his exact words and not something colorful you put in his mouth.

Gail Sheehy once wrote an article on a hooker named Redpants for *New York Magazine* that grew into the book *Hustling*. Redpants was a "composite of several different girls at various stages of their involvement" with prostitution. Sheehy's author's note explaining her method was omitted when her story went to print, with the result that some of her audience, finding out, felt betrayed, lied to. The use of a composite character is a dubious device for the writer of nonfiction because it hovers in a gray region between reality and invention, but if it is employed the reader should be made aware of the fact early.

The reason for sticking absolutely to the facts goes beyond honesty to the believability of your byline. If there are errors in your story or invented touches, be sure somebody somewhere will know about it. If these lapses occur often enough, your credibility will be gone. You will be suspected of embroidering even the straight story, and your bad example will further dilute the credibility of all the other writers of nonfiction. If you like to improve on reality and dress up quotes to make a better story, perhaps you'd better get back to that Gothic romance you were thinking of writing.

Skepticism for received opinion— and one's own

Trust nobody.

The copy you turn out is your best testimony to the truth, so you have to be very careful what you believe. Even if your sources are honest — and some of them won't be— they have a way of getting matters mixed up. You're going to need corroboration to protect yourself not so much from mendacity as from human error.

Legend are the eyewitnesses at the scene of any serious situation. One will tell you the mugger was a fat man in an Afro who left in an emerald green sedan; another will insist he was skinny bald guy who escaped on foot. Both are absolutely convinced they are right. Chances are fair the mugger was a woman who took off in a taxi. This is the kind of thing that keeps detectives and reporters amused.

The Secretary of State himself may tell you a particular official made a personal deal in Durango with El Taco, a notorious Mexican gunrunner; you had better check. Who knows where the Secretary heard it? Or why he's telling *you*? Meanwhile the official turns out to have been half a continent away for the tuna boat festival in Teeming Sump, Maine. Prudent doubt is not suspicion but simple good sense.

Chicago Daily News reporter Ben Hecht was assigned to interview a young man who achieved some celebrity in a 1922-shot-out on North Campbell Avenue. Hecht began the story this way:

> Carl Wanderer, fresly shaved and his brown suit neatly pressed, stood looking over the back porch of his home at 4732 North Campbell Ave. His wife, who was murdered last night by a holdup man in the doorway downstairs, lay in their bedroom.
>
> Wanderer looked at his gold watch, and his hand was steady. He smiled blankly at the back porches in front of him and, with his eyes grown cold, repeated, "Well, I got him. I got him anyway."
>
> At two o'clock this afternoon there are scheduled two inquests, one over the body of Mrs. Carl Wanderer and the other over the body of the stickup man. Wanderer, standing two feet away from the man who had killed his wife, opened fire with his .45.

Wanderer was a recently-discharged veteran with a *Croix de Guerre* and a Distinguished Service Cross. One night on his way home from the movies he and his pregnant young wife were accosted by a ragged gunman who attempted a holdup. Wanderer and the gunman blazed away at each other — the wife and the gunman were killed. Wanderer was immediately lifted aloft on great winds of public approval that hailed him as a tragic hero.

Hecht smelled a rat. His story showed a strangely unmoved man and some loose ends. "His hand was steady," indeed; Hecht's instincts were right. Police proved both guns were Wanderer's. The veteran had hired his "assailant" in order to stage-manage the elimination of an unwanted wife.

That same skepticism for one-source information should extend to an honest element of self-doubt. Don't preconceive a story; if you go in expecting to get a certain slant, you may insist on it when it isn't there.

And always struggle with the certainty that you haven't got the whole story.

The Whole Story — absolute truth in the abstract — is stubbornly elusive. People can live whole lifetimes with their mates and never understand them utterly; it would be arrogance to expect, then, that one can plumb the depths of strangers in a few hours or weeks. This awareness of human limitation should push the writer to be as thorough as possible. If he can't preserve the final truth, he can come to earn a piece of it.

Reporters are often assailed for not being objective. Well, real objectivity is possible only to a machine, and the subjective hand has to turn it on. Take a scene of a riot. At one corner of the park a bearded youth throws a broken bottle at a cop. At another a heavy-set trooper beats an unarmed young woman with a nightstick. Which is the objective vision? Include both; but what about the camera crew filming all this, revealing each figure a famous actor?

David Brinkley once properly pointed out that no one ever accused him of bias who agreed with him. As a journalist, he was arguing that bias is in the eye of the beholder. Indeed, reporters have prejudices and blind spots like anyone else, but it is their job to be aware of them and attempt to overcome them in their coverage. Because of this, it is a good idea not to write about people or groups one is too close to; a straight story on one's own mother or fraternal order can be extremely difficult.

What reporters work toward is not objectivity but *fairness*. In showing all sides in just balance, the reporter leaves judgment to the proper tribunal — his audience.

A reporter's instinct is, contrary to popular belief, not always to tell all. Suppose you were cruising in a squad car as part of the research on police work. One of the officers you're with lets drop that two armed escapees from out of state are expected to be passing through town, and the sister-in-law of one of them is being staked out. They've already killed two motorists. The cop asks you not to print — if you did, the fugitives would surely see the story and bolt. Lives are more important than stories, so you don't.

But when the two are captured, you jolly well might expect the favor to be returned with a tip.

The ethics of representing yourself as anything but a reporter can be worrisome, and they should be. Those who get information by posing as insurance investigators, census takers and the like are getting it under false pretenses — their subjects don't know they are talking for print. The limits are ill-defined in cases where a reporter's quarry has gone beyond the law, or where the public's right to know seems to outweigh too-strict reportorial prudence; once you have crashed a closed Klan meeting, it is unwise to doff the hood and identify yourself as an investigative reporter.

Defining the feature

A feature story is a hunk of overheard humanity that may or may not have the news value of the large events appearing on the front page. *The Final Days*, that lengthy exegesis of the end of the Nixon administration by Bob Woodward and Carl Bernstein, is a feature story. So is the taut, wry humor column that Art Buchwald does. Feature stories attempt to engage or amuse a reader. They approach excellence when they also inform him.

Feature writers are less concerned with formula writing than their hard-news counterparts. They rarely resort to inverted pyramids in putting together a piece; when editors cut a feature, they don't do it from the bottom.

Of course every feature writer does such judicious work he regards it as uncuttable.

Feature writers also concern themselves more with style — that is, "fine" writing — than do other reporters. They are given greater freedom in their use of the language. The results aim at color as well as clarity.

A feature story is nonfiction written with the liveliness of good fiction. It employs plot, character, dialog, even symbolism. It attempts to provide a moving picture in prose of something real.

The best way to describe the unconventionality of the feature and the sensitive mind behind it is to point to the funeral coverage for assassinated President John Kennedy. Legions of pressmen from all over the world moved in on Washington on a cold November Sunday to cover the long street procession, the riderless horse and the scores of dignitaries in attendance.

Two miles away Jimmy Breslin was standing on a hill at Arlington National Cemetery, interviewing the gravedigger.

"I'd like to have everything, you know, nice," Clifton Pollard told him. "He was a good man."

Breslin's short story on the attentive ministrations of one sad

American working man said more about the deep national feeling over the President's passing than many a lengthy account of the cortege.

A Page from a Reporter's 1930's Notebook
by Dorothy McCardle

[The following is a feature story by a skilled Washington Post *reporter who displays the twin virtues of intense awareness and personal assertion. Notice the news peg: Mrs. McCardle isn't writing at whim, but because the Lindbergh kidnapping has become again a current concern. Whether she is describing the commotion of a town in the middle of a media event, the early-morning howl of a hound, or the tight smile on an accused kidnapper's face, Mrs. McCardle sets us inextricably inside the scene. She does not allow herself to be told where she can go; she eavesdrops; she asks questions. Watch her work.]*

The questions linger on. After all these years, people are still asking whether Bruno Richard Hauptmann really kidnapped and killed the Lindbergh baby. If he did, did he do it alone?

On the stormy night of March 1, 1932, Charles A. Lindbergh Jr., the 20-month-old first-born of the American flyer-hero and his wife Anne Morrow Lindbergh, was snatched from his crib in his parents' new home on the top of Sourland Mountain, N.J.

The nation was shocked by the audacity of the crime. There was universal mourning for the little boy whose body was found some two months later in a wooded area not far from the Lindbergh home.

The tiny form was still recognizable to the young father asked to identify him. The world grieved with the parents whose anguish was so silent and unobtrusive.

News peg— The tragedy was re-enacted for the first time as a drama Thursday night on a three-hour NBC television special.

The broadcast brought back vividly events of the tragedy, from the kidnapping to the electrocution of Hauptmann four years after the crime. And it raised many of the old questions.

But in the jury's mind, there were no unanswered questions. And most of the 600 news reporters who covered the six-week trial agreed with the jury.

I was a member of that press corps, covering the case for the

Philadelphia Inquirer.

I had been a crime reporter on the *Inquirer* since my early twenties, but I did not get into the Lindbergh story until the baby's body was found in May, 1932, a little more than two months after the kidnapping.

I was about to go to dinner with Carl W. McCardle of the *Philadelphia Bulletin* when the news that the baby's body had been found flashed into the office.

My plans shifted immediately, of course, and with Carl, whom I would marry two years later, I drove to the village of Hopewell. (I had missed covering the actual kidnapping March 1 because of illness.)

But now, with the long search for the missing child over, I was determined to make up for lost time on the story. As we drove into Hopewell, the village looked like a gold rush town.

Detail— The one hotel was jammed with reporters, photographers, telegraph operators, police and the merely curious. The click of typewriters and the crackle of telegraph lines began sending thousands of words around the world.

We wanted to get to Sourland Mountain, to the Lindbergh home, but the other reporters who had been there before us told us that we could only get our news at the gate to the property. Regardless, we decided to try. We did, only to get as far as the gate and be turned back.

Persistence— But the house was directly behind the gate, and as police cussed at us for our nerve— and even threatened to arrest us— we were watching the house, trying to figure out another approach.

A chill spring rain was coming down as we drove off in another direction. We finally parked and began to find our way through the soaking underbrush. It was about 1:30 a.m. when we found the telephone lines lying on the ground. We used them as a guide to the house through a thin woodland.

Detail— Every time a twig or branch snapped, we froze and listened. We were shivering with the cold and wet, our shoes slogging along through the mud and wet grass.

It occurred to me as we trudged along that this must have been the route taken by the kidnapper that stormy March night two months before.

Finally, we emerged from the woods, crouched down and ran behind mounds of earth thrown up around a high wall at the rear of the house.

Straight ahead behind the wall, a window was raised a few inches in a downstairs room, where a man was sitting and talking to New Jersey state troopers. We recognized Lindbergh from his hair and jacket. Then glancing upstairs, we could see the figure of a woman pacing back and forth. It looked like Anne Lindbergh.

The house was ablaze with lights, except for one room upstairs. It was dark, and we sensed it must be the nursery.

As we hid and shivered at the thought of imminent discovery, we could hear snatches of conversation coming from the other side of the wall.

Lindbergh was telling the story of his fruitless search for his child by plane and boat at sea, lured by false clues, at the very time the body was found in a rude open grave not far from home.

We were so engrossed in the tragic story that we lost track of time, until we realized suddenly that it was dawn. The night — and our protective cover — was over.

So we crawled back through the woods and hid behind trees nearby for a final look at that house of grief. No lights now showed. The downstairs conference was over, and everyone seemed to have gone to bed.

Perception— As we ran along back toward the car, there rose a high thin wail of some lonely hound. That plaintive wail accentuated the sorrow we had just witnessed. It was after six o'clock in the morning when we got back to Hopewell.

It was more than a year before Bruno Richard Hauptmann, the German immigrant, was finally arrested for the crime. He was arrested in September, 1934, but his trial did not begin in Flemington, N. J., until January 2, 1935.

At the trial that lasted six weeks, there was nothing but circumstantial evidence, but that was overwhelming. There was no confession, but the tight-lipped German carpenter was not the kind to talk.

During the trial I talked to Hauptmann twice— as much as one could talk to this strange dour man who cultivated secrecy all his life. I spoke with him once more, two days before his death.

Our first exchange came during a brief intermission in trial proceedings. I asked him a question as state troopers stood around him. But I could not understand the gutteral words through his heavy accent. So a trooper interpreted for me.

"He says he wants your address and phone number," said the trooper.

Hauptmann leaned his full length back in his chair and from behind drooping lids eyed me up and down suggestively, like a man in a common bar, not at a bar of justice. A tight little smile hovered around his mouth.

The second time I asked him a question was right after the testimony in the courtroom on the condition of the baby's body when it was found. It had been mutilated by the small wild animals of the area. Nearby was an old burlap bag, as if someone had dumped the body and then ran to escape detection.

I was writing a human interest story, and wanted to get a Nerve— comment, almost any comment. "Did you forget your bag when you dumped the baby in the grave?" I asked Hauptmann.

His leer turned to a look of rage, and his gutteral voice could be heard around the room as he half shouted at me: "You, you get out of here!" He was stuttering in his fury.

Two days away from death, he had the same secret smile and the same leering glance that tended to make women uncomfortable. He was in the Flemington, N.J., jail, waiting to be taken to the Trenton death house for his execution. He still intoned he was "innocent."

The man had been secretive all his life. To get to the United States, he had stowed away twice beneath loads of coal in the holds of ships. He finally made it here and made his way, somehow, with odd jobs — and no passport. He successfully eluded immigration officers and police.

In his own country, he had a police record which was brought out at the trial. In this country, he had found off-and-on jobs as a carpenter in the Depression. When money was scarce he depended on his wife who gave him her wages and tips as a waitress. When he had money, he did not share with his wife. He was a loner who never trusted anyone.

His voice was unforgettable.

It was that guttural voice, heard when the kidnapper came for the ransom money in a Bronx cemetery, that was identified by Col. Lindbergh and Dr. John F. Condon ("Jafsie"), the man who served as a go-between in the crime.

Hauptmann was finally arrested through a trail of ransom bills. The one he used to pay for gas at a New York service station led to his home. There was a suitcase full of the ransom money in his garage. Part of it was accounted for by Hauptmann's splurge on the stock market.

The wood of the famous ladder left behind by the abductor after he had climbed to the baby's room was similar to that of wood in the attic of the Hauptmann home and in the lumber yard in the Bronx where he worked. Nicks in the rungs of the ladder corresponded to those made by Hauptmann's carpenter's plane.

The handwriting on the ransom notes was studied by the experts who matched it with Hauptmann's poorly spelled scrawls under other and more normal conditions.

After the mass accumulation of evidence in the long trial, the jury came up with a first degree verdict. The judge promised the death sentence.

But the case was not over.

It dragged along for more than a year. Hauptmann's lawyers sought various delays, and the officials of the State of New Jersey tried to make a political football of the case by issuing reprieves for various reasons.

I was in on the finale, the night that Hauptmann finally went to the electric chair April 3, 1936, in the death house in Trenton, N.J.

However, no women reporters were allowed to witness the execution. John McCullough, the veteran *Inquirer* reporter, who had been the main reporter at the trail, watched the execution.

As the paper's so-called "sob sister," it was my job to stand outside and watch for John's signal that it was all over. And then I rushed to the telephone to inform my office and to write a story.

When I had written the last word, I decided I could not possibly spend another night on this story. I was cold, tired, hungry, so although it was two o'clock in the morning, I decided to go home.

"Drive home alone at this hour?" asked one of the reporters.

Strong "Yes, alone," I said.

summary finish— As I drove from Trenton to Philadelphia, the moon had risen as a magic lantern. I pressed down the accelerator and began to sing. I sang and sang, light, lilting tunes as a kind of requiem to all the tragedy of the past many months, and as if to lift the sadness that had touched the world for so long.

Jinx Wins Out in 6th at Latonia
by William Ruehlmann

[I knew nothing about horse racing when I went out after this story for the Kentucky Post. *The idea was to follow around the best jockey at the track, from the time he arrived there until he left, relying on proximity and plenty of questions to convey to race fancier and layman alike the sights, smells and textures of the course.*

The story turned over in front of me when a horse was killed.]

Summary lead— Last night at Latonia Race Course a rider's fortunes soared as a horse's ended disastrously.

At 9:15 p.m. Jim McKnight, 23, waited quietly in the jockeys' room for the sixth race. The five-foot four-inch, 110-pound professional had already had a fair evening, finishing second and fourth in two earlier contests; only nine days before, he had collected an incredible five wins on a single card.

At the same moment, across the track in a low-slung yellow brick barn, trainer Robert McElroy, 69, supervised the final grooming of Bright Blend, a big six-year-old filly who won just two weeks ago at Commonwealth.

Earlier in the evening, surrounded by varicolored silks that **Direct** hung from the jockey room ceiling like bright flags, McKnight **quote** had commented on the attitudes of his audience.

as angle— "People expect too much of a rider," he said. "In the event of a loss they tend to blame the rider, not the horse. They don't understand what can happen in a race.

"You've got to remember we're not riding a bunch of ponies. Each one is a thousand-pound animal with a mind of his own." It was a statement that would prove grimly prophetic.

At 9:25 p.m. McKnight moved across the locker room to have his weight certified by Clerk of Scales Orene Hampton.

McElroy was escorting Bright Blend across the race course to the number eight stall in the paddock.

Full names of all principals—

At 9:30 p.m. custodian Charlie Jaeger called out the jockeys. McKnight mounted the three entry, Abrocrozier, and Ed Snell seated himself on the back of Bright Blend.

The race seemed jinxed from the start.

At first they filed out obediently enough past Paddock Judge Collett Griffin, but the horses had barely completed the half-course post parade and were taking their places at the starting gate when entry six, English Regency, reared. Throwing off jockey Rafael Gaston, the scratched horse ran his outriders a stubborn track-long chase.

Starter Jimmy Long lined up the remaining entries in the long green-and-white steel starting gate and pushed a 12-volt trigger button. Cages clanged open, and the race was on.

Detail—

Bright Blend took an immediate lead in the back stretch as the pack strung itself out along the rail. Beyond the chill black infield lake with its limp windless flag, the clubhouse loomed like a great illuminated aquarium in which thousands of heads bobbed. The cry was taken up: "Come *on* . . . COME *ON!*"

Detail—

Bright Blend held her lead through the far turn.

The horses and their riders moved with one fluid motion, like brightly colored centaurs loping along a giant ring. The far side of the course was too distant to hear them and they ran silently, as if from a dream, but as they approached there was a heavy thud of hooves drumbeating the loam track, a squeaking of leather strained tight at the bridle and back.

Then, suddenly, Bright Blend was down.

The field shot by as spectators craned for a view of the fallen horse and rider; an ambulance hastened along the outside track. And McKnight hurtled past the white pole at the finish line, showing a close third in the five-and-a-half furlong race.

Meanwhile McElroy was striding disconsolately down the dirt surface in the other direction, his knit-capped head bent forward.

"Oh man," he said. "Oh hell. It's broke."

"She was out in front going around the back side," an un-hurt Snell said later. "I felt her getting tired. Then she just pop-ped her knee and went down."

Bright Blend was loaded on the back of a trailer gently, steadied by the firm hand of a groom.

"Aw man," McElroy said. "They're gonna have to put her down."

The trailer with Bright Blend drove away slowly. McElroy watched it go.

At ten p.m. the jockeys were summoned again for the seventh race. The ritual began once more, fiberglass whips flashing around the white-lit ring, drumming hooves sending up great looping sprays of loam eight feet into the air. This time McKnight finished first, his forty-second victory of the year, and it was his picture track photographer Jack Pille recorded in the winner's circle.

The name of McKnight's mount was Luck Ahead.

But luck had run out for Bright Blend, who lay that moment half a mile distant at the end of an unlit road, her large brown eyes open and sightless forever.

"Any time you win a race it picks up your spirits a little," admitted Jim McKnight in the jockey's room.

Back at the barn, Robert McElroy took a long breath.

"I hated to lose her," he said.

2. Focus

Abstraction

It is harder to see the earth's landscape from a thousand feet up than from a fixed point on the ground. The buildings of a large city become indistinct observed beyond the wing of a Whisperjet, and a gun-cotton carpet of clouds often intervenes.

The same is true of language. High altitudes of rhetoric provide poor pictures of what one is talking about. Try telling a friend about your pet dog Igor only in terms of his traits as a "carnivore." His peculiar qualities as Igor — shedding on the sofa, stealing your socks, chewing up the process-server — are completely lost to the more general qualities of his class.

"Carnivore" is an abstract term. Igor is a concrete one. The best writing will be concrete, because it is more interesting to read specifically about the ten-year-old kid down your block who built a nuclear reactor than it is to read about "gifted children" in general.

Concrete writing calls for the kind of vision we talked about in chapter one. You can't write about what you can't see. The writer's eye is a cutting torch that burns through fogs of rhetoric to the truth. That eye does not see "the distinguished councilman from East Quagmire"; it sees a middle-aged man with large hands and a tendency to sleep during the speeches of the opposition.

Don't be fooled. The "high style" some mistake for profundity is really nothing more than a retreat from clarity. One politico long noted for alliterative language referred to his critics as "nattering nabobs of negativism"; what he meant was these were people who disagreed with him. Some resort to abstract terms as a method of making rather simple-minded ideas sound complex— and so we get lofty references to "cosmetic embalming" instead of the ways one makes a corpse look good.

On the other hand, concrete writing illuminates complicated matters. Robert Frost, who said complex things simply, dealt with bureaucratic distance by recounting the funeral arrangements for an ant in his hive. Albert Einstein once explained his Theory of Relativity to someone on a moving train by asking, "When does the next town get here?" If it can't be stated clearly and simply, an idea is not profound. It is merely unformed.

The language of Vaguespeak

Abstract writing is bad writing, and, as we've noted, it is not always inadvertent.

Professionals — that is, those people who refer to each other as "colleagues" instead of co-workers — frequently resort to jargon in describing what they do and how they do it. This is often a defense; in creating abstract terms for one's pursuits, it is possible to have those often trivial preoccupations perceived by the uninitiated as somehow mysterious and very difficult indeed. Thus one professional winner of a $35,000 Ford Foundation grant described his project as an attempt, "in a primary sense, [to] meet the need to provide an academically 'airtight' environment within which a 'think-tank' (what we prefer to call) 'cellular' approach to the intensive study of communication theory and arts can be undertaken by *communication specialists* and *scholars* free of academic contingencies which too often dilute and blunt evolving, embryonic researchers."

He admitted privately he wasn't precisely sure what the sam hill he was up to.

Author Kurt Vonnegut has said succinctly, "Anyone who cannot explain his/her craft to a 14-year-old is a mere talking pretender. The hell with these inarticulate meditators and writers!"

Still, a psychologist will not tell you little Sedgewick is overactive; he will announce "your son has been adjudged hyperkinetic." A public relations executive will not tell you you look like a meatball on TV; he will regret you lack "positive reference inputs." Even police officers don't catch crooks— they "apprehend alleged perpetrators."

Advertisers are not as concerned with pretense in their willful use of abstraction as they are in misdirection. One fast food chain is sold by the slogan "We do it all for you," indicating an absolute frenzy of effort to please the customer; any concern in this direction is of course not altruistic— fact is, they are doing it all for *themselves,* to make *money.*

One cigarette ad suggests the consequence of taking a single puff on one of its mentholated cylinders is to transport the smoker to "a wonderful world of softness, a wonderful world of freshness," an interesting region to gain merely by sticking burning leaves in one's mouth.

Politicians of course retire the trophy for using abstract language in a deliberate effort to subvert the truth. Having employed the word "recession" for years as a rather immaculate reference to higher prices and fewer jobs, an entire Washington administration still found the term too unsavory (since it denoted a situation that was even more so). Cabinet officers began calling the economic predicament they found themselves in "stagflation." A former commerce secretary wouldn't say the economy was in difficulty; rather, it was "waffling sideways."

Which is a poor description of an economy, but a good one of this kind of linguistic behavior. Wartime brings particularly grim examples of official abstraction; figures in power do not so much falsify the facts as launder them. When the other side stages an armed assault, it is a "sneak attack"; when our side does the same thing, it is a "protective reaction raid." Bombing is "air support"; a blown-up village is "effective ordinance delivery." The utter capitulation of the enemy is "a just and lasting peace."

And of course a politician caught in incongruities of testimony has not lied; he has "misspoken himself."

George Orwell, that highly prophetic novelist-journalist, argued that political language "is designed to make lies sound truthful and murder respectable, and to give the appearance of solidity to pure wind."

A reporter must remain absolutely unsuckered by these constructions and certainly should never employ them, inadvertently or otherwise. Because such abstract communication can not only obscure reality but distort it as well, the reporter cleaves to the concrete in an effort to make things clear. What emerges from such an effort may be ugly, but it will be reliable. To that end, Orwell offered his sound advice:

"Never use a long word where a short one will do."

Seeing the war through the single soldier

Recounting tactical movements of troops in the course of a campaign will convey little of the reality of battle to a reader. But show that reader one soldier on one patrol; reveal that soldier's solitary, personal encounter with gore and glory, disaster and dread; and you can drive home something of what it all means. The soldier's actions are concrete. The doings of his battalion are abstract. It is the difference between a casualty count and somebody's dead body.

This is the way in which overwhelming subjects can be made manageable and interesting. Suppose you are assigned a story on swindlers in your city. Citing statistics would have all the impact of a "No Shooting" sign in hunting season, while it would be tedious to set down the situation of every victim. But an intensive account of one aged individual on welfare who lost his food stamps and savings to the old "pigeon drop" ploy will convey the tragedy of the mark as well as the method of the con artist. That story better than any other will say it: beware of geeks bearing grifts.

Seek then the paradigm, the example that will sum up your subject. That takes your camera from the abstract to the concrete, from the ill-defined wide-angle long shot to the crisp concise closeup. Instead of rattling on about the meaning of courage, Ernest Hemingway wrote about an old man and a fish; instead of railing at the insensitivity of racism, Mark Twain told of a southern white boy's loyalty to a fugitive black slave.

Charles Dickens, who started out as a reporter (he was so fast he would have the story scrawled down and done in the time it took his carriage to go to the press office), dealt with the bleak circumstances of the condemned of Newgate by focusing upon a single cell:

> It was a stone dungeon, eight feet long by six wide, with a bench at the upper end, under which were a common rug, a Bible and a prayerbook. An iron candlestick was fixed into the wall at the side, and a small high window in the back admitted as much air and light as could struggle in between a double row of heavy, crossed iron bars. It contained no other furniture of any description.

This stark, arid little room frozen forever in clean prose becomes an emblem for all such little rooms of Dickens' day and our own, utterly empty, severe — and immediate in a way no more general description could make them.

Jack London, another reporter of great reputation, went into the blighted East End of England's capital just after the turn of the century to reveal the extent of human deprivation there. He selected the follow-

ing moment to sum up the situation of all elderly laborers who had outlived their employment, showing instead of bewailing the pass to which
a carter and a carpenter had come on their way to the workhouse:

> Both kept their eyes upon the pavement as they walked and talked,
> and every now and then one or the other would stoop and pick
> something up, never missing the stride the while. I thought it was
> cigar and cigarette stumps they were collecting, and for some time
> took no notice. Then I did notice.
>
> From the slimy, spittle-drenched sidewalk, they were picking up
> bits of orange peel, apple skin and grape stems, and they were
> eating them. The pits of greengage plums they cracked between
> their teeth for the kernels inside. They picked up stray crumbs of
> bread the size of peas, apple cores so black and dirty one would not
> take them to be apple cores, and these things these two men took
> into their mouths, and chewed them, and swallowed them; and this,
> between six and seven o'clock in the evening of August 20, year of
> our Lord 1902, in the heart of the greatest, wealthiest, and most
> powerful empire the world has ever seen.

Very specific — thus very powerful. London went on to synthesize the
myriad inequities of English law in the administrative language of one
municipal report:

> Lambeth Police Court, London. Before Mr. Hopkins. "Baby"
> Stuart, aged nineteen, described as a chorus girl, charged with ob-
> taining food and lodging to the value of 5 s. by false pretenses, and
> with intent to defraud Emma Brasier, complainant, lodging-house
> keeper of Atwell Road. Prisoner took apartments at her house on
> the representation that she was employed at the Crown Theatre.
> After prisoner had been in her house two or three days, Mrs.
> Brasier made inquiries and, finding the girl's story untrue, gave her
> into custody. Prisoner told the magistrate that she would have
> worked had she not had such bad health. Six weeks' hard labor.

The single item makes the best subject. Keenly seen, a flagship can
conjure up the entire fleet.

Detail

Mass transit: a subway.
It roars through the electric-lit subterranean mesh, a metal snake

rattling to the scream of wheel on rail while the waiters hang inside from steel hooks and stare straight ahead or into the morning paper. There are only so many seats, and at the stops they shove for them, push, especially the old, like willful cattle insisting on some rightful stall in the stockyard, save in a corner where a wino in a hunter's hood coughs of the Apocalypse and demands a dime for Jesus.

The preceding was a parlor trick. Just as subjects can be made concrete by example, so any scene, situation or state of mind can be portrayed most strongly by the sensitive selection of vivid visual detail.

Dorothy Parker once transfixed the cheap gaudiness of an entire era with nothing more than a doughnut for a dart:

> I can't talk about Hollywood. It was a horror to me when I was there and it's a horror to look back on. I can't imagine how I did it. When I got away from it I couldn't even refer to the place by name. "Out there," I called it. You want to know what "out there" means to me? Once I was coming down a street in Beverly Hills and I saw a Cadillac about a block long, and out of the side window was a wonderfully slinky mink, and an arm, and at the end of the arm a hand in a white suede glove wrinkled around the wrist, and in the hand was a bagel with a bite out of it.

The relentless literary focus that continues all the way to the end of this passage leaves the reader with a powerful mental picture. Out of the thousand items that might have embodied that famously surreal section of southern California, Miss Parker chose the one that seems exactly right.

In setting down any subject, a writer has a bewildering array of material to choose from. But it is the writer's job to pick among the pieces like a riverbed ragman, searching out the few salient items that will be of the best value in his evocative transaction with the reader.

Truman Capote has explained this painter's process of seeking the particular surfaces that might illustrate an entire environment on the canvas of a printed page:

> When I was a child I played a pictorial game. I would, for example, observe a landscape: trees and clouds and horses wandering in grass; then select a detail from the overall vision — say, grass bending in the breeze — and frame it with my hands. Now this detail became the essence of the landscape and caught, in prismatic miniature, the true atmosphere of a panorama too sizable to en-

compass otherwise. Or if I was in a strange room, and wanted to understand the room and the nature of its inhabitants, I let my eye wander selectively until it discovered something— a shaft of light, a decrepit piano, a pattern in the rug— that seemed of itself to contain the secret. All art is composed of selected detail, either imaginary or, as in *In Cold Blood,* a distillation of reality.

What is the single thing that can call up the larger whole with such precision? Quite simply, the most interesting thing. The most remarkable thing. The thing that rivets the attention.

Watch Raymond Chandler capture the mood and texture of a tense urban summer's night in just 66 words that make an ordinary breeze burn:

> There was a desert wind blowing that night. It was one of those hot dry Santa Anas that come down through the mountain passes and curl your hair and make your nerves jump and your skin itch. On nights like that every booze party ends in a fight. Meek little wives feel the edge of the carving knife and study their husbands' necks. Anything can happen.

A lesser writer would have elaborated on the heat, gone on about the possibility of violence, brooded over the buildings and the beach. But Chandler conjures a whole world by describing a hot wind.

In the course of selecting detail, one should remember to save the overwhelming, most specific for the end. The attempt is to build toward an impression that is absolutely immediate in the screening room of the reader's mind. Mark Twain once wrote of traveling down San Francisco's 3rd Street on an October afternoon the moment an earthquake hit. Anyboyd but a writer would have taken cover; instead, Twain was carefully cataloging his impressions in order to convey this tight, beautifully built historical chromo:

> One could have fancied that somebody had fired a charge of chair rounds and rags down the thoroughfare. The streetcar had stopped, the horses were rearing and plunging, the passengers were pouring out at both sides, and *one** fat man had crashed halfway through a glass window on one side of the car, got wedged fast, and was squirming and screaming like an impaled madman.

The plight of the unfortunate fat man is an immortal picture of human

*Italics mine.

panic. Twain had a further detail that tops it: "One woman who had been washing a naked child ran down the street holding it by the ankles as if it were a dressed turkey." Reports of national disasters pass through the imagination with the empty impetus of stock market reports, but the situations of these two people stun even the jaded modern mind into sensibility.

In describing a dynamo, pick *one* gear and show it spin.

Show, don't tell

Professional comedians know that if you ask the members of any audience to laugh they will sit very still and look at you. If the wait is long enough, they will begin to address you in a way that is not deferential. Then they will begin to throw things.

The only way to make them laugh is to say something funny.

The dramatic actor knows the same is true when you try to make an audience cry. If what you're saying isn't genuinely sad, all the organ music in the world won't make it that way.

A writer is a performer who must never ask for the reader's emotion. He or she must earn it. Ernie Pyle once wrote a war report describing conditions in the London underground; it wasn't his best work. Although it was cleanly written, Pyle let his feelings intrude:

> In my first days in England I had seen terrible bomb damage. I had seen multitudinous preparations for war. I had talked with wounded soldiers. I had gone through London's great night of fire-bombing. I had listened for hours to the crack of guns and the crunch of bombs. And although I didn't especially know it at the time, none of these things went clear down deep inside and made me hurt.
>
> It was not until I went down seventy feet into the bowels of the Liverpool Street tube and saw humanity sprawled there in childlike helplessness that my heart first jumped and my throat caught. I know I must have said to myself, "Oh, my God!"

Contrast that passage with this one by Michael Herr:

> The first dead I saw in Vietnam was a Cambodian mercenary serving with the Special Forces in the Seven Mountains Region of the Delta. He had accidentally shot himself in the head while cleaning his .30-calibre rifle. Mercenaries live in a compound with their families, and this one had his parents, his grandparents and his

wife with him at the time. The medics bandaged his entire head so that he looked like something you'd see in relief on an old temple wall, some dead prince, very dignified in repose. The women squatted over his body, and their moaning built up into a terrible wail, falling off and beginning again, hour after hour. Some blood and brine had seeped through the bandages and filled a dent in the canvas, so that when they carried him from the stretcher some of it spilled over my boots. "Sorry," one of the medics said. "Got some on you."

The difference between the passages is crucial. In the first, we are confronted with abstract "humanity"; in the second, we are shown the concrete situation of one wounded man. Pyle relies on his own emotion; Herr engages ours.

Herr does not cry "Oh, my God!" Such is his skill that he makes *us* do it.

Avoiding bias

Responsible writers avoid passing on their prejudices cheaply by taking great care in their use of adjectives and adverbs. "Dear Mr. Babcock with his cute walk" and "that limping son-of-a-bitch Babcock" are the same man viewed variously by vastly different perceptions. The reader should be allowed to make his own estimation based on the man's deeds, not on the received opinion of the writer.

Erma Bombeck, a wry observer of all matters domestic, once noted that some mothers had quite an opposite vision of their children from her own. These mothers of so-called "super children" simply referred to their doings in different terms:

NORMAL KIDS	SUPER CHILDREN
Forgetful	Preoccupied
Fat	Healthy
Sloppy beasts	Academically geared
Weirdo who won't get a haircut	Nonconformist
Lazy bum	Deep thinker
Flunked out	Victim of a poor teacher
TV addict	TV critic
Cut from the team	Saved from a prejudiced coach
Forgot me on Mother's Day	Is saving his money for my operation
Oversleeps in the morning	A recessive gene

The tendency Mrs. Bombeck has pointed out amusingly can have grim, even vicious consequences. Writing grounded in interpretation rather than observation becomes a kind of literary Rorschach test; it tells more about the author than the subject.

For example, here is part of William Howard Russell's dispatch on the famous Charge of the Light Brigade which appeared in the London *Times* November 13, 1854:

A more fearful spectacle was never witnessed than by those who, without the power to aid, beheld their heroic countrymen rushing to the arms of death. At the distance of 1,200 yards, the whole line of the enemy belched forth from 30 iron mouths a flood of smoke and flame through which hissed the deadly balls. Their flight was marked by instant gaps in our ranks, by dead men and horses, by steeds flying wounded or riderless across the palin. The first line was broken — it was joined by the second. They never halted or checked their speed an instant. With diminished ranks, thinned by those 30 guns which the Russians had laid with the most deadly accuracy, with a halo of flashing steel above their heads and with a cheer which was many a noble fellow's death cry, they flew into the smoke of the batteries. . . .

It is unnecessary to note that Russell was an Englishman. Russell calls the British contingent his "heroic countrymen," "noble fellows" engaged in valorous swashbuckle; a more objective observer might have called attention to the criminal stupidity of the officers who led them. Russell's war correspondence is not only partisan, but is responsible for a glittering vision of war — "halos of flashing steel" rather than rent and broken young corpses. It makes for stirring but unreliable reading.

On February 15, 1898, the U.S. battleship *Maine* exploded in Havana harbor. The ship had been there to protect American citizens from the riots against Spain there; now 250 sailors were dead. Typical of *New York World* stories on the matter was this one:

HAVANA, Cuba, 10 a.m., by way of Key West, Fla., Feb. 23—
There is not one chance in a hundred but that the *Maine* was blown up deliberately.

Whether a mine detonating key was mistaken for a testing key or whether a mammoth contact torpedo broke its moorings by accident, the awful, astounding thing is that up to now there have been discovered fifty actual, positive physical proofs of the tragic act.

Against it are only a few theories and suppositions.

An official U.S. court of inquiry was still making no accusations after six weeks of investigation, but days after the event the *World* was concluding the Maine had been mined by the Spanish. What the *World* was really saying was that it did not like Spain — but evidence is more important than any assertion of approval or disapproval, and the paper had none.

When screen lover Rudolph Valentino died suddenly a good deal of fuss was made over his passing. Not the least audible of the immediate mourners was an actress who collected her share of copy over displays of public woe. Standard coverage — a sidebar in the *Los Angeles Record* of August 23, 1926, that began:

> Unconscious and hysterical by turns, crying out her grief over the death of Rudolph Valentino, Pola Negri, reported fiancee of the dead film star, was under the care of two physicians in her Ambassador hotel bungalow today.
> The Polish film star's grief was touching.
> Informed of Valentino's death by newspapermen, Miss Negri fainted.
> Frantically her maid, crying out for aid, summoned the hotel house physician. A few moments later the star's private doctor arrived. Restoration returning her to consciousness, Miss Negri wept bitterly. The star was completely unnerved. A few moments later and her grief turned to hysteria.

There's a lot of unearned sympathy for Negri here. Note the writer's conclusions — her grief was "touching," she was "completely unnerved," etc. A more jaded commentator might not have seen a "star" in agony but rather a practiced poseur milking the moment for the press in typically exaggerated silent film style.

Damon Runyon, that wonderfully spare writer of hard-boiled Broadway fiction, sometimes flexed his muscular prose rather too ruggedly in the public prints. His lead for a celebrated trial over the International News Service April 19, 1927, did not go easy on the adjectives:

> A chilly-looking blonde with frosty eyes and one of those marble, you-bet-you-will chins, and an inert scare-drunk fellow

that you couldn't miss among any hundred men as a dead setup for a blonde, or the shell game, or maybe a gold brick.

Mrs. Ruth Snyder and Henry Judd Gray are on trial in the huge weather-beaten old courthouse of Queens County in Long Island City, just across the river from the roar of New York, for what might be called for want of a better name The Dumbbell Murder. It was so dumb.

They are charged with the slaughter four weeks ago of Albert Snyder, art editor of the magazine *Motor Boating,* the blonde's husband and father of her nine-year-old daughter, under circumstances that for sheer stupidity and brutality have seldom been equaled in the history of crime.

So who needs a jury?

Like jet pilots running low on oxygen, writers can become light-headed when they soar too long in the thin atmosphere of their own views. I've done it myself. I once did a rescue squad story that ended like this:

> They don't romanticize their reasons for taking this job. Jim Reed will tell you he fell into it after seven years of driving a Coke truck, and Dick Sullivan will say it was just the best job he could find. But there is certainly something rare about these two skilled men who make their living saving lives.

The benediction was hardly necessary. I had already *shown* they were good, but I had to go ahead and *tell* it to make sure the proper "bless 'em both" rode high in the hearts of the audience. I should have killed that paragraph and left the reader to draw his own conclusions from the data that gave bones to the story instead of fat:

> 3:25: p.m. The hood stays warm all day on the life squad ambulance. This time it's a boy struck by a car at 12th and Holmes Streets. Reed lets the engine out that extra little bit he reserves for critical trouble.
>
> The siren is stopped two blocks short as usual to avoid further exciting the patient and collecting a crowd; the code "2-6" is read over the radio to indicate the men will be away from the mike. Reed and Sullivan sew through the swarm around an eight-year-old boy with a broken nose.
>
> Reed crouches before him and has him go through a number of

stretches and reaches. The nose is all that has been broken. The young driver of the car that hit him stands by with a nobody-home look on his face as the police pull up and the mother of the boy comes running from down the street.

Sullivan moves to intercept the frightened woman as Reed walks the boy away from the blood to the ambulance. Reed calms the mother with one of his easy jokes and Sullivan hops into the cab.

A driver sticks his head out of his late-model machine and addresses Sullivan.

"Kid got hit by a car, huh?"

Sullivan looks at him.

Reed gives the go-ahead from in back and Sullivan takes off.

Why embroider on that? If the skill that impressed me wasn't implicit in the material, all the stops on the organ couldn't get it across for me.

Lines like the following from an advocate press irritate rather than illuminate:

WASHINGTON — The FBI was placed on trial this week as congressional committees held public hearings on the secret Cointelpro operations. The verdict in the minds of millions of Americans was "Guilty."

There is no evidence to suggest that writers reliably read minds. Nor are public hearings trials. Nor do millions of unpolled people agree utterly about anything.

Such devices are employed by propagandists, not feature writers. But feature writers *will* attempt to leave an impression — a fair one, supported by unvarnished facts. In the following fragment from a news brief in *Rolling Stone* there are no judgmental constructions, but powerful reverberations go out from it like fissures from a fault line:

In a brief speech, Ambassador Emory C. Swank told the Cambodians: "It was a mistaken American bombing and we desire to compensate, insofar as possible, the survivors of the tragedy."

Compensation came in the form of payment. Surviving relatives of the dead were each paid $400.

Nothing more is necessary.

Making the blue pencil superfluous

Write lean.

Hemingway had on a red plaid wool shirt, a figured wool necktie, a tan wool sweater-vest, a brown tweed jacket tight across the back and with sleeves too short for his arms, gray flannel slacks, Argyle socks, and loafers, and he looked bearish, cordial, and constricted. His hair, which was very long in back, was gray, except at the temples, where it was white; his mustache was white, and he had a ragged, half-inch, full white beard. There was a bump about the size of a walnut over his left eye. He had on steel-rimmed spectacles, with a piece of paper under the nose-piece. He was in no hurry to get into Manhattan.

The preceding paragraph by Lillian Ross defies cutting. Every word counts. Any deletion at all would either deprive us of interesting information or impede the measured rhythm of her prose.

Such spare copy has been cast, recast and polished. In that condition it goes to an editor.

The editor should be regarded as a sort-of sage. Even though the writer feels his piece is unimprovable, the editor may have suggestions that must be weighed. He or she comes to your material as an objective outsider just as interested as you are in turning out the best possible final product.

I said *sort-of* sage. Editors can be dead wrong. Go ahead and scrap if you feel your story has been misassessed. But if the editor has spotted a weakness, be smart enough to do something about it with good grace.

Delete excess.

Anything inessential — a paragraph, a line, an unwieldy word — should be cut. Tedium should be avoided absolutely. A safe rule of thumb: Whatever bores you will most assuredly bore a reader. Insist on tightness; stay away from the kind of overwriting that always calls a car a "sleek low-slung limo."

Writing is probably more closely allied to sculpture than any other art. After a sentence has been crafted, it is not inviolable— it is merely the roughcast of what remains to be carved on some more. From the heavy stone of imprecision emerges a chiseled thing that, out of much effort, gives the appearance of ease. At precisely the moment when one touch more might destroy it, the sculptor stops.

The original: *The men testifying at Watergate hearings did not look at all like the enemies they had identified for us.*

The revision: *The well-groomed men testifying at Watergate hearings had the clean-cut image and purpose of what we had perceived to be*

conventional American heroes, not villains.
The finishing stroke: *The immaculate men who testified at the Watergate hearings were not wild-haired demons out of motorcycle sagas but scrubbed, crew-cut Haldemans, bright, bifocaled Deans, men whose very purity of purpose revealed the ragged outer edge of American rectitude, the edge Melville saw in the whiteness of the Whale.*

But don't overrevise. A too-finicky diamond cutter can carve away the whole gem. Remember you are working for quick refinement, for the feature game is played at speed. If you are any good, you will never be quite satisfied with what you have done. Still you'll go immediately on to the next project with the intention of making that one your best, like Stephen Crane's runner in search of the sun.

A Night in a Squad Car Out of "Two-Four": Trouble Partners, Trouble in the Street
by Mary Breasted

[Police officers do not normally enjoy the presence of reporters, especially on patrol. The relentless attention of a third party can be inhibiting to certain habits, and a reporter is one more person to worry about in the event of danger. But rides with police make for sure-fire stories when you can get them, even it nothing happens; cops will reveal something of themselves in the course of an eight-hour shift. Once the initial suspicion has worn off, they are as flattered as anyone by the presence of an interested audience.

Mary Breasted's New York Times night run story begins abstractly and becomes quickly concrete. The experience of one weekend becomes exemplary of regular police routine. She concentrates particularly on a single incident — a typically explosive domestic disturbance call — and follows it through with an alert eye for detail.

The result is this powerful look at urban reality.]

Summary lead— Life in a police radio car is a journey between tedium and terror. It is heartburn and cigarettes mixed with too many cups of take-out coffee. It is holding a front-seat on the world, manning a mobile information booth, driving a taxi for the destitute and being a slow-moving target for the deranged.

It is a state of readiness, a series of interrupted conversations. And, always, it is the inner ear poised for that crackling of the city's nerve ends that is the radio dispatcher down in "Central" where the 911 calls come in.

The partners
as
paradigm—

Detective Third Grade Alfred Genova and Police Officer Harold Dice have been partners in a radio car on Manhattan's West Side for so long they feel as if they are blood relatives. Officer Dice is godfather to the Genovas' youngest child, and he calls his partner's mother-in-law "Ma."

Quite tall, 6 feet 3 inches in his stocking feet, Officer Dice is 26 and looks it. His face is smooth, his cheeks faintly rosy and his eyes are bright and clear. Officer Genova, who stands 5 feet 9 inches, has dark rings under his eyes and hair that is prematurely gray. He is 32, but he looks 42. Officer Dice defers to his partner on "jobs," responses to radio calls.

They are perfect partners, and they hate to be separated. Both Queens residents, they commute to and from work together. They won the department's coveted honorable mention citation together. Officer Genova makes jokes about their being in love.

Typifying
the
larger topic—

Their captain calls them two of the best men in the 24th Precinct, but in many ways they are typical of New York City policemen. They are sons of blue-collar workers, firm believers in the work ethic, and they say they still work as hard as they can at being good police officers. But they are discouraged and losing enthusiasm.

The point—

The new work schedules that set off recent angry police demonstrations have disrupted their lives and made them feel that the city, which asks them to keep the peace, does not appreciate them.

But some of their discouragement has built up over the years. For with or without the new chart, or schedule, they are subject to dangers of their job and frustrating changes of schedule. In uniform they feel themselves isolated, conspicuous.

Friday, Oct. 15, was their ninth straight day of work, they said, because the chart change gave them only one day off between five-day tours of duty, and their last day off had been consumed by an obligatory court appearance, for which they were paid.

Proximity—

Working the 4 p.m.-to-midnight shift that Friday, they

started at a leisurely pace. They bought coffee at a doughnut shop on Broadway and drove to a favorite resting spot, 107th Street and Riverside Drive, where the yellows and fading greens of Riverside Park trees were luminous in the late afternoon sun.

Lighting up cigarettes, they talked about their family backgrounds, and that inevitably led to discussion of a police officer's unpredictable schedule. Every arrest, they said, meant a disruption— a schedule change or a day off spent in court.

Quotes
for immediacy— "You can't socialize," Officer Genova said. "Say, you get invited to a wedding three months ahead, and then the time comes, and you have to go to court. Your wife wants you to go, and most of the time she goes by herself. . . . Harry's wife, she couldn't take that."

"We went out before," Officer Dice said. "She knew what it would be like— but still. . . ."

Officer Dice is now divorced.

"After a while," he added, "all your friends are police officers. Because— the old crowd— you just don't see them."

Officer Dice put the blue-and-white car in gear. Officer Genova told "Central" they were resuming patrol, and slowly they began to cruise.

Detail— The 24th Precinct, less than a square mile in size, runs from Riverside Drive to Central Park West and from 86th to 110th Streets. It has a population of about 116,000 that ranges in wealth from those in the Eldorado at 300 Central Park West, where monthly rents may exceed $2,000, to destitute residents of single-room occupancy hotels living off Social Security checks.

In the northeastern section of the precinct, there are tenements and walkups crowded with poor Hispanics and blacks. "We get a homicide a week up there," one of the sergeants said at a later point. "And sometimes it's like civil war, with the Dominicans on one side shooting at the Puerto Ricans on the other side of the street," Officer Dice added.

The patrol car had turned onto Broadway, where the partners waved to a store owner, who waved back and smiled.

"He's been hit about seven times this year," Officer Genova said quietly. The talk turned to department citations and medals, which both partners bore above their shields. Officer Genova, who is much decorated, had been promoted to detective third grade as a reward for his work. This meant about $2,-400 more than a uniformed man with the same seven years' experience, or $18,500 a year. Officer Dice earns $16,000 a year. Neither figure includes overtime.

The partners recalled how they had won their honorable mention citations. They had gone to assist a wounded officer, who, in turn, had answered a "domestic dispute" call.

The suspect or "perp" (short for "perpetrator" in police jargon), was an armed state probation officer who had gone berserk in his home. He was ultimately captured unharmed, but Officer Genova was wounded in the hand during the incident.

The "domestic dispute" call is among the most dreaded of all, the policemen said, for it summons them to situations of unpredictable violence with victims who are seldom grateful.

The subjects observed in action—

It was exactly 5:30 p.m. when the radio dispatcher announced: "Twelve West 107th St. Male trying to throw a female out the window. Fifth floor, bedroom."

They fell silent. Officer Dice, the driver, switched on the blinking lights, the siren. In seconds, they were there, dashing through stoop-sitters, racing upstairs, their hands on their guns.

A thin young woman, weeping, wearing one shoe, appeared on a landing.

"Where is he?"

"He went up there." She pointed toward the roof.

"Does he have a weapon?"

"No."

Leaping up the stairs again. They were out on the roof, seeing nothing, no one. Little boys popped into sight on the opposite roof.

"He went that way, that way!" they shouted, pointing westward over the rooftops.

One after the other, the two partners mounted the wall between roofs, handspringing, legs to the side.

Detail—.

The weeping young woman came out onto the roof, holding her shoe in one hand, holding her jaw in the other. Her lip was bleeding, and her hair was bedraggled.

Soon the two partners gave up their search. Slowly they walked downstairs with the woman, who they learned was 21 years old.

She explained through her swollen cheeks that her boyfriend had come home drunk, they had fought, he had beaten her with a broom handle and bashed her against the bedroom window, breaking the glass, terrifying her and stirring someone — the call was anonymous — to phone the police.

"We'll take you to the hospital," Officer Genova told the woman. He and his partner waited while she went upstairs to fetch her 2-year-old child, who had been alone in the apartment during the chase.

"Thank God you came," she said, settling into the back of the car, her daughter's tiny hands clinging to her.

She had been living with the man for three weeks before he beat her, she said.

"Why do you stay with a man like that?" Officer Genova was to ask. He got no answer.

The officers brought her to the emergency ward at St. Luke's Hospital, quickly told her they would escort her back to the apartment should she be afraid to return alone, and then they left.

Twice in the next hour the partners were called to 105th Street between Columbus and Manhattan Avenues in pursuit of a "man with a gun." They found nothing.

The block's stoop dwellers, blacks and Puerto Ricans, looked at the police car hostilely. "We were shot at on this block a few years ago," Officer Genova said. It was a block buzzing with drug sales.

Later, when the officers returned to the precinct to file a report on a street argument they had helped to break up, they again encountered the young woman of 107th Street. She asked them to escort her home.

She had no keys, so Officer Dice had to worry the latch back with his knife. The young woman gathered clothes for the night, planning to stay with a relative. Officer Genova played with her daughter, hiding a button in his big fists, making her guess where it was.

Irony— Flowers, still wrapped, lay on top of the refrigerator. "For my funeral," the young woman joked bitterly.

Officer Genova carried her child down the stairs and the partners offered to take her to a cab or a subway station. Slowly the car pulled up the block, and just at the corner, a young man in a light blue shirt came dashing alongside, looking into the police car.

"That's him," she said calmly.

"Do you want us to arrest him?" asked Officer Genova.

"Yes," she said. "Well, not exactly. Just to tell him to take his things and leave."

"Look, we can't solve your marital problems. Do you want us to arrest him?"

There was a pause. "Yes," she said.

So Rocky Parker, 25, frightened, weeping, saying, "I haven't done nothing wrong," was handcuffed, driven to the station in another squad car and held for the night.

When the two officers entered the 24th Precinct station, it was mild bedlam.

Revealed drama— Mr. Parker, being booked at the desk, bobbed and twirled in a circle calling out to her, "Goomie, Goomie, PLEASE! Goomie, don't do this to me!"

"You have choked me half to death," said the young woman, from across the room. "That's how come I have these marks on my neck."

Officer Genova, holding his prisoner's elbow, was shouting frantically: "You have the right to remain silent, do you understand that? You have the right to have an attorney present—"

"If somebody has *what?*" came a voice through the din, the voice of Police Officer Frank Cohen, who was answering the phone behind the desk. "If somebody has sex with your *dog?*" he said in amazement. A moment later, he cupped the receiver and said, "I've been a police officer for 20 years and I've *never* heard anything like this!"

Detail— Finally, Officer Genova led Mr. Parker away and up to the second floor where the detectives worked. All the way up, the prisoner sobbed and blurted out his version of the fight — "I brought her *flowers!*"

When Rocky Parker was finally arraigned at 6:15 p.m., the day after his arrest, he pleaded not guilty and was paroled in his own recognizance.

Because of the Parker arrest, Officer Genova's shift was changed to an 8 a.m.-to-4 p.m. tour. He reached home in Queens at 12:50 a.m. Saturday and reported to work seven hours later.

He was assigned to foot patrol for two hours, then to the courthouse at 100 Centre St. Sixty-two cases were ahead of his.

He spent most of the day in the litter-strewn complaint room, sitting on a grimy plastic chair and recalling the days when he used to "get angry about all this." He was waiting for various clerks and prosecutors to do the paperwork on the Parker case. All around him, police officers were reading, sleeping, griping to one another about the Commissioner and the new chart.

The "tour" change meant the partners were separated Saturday night, and the next night a family emergency kept Officer Genova at home. But the rest of the weekend was relatively uneventful.

On Sunday, the stationhouse pundits speculated that the World Series games had stopped crime in the "two-four." There was not much else to talk about— except the alleged dog rapist, who had denied the crime, although the dog had injuries that seemed to support the allegations.

The case was already added to the precinct's list of bitter comic stories.

On Sunday night, Officer Dice left work early, with his sergeant's permission, to go to the hospital where Officer Genova's brother-in-law was dying.

"To me," Officer Genova had said, brooding during a long wait at 100 Centre St., "that's the most important thing, your family."

They left, though they did not phrase it exactly so, isolated from the rest of the world, from everyone except friends on the force, their relatives and maybe a few old, old friends who did not see them in uniform. Once, on that Friday evening they had patrolled together, a woman had waved to them and smiled

The point driven home— from a van.

"Must be out-of-towners," Officer Genova had said. But the van had then pulled ahead, revealing its license plate.

"New York," he said. "I don't believe it!"

"Well," said his partner brightly, "New York's a big state."

Ambulance Duty Provides a Wide Range of Experiences
by J.Y. Smith

[Another ride: J.Y. Smith of the Washington Post *begins immediately with a standard rescue squad situation, then follows the ambulance through a night and a morning, stopping at the White House on the way. His story is not a fragmentary entry-book account, however; he has a point to make, and the cases he records create a pattern.*

Note the ironic, well-observed details of the police officer's distress at a scratch and the woman hit by a baseball bat.]

The story shown, not told— The man was sprawled on the floor of the fast-food restaurant at 14th Street and New York Avenue NW. His hand rubbed the left side of his body.

"I've been shot," he said. 'I've been shot right here in the gut. I've got to go to Veterans'."

Pvt. Duane R. Parker of D.C. fire department ambulance No. 6 recognized the man immediately.

The problem as paradigm— "He's one of our regulars," he said. "Every time we pick him up he says he wants to go to Veterans' Hospital. If he got shot, it was in World War II."

Parker, who is 25, checked the man's pulse and respiration. He smelled his breath, which was heavy with the odor of alcohol, and said, "OK, Edward, get up. We're going to the hospital."

"What's the matter with him?" said the restaurant counterman.

"He's drunk," said Parker. "You ought to call the police and they would take him to Detox." (Detox is the D.C. detoxification center for alcoholics at 619 N St. NW.)

"I didn't know," said the counterman.

"That's OK, we'll take care of him," said Parker. "Come on, Edward, get up." Turning to his partner, Pvt. J.N. (Nick) Manthos, 28, Parker added, "I don't know how many times

I've seen this guy."

Parker and Manthos were near the beginning of an eight-hour shift on Ambulance No. 6 one recent evening. Before it was over, they would see things, many of them familiar, but all of them different, for a public ambulance provides an extraordinary window on the life of a city from its richest and most opulent quarters to its saddest and most forlorn.

During two consecutive shifts, from about 3 p.m. to 7 the following morning, the men on No. 6 answered calls in various parts of the city, including a stop at the White House.

For Parker and Manthos, their first problem was Edward, lying on the floor of the fast food place.

"Come on, Edward, get up," said Parker. Manthos unfolded a wheelchair.

"I been shot, I need to go to Veterans'," said Edward.

"We're going to George Washington," said Parker. Outside, they put Edward on a stretcher, then into the ambulance, and drove to the George Washington University Hospital emergency room entrance near Washington Circle.

They went to the hospital instead of the Detox facility because regulations require that the ambulance take all patients to a hospital. At GW, Edward was placed on a bed and secured there with a sheet tied around his middle so that he would not fall while he slept it off.

The problem again— "That was a taxi run," said Parker as he drove back to the firehouse at 23d and M Streets NW, where No. 6 is based.

A few minutes later, Parker had the lights and the siren going again. He was responding to a call that came in at 5:37 p.m. for a sick man on a Metrobus at 18th Street and Pennsylvania Avenue NW.

The rush-hour traffic on Pennsylvania Avenue was heavy. Manthos was sitting in the passenger seat up front and watching for vehicles on the right that Parker might not see. Parker was playing variations on the siren's basic scream, making changes— whoops, growls, undulations— by pushing a button on a box to the right of the driver's seat.

The Metrobus, a westbound No. 30, was parked by the curb. The passengers who had been standing in the aisle had moved out onto the sidewalk to wait for the situation to be taken care of.

Proximity— A man who appeared to be in his 20s had collapsed between two seats. His feet were sticking out into the aisle. One arm was stuck between the end of the seat in front of him and the side of the bus.

Manthos examined him. It appeared to be another case of alcoholism. He asked the man to get up.

"Leave me alone, man," said the man on the floor. He began to curse Manthos. The people on the bus looked uncomfortable.

Manthos and Parker got the man to his feet. The man cursed and fought them. He refused to get off the bus or into the ambulance. Since the regulations say that the attendants can transport no one who refused their services, the two men began to leave. This caused some consternation among the passengers and the bus driver.

The problem again— "There's nothing we can do," explained Manthos. "If he doesn't want to go, we can't take him."

Several passengers protested that the least the firemen can do is take the man off the bus.

Manthos shook his head. "You ought to call the police," Manthos told the bus driver. "He ought to go to Detox."

A police scout car arrived, and the officer boarded the bus and asked the man to get off. The man started cursing and struggling with the policeman. The officer twisted his arm behind his back and forced him off the bus. Several passengers expressed disapproval.

The policeman pushed the man against the hood of his cruiser and patted him down to search for weapons. Then he put him in the back of the scout car, which had a wire screen separating the front and back seats.

Parker and Manthos got into No. 6 and headed for the fire station. A block from the bus, they got a radio call to return to the scene. Parker snapped on the lights and the siren and made a U-turn.

It was the policeman who had summoned them back.

"Listen," he said, leaning in the window on the driver's side. "What ambulance is this?"

"No. 6," said Manthos.

"OK," said the officer. "I need to know that and also, in your opinion, is this guy drunk?"

"To the best of my opinion he is drunk or coming off some kind of drug," Manthos said.

"OK," said the policeman. "I need to know that. Listen," he Detail— adds. "This guy scratched me. Do I need a tetanus shot for that? I don't know what this guy's got under his fingernails."

"You take him to Detox. They'll fix you up," said Parker. He turned the ambulance around and headed for 23d and M Streets NW and the station.

"You always get stuck in the middle," Manthos said later. "That's what I don't like about this job. You always get stuck in the middle and you can't win. When you can save somebody, then you feel pretty good, but this stuff. . . ."

Manthos, who had been a fireman for five years, said the eight weeks of training he received in first aid procedures before being assigned to the ambulances were excellent preparation for medical emergencies, but not for the other problems an attendant must face.

"I doubt that there's any way you could be prepared for it," he said. "You just have to do it."

Service on the 11 ambulances operated by the D.C. fire department is generally unpopular. Battalion Chief Joseph R. Shelton, 42, says it is necessary to "draft" men to do the work. So most firemen have to put in one year on the vehicles during their first five years on the department. Many who are doing it Typifying now can tell you the exact day when their year will be up.
the larger
topic— Part of the problem, said Shelton, is the number of "taxi runs" the men have to make. So far this year, the fire department ambulances have responded to more than 70,000 calls. By one city estimate that some fire officials think is conservative, 60 per cent of them have been "taxi runs."

A "taxi run" is one in which the patient might well be able to get to a hospital without an ambulance, one not involving an emergency such as a heart attack or a serious injury, or it is a run that should be handled by another city agency, such as the police department.

There is no way to screen the calls until the ambulance arrives on the scene. Even then, regulations say that the ambulance must take a patient to the hospital if that is what the patient wants.

Before they got back to the fire station from the bus incident, Parker and Manthos were off on a "sick woman" call to Vermont Avenue and 11th Street NW.

The woman, who is 23, was standing in front of her house supported by friends and relatives when the ambulance arrived. She was in obvious pain. The ambulance men asked the nature of the problem.

"She went to the doctor and he took her blood pressure and said she ought to go to the hospital," said a woman next to the patient.

Manthos and Parker put the woman on a stretcher and lifted her into the ambulance. The woman who had spoken about the trip to the doctor also got in. Whenever there is room, friends and relatives are welcome to ride to the hospital because they may be able to assist the patient and also provide pertinent information about sickness or injury.

"Where are you going to take her?" said the woman who was coming along.

"To Howard," said Parker.

"No you don't. No you don't, you're not going to take her to Howard," said the woman. "You take her to the Washington Hospital Center. I've been there and she'll be fine if you take her there."

"Howard is the closest hospital," said Parker.

Several bystanders loudly expressed the opinion that the woman should not go to Howard.

Manthos asked the accompanying woman who she was and she said that she was the patient's sister-in-law.

"OK," said Manthos, holding out a clipboard and a form to the woman. "You sign this here. This means you take responsibility if she dies on the way to the Hospital Center."

"That's all right," said the woman. She signed.

Four more calls followed, and about 11 p.m. Parker and Manthos were relieved by Pvt. John W. McDonald, 22, a veteran of 2½ years on the fire department who volunteered for ambulance service because life was too quiet in the firehouse where he was stationed, and Pvt. Robert S. Turner, 25, a five-year veteran who looks forward to reassignment in two months.

The first call for McDonald and Turner was to a high-rise apartment in the 2400 block of Virginia Avenue NW, near the Watergate. A 69-year-old man had suffered a seizure. A neighbor who is a physician was attending him when the attendants arrived. They loaded the patient into the ambulance and took him to George Washington.

They did not get back to the fire house, which is only three blocks from the hospital, before they got a radio call for a woman in the 1700 block of Lamont Street NW. The report said she had been bitten by a dog.

The problem again— Turner, who keeps a small unlit cigar in the corner of his mouth when not actually working, said he thought he recognized the address. Like Parker, he was acquainted with Edward, and his thought was that this was a similar case.

The woman resides in a first-floor apartment in the front of the building. The sounds of a television set came though the door, but the only response Turner got when he knocked was the barking of a dog.

So he went outside and climbed on a railing to look in the window.

A woman with her arm in a cast was sitting in an easy chair watching television. A small dog sat at her feet.

"I know her," said Turner. "We took her in when she broke the arm."

The woman was drinking what looked like a glass of whiskey. She refused to answer any of the knocks on her door or window, or Turner's shouts that the ambulance had arrived.

So the crew got back in the ambulance and drove away.

They made it back to the firehouse before they got the next call. It was for the White House. The dispatcher told them to go to the main gate on Pennsylvania Avenue and not to use the emergency lights or the siren. Since it was just after midnight, there was little traffic and they made the trip in a few minutes.

It turned out that a guest had been taken ill at a party President Ford gave in honor of Martha Graham, the great modern dance innovator. A White House doctor had treated her by the time the ambulance arrived and made arrangements for her to be admitted to George Washington.

A few minutes later, Turner and McDonald wheeled the patient out of the White House on their stretcher. She was accompanied by her daughter, who said the woman was 73, a resident of New York, and a friend of Martha Graham. The woman was frightened— what sudden illness in a strange city is not frightening?— and her daughter assured her that she would not die.

At George Washington, the patient was admitted. Her daughter asked Turner how much the ambulance service cost.

"Nothing, m'am," he said. "It's absolutely free. It's free for everyone."

"Well," said the woman, "this is certainly a well-run city. It's much better run than New York. But then, of course, it's the capital, and I suppose you would expect it to be well-run."

By 1 a.m., the ambulance was back in the fire house. Only seven of the fire department's 11 ambulances are kept in service after midnight. It was quieter, but in a way the night was young, for the time of despair —the hours between midnight and dawn—were just beginning.

At 1:41, No. 6 responded to a call for a man who had been hit in the face with a candle-holder in a nightclub on the "Georgetown Strip" along M Street NW. The man said he had no idea who had hit him or why. Turner and McDonald took him to Georgetown University Hospital.

At 2:27 a.m. there was a call to the 1100 block of 8th Street NW, a decaying street in the Shaw area. Police are reported to be on the scene. A woman is said to have been injured. At that hour, there was little need for the siren. Turner drove there quickly with only the emergency lights going.

A dozen people were standing on the sidewalk. It was difficult to see who the patient was. A man sat in the caged-in rear of a police squad car.

"She's the one," said a woman, indicating a 19-year-old girl standing with some friends. "He beat her."

Turner asked the girl what had happened.

"He beat me," she said. "He beat me with a frying pan."

Detail— "You ought to take me to the hospital," said the first woman. "I got hit with a baseball bat."

"Do you want to go to the hospital?" Turner asked.

"No."

"When did you get hurt?"

"Last summer," said the woman.

Turner continued to examine the 19-year-old. There were no cuts and she remained standing. He helped her into the ambulance.

The man in the back of the police car was pleading with her through the wire mesh covering the window.

"Baby, please don't make them take me to jail," he said. "Baby, please don't make them take me to jail."

On the front seat of the police cruiser lay a heavy iron skillet.

In the ambulance, the girl said the man was her boy friend and that he had just got out of jail.

"He thought I was running around," she said.

On the way to Howard University Hospital, No. 6 got a call for a man suffering from a "seizure" in an apartment in the 1100 block of 13th Street NW. This is roughly on the way to Howard, so the attendants decided to respond before taking the girl in.

They went to the sixth-floor apartment and knocked on the door. There was no answer. Turner knocked again and announced loudly, "Ambulance. Ambulance here."

There was another moment of silence and then a man's voice said angrily, "I'm coming, I'm coming. Wait a minute and I'll be there. I've got so much to do I can't get it all done at once."

Suddenly the door opened and there was a man in a wheelchair with his pants down around his ankles.

"Come in, come in," he said. "He's the one who needs to go to the hospital," he said, indicating another man sitting on a day bed.

The man on the bed looked surprised. "I don't need to go to the hospital," he said. "He does."

"Oh yes, of course I need to go to the hospital," said the man in the wheelchair. "Lord yes, of course I need to go to the hospital."

"Do you want to go to the hospital?" Turner asked.

"To Veterans' Hospital?" said the man.

"No, we're going to Howard," said Turner.

"Well, the only place I want to go is Veterans'," said the man.

Turner asked him what was the matter.

"Well, my stroke has been coming back on me," he said. "I think it's been coming back on me all day."

"We'll be glad to take you to the hospital," said Turner.

"When did you have your stroke?"

The problem again— "Three years ago. Maybe I'll go to the hospital tomorrow. I've got too much to do around here right now."

Later, on the way to another call, Turner suddenly swerved the ambulance, jammed on the brakes, got out and began chasing a youth who was being pursued by a policeman. McDonald joined the chase. The youth disappeared in an alley with Turner on his heels. He reappeared in a moment alone.

"I got about 10 feet from him and then he went into second gear and just disappeared," he said.

The policeman said he appreciated the effort. He said he thought the youth might be responsible for several recent burglaries in the area, which was near 4th and V Streets NW.

The last call of the night came in at 5:34. It was for an elderly woman in a high-rise in the 2400 block of Virginia Avenue NW. She had fallen and broken an ankle.

Turner and McDonald took her to George Washington. At the hospital, they noticed that Edward, the alcoholic, was no longer there. Turner asked a hospital clerk what had happened to him.

Coming full circle— "They took him to Detox," he reported as he came back to the ambulance.

3. Form

Grammar and diction

Architects must know how to design a structure that won't collapse before they concern themselves with making it beautiful. The same is true of writers. The rules of grammar are not pedantic restrictions but necessary aids in communicating meaning.

The net in tennis may be a nuisance, but it makes sense of the game.

So the serious craftsman will want to know where the commas should go. He will learn when to use "who" and "whom." He will master sentence structure.

An excellent source for this information is *The Elements of Style* by William Strunk Jr. and E.B. White (New York: Macmillan, 2nd Ed., 1972). This concise paperback distills matters of composition and usage down to 78 pertinent pages.

Two other books should always be at the writer's elbow: a dictionary and a thesaurus.

Larry Claflin, a sportswriter for the *Boston Herald American*, recalled his early days in a city room when he would casually call out from his desk for the spelling of a word. "I know, but I'm not telling you," his editor would growl. "There's the dictionary. Go use it."

At first Claflin couldn't understand why his mentor wouldn't simply spell the word for him. But then he realized the ritual of walking over and looking it up helped to cement the word in his memory — and instilled a life-long habit of doing his own homework.

Many writers are not great spellers, but they do not let that show in their work or leave it for the copy desk to clean up. If they are unsure about the number of *i*'s in "liaison" or *r*'s in "harass," they check.

The thesaurus can help a writer locate the exact word that eludes him or find a fresh one to put in the place of a word he has overused. This book should be used sparingly, however, to avoid jazzing up every other adjective with fancier language that will only sound artificial.

Such discipline is required of feature writers especially because newspapers and magazines are the last repositories of the English language. If the diction of the most widely-read printed media becomes sloppy and imprecise, so will that of readers learning by example. Syndicated columnist James J. Kilpatrick has articulated the high calling of the communicator:

> We of the print and broadcast journalism are custodians of the word. Long after the educators have done their job, for good or ill, we provide the conduits by which our language transmits understanding. If literacy, in the largest sense, is to be preserved, we are the ones who must preserve it. And we have a high obligation, too often subordinated, to write well, to speak clearly, to defend the best usage and not the slipshod usage, to serve as good and faithful stewards of the trust reposed in our profession. Such a trust must be lovingly cherished.

Truth badly stated does not communicate itself. It is useless, like the illegibly scrawled message of a seer.

Therefore a sentence should be composed with care. Ideas come at random, but they are given order by placing the words that stand for them on a page judiciously. Does an introductory subordinate clause clarify matters or clutter them? Does an appositive really add information or just pump up the prose? Does this or that phrasing make a difference?

Compare these three sentences:

His bag was hassling over not much.
The guy made a big deal out of his work, which wasn't heavy duty.
He seemed busier than he was.

Or these:

Dying, I'm running out of stuff to say.
What comes next I can't tell you, because small talk is tough when the old kidneys are giving out.
The rest is silence.

Or these:

I'll let you address me as somebody symbolic, from the Bible, like.
Truth to tell, my last name escapes me.
Call me Ishmael.

The last lines in each set are precise; the others are backchat (with apologies to Geoffrey Chaucer, William Shakespeare and Herman Melville).

Sentences are set down in distinct units of thought. A paragraph might be a single word—

Beans.

— or a pageful of sentences, but whatever it contains should be inseparable. One never indents without purpose. The following paragraph would be better broken down into smaller ones as marked to make the information in it coherent:

What does a fireman do when he isn't answering a call? [The trucks of Pumper Company One are washed daily, the wheels and wheel wells after every run. This is not done for cosmetic reasons but to prevent corrosion and make clear the condition of the tires. The air bottles must be pumped up, those vast tanks from which the smoke masks are filled. The hundreds of yards of hose, accordion-folded on the five-hundred-gallon pumper, must be changed regularly to keep the rubber from cracking. Paper work, including maintenance and run reports, makes its daily bureaucratic demand, and there are one thousand area fire plugs that must be checked biweekly. [Fire inspections are constant. [Much time is spent on drill and the methodology of firefighting. A fireman knows one gallon of gasoline has the destructive capacity of fourteen sticks of dynamite. He knows that the fumes from burning vinyl are lethal, that a stairwell acts as a natural chimney, and that a man can bleed to death in less than one minute. ["If you see a fireman cutting a hole in the roof of a burning building with a power saw, it doesn't mean he's taken leave of his senses," Captain Clarence Vastine said. "He's relieving the pressure of superheated air so the others can work inside. The extremely high temperatures of a working fire require ventilation."

Huge unbroken paragraphs rush over readers like waves of heavy traffic. More manageable paragraphing enables a reader to follow the line of thought from one idea to the next. Variety in paragraph length helps to set up a prose rhythm. Notice how the paragraph construction in the following passage picks up the pace and sustains it:

> Patrolman Tom Schoenecker spots a green 1965 Chevy II with a red front right fender at 19th and Russell Streets. The car is registered to a walkaway from work-release. Its driver is a blond wooly-headed 20-year-old who stares straight ahead; beside him is another youth in a tassel cap who does the same.
>
> Schoenecker circles the block and comes up behind the car, blue lights and spotlight shining right into the Chevy's rear-view. The Chevy runs a stop sign and Schoenecker hits the siren.
>
> "We got a chase," he says.
>
> The Chevy climbs the long hill to Ida Spence Project flat out and fishtailing in the chill evening rain. Schoenecker keeps his squad car just inches from the back bumper of the Chevy. He reaches a hand out before the German shepherd in back, snapping his fingers in a quick rhythm.
>
> "Let's go, Vonner," he says, readying him for a run. *"Let's go, boy."*
>
> The Chevy careens left at Alden Court and roars past the rows of shrubless project houses. The paving ends at a 10-foot drop to a grassy clearing in the woods below, but the Chevy does not stop, gunning the engine at the edge.
>
> It sails out airborne like a stunt vehicle in a Don Siegal film. Schoenecker stops the squad car at the brink and throws open his door and Von's.
>
> The Chevy lands axle-deep in mud. The wooly-headed youth makes for the woods on the left; the one with the tassel cap sprints right.
>
> Schoenecker and Von start down the hill at a dead run.
>
> All four disappear into the trees. A crowd gathers, mostly kids. "He's got the dog on him!" breathes one. After a long time the crowd begins to pull back from the tree line.
>
> *"Here comes the dog."*

Vigorous prose rises and falls like human breathing. It can't huff on forever at high speed or it will carry a breathless quality; nor can it long survive at a soft sustained sigh.

Short single-sentence paragraphs following longer ones carry a sense of emphasis, like this:

> At 6:30 in the morning Covington Chief of Detective Jess Sanders stood at the booking desk in a ski coat and hunting jacket paging through a criss-cross directory as his men drew shotguns and flak jackets.
> "It looks like a whopper," he said.

Or this:

> "They work like maggots in these alleys," observes night watch lieutenant Jim Summers as he prowls the brick backroads of Covington. There are repaired pry marks on the windows, new padlocks on the doors. Twice Summers breaks up packs of kids like fugitives from *Oliver Twist*, their eyes all innocence and their probation records pat. "Head home," advises Summers, and they split.
> But they gather again.

Since one-line paragraphs are emphatic, too many strung together lose their effect and create the dull repetitive quality of a military drumbeat. These sentences could better be incorporated in one complete paragraph:

> For five years Fire Department Master Mechanic Bill Glindmeyer was the tillerman on an aerial truck.
> That's the man who steers the hind end of a hook-and-ladder, an individual who might be compared to a determined flea at the tip of a fiercely-wagging tail.
> In those days there was no radio communication as there is now between the tiller and the cab of the truck.
> All Glindmeyer had to warn the driver of trouble was a panic button that lit a small red light in front.

A writer, then, embarks on his labor with deliberation. Like any reliable carpenter, the wordsmith is always in complete command of his equipment. He never sets pen to paper casually. The words suit, the sentences scan, the paragraphs convey sense each one to the next.

Season, but don't overspice

Literary folk love language. They love the flexibility of it, the endless ease with which it expresses itself in fresh and startling ways. Someone centuries back was confronted with a flower. Having the soul of a poet, that individual called it the "day's eye" or *daisy* because the daily bright yellow opening and closing of it reminded him of the sun. That endlessly allusive vision does not restrict itself to poets but to anyone with a lively sense of wordplay. Street slang comes from the same impulse — thus we get "sneeze" for cocaine and "rainy-day woman" for marijuana cigarette.

Because of this love of language, writers avoid repeating expressions that have gone stale from overuse. Including cliches in your writing is like furnishing a new house with the worn overstuffed creak-all from some dead doctor's waiting room. Good writers do not *buck up, knuckle down* or *freak out*. They do not *comment on the human condition* or *provide penetrating insights into the contemporary scene*. And above all, oh above all, they most emphatically do not *Tell It Like It Is.*

Only broadcasters do these things.

"Make it new," urged Ezra Pound. If you want to salt your material with figures of speech, create your own. This facility comes through practice; start looking at the world in terms of how you would describe it. Associate what you see with vivid verbal images.

Similes and metaphors sharpen the senses. By revealing striking similarities between seemingly unlike things, figurative language makes the ordinary interesting. A spare garrison soldier has the keen carven face of a caged hawk. A dimestore Santa sports a spun-glass beard. A smirking talk show host has dimples deep enough to drop a marble in.

Silent senior citizens sit in a nursing home day room like chessmen between moves. The lime green dial of a radar scanner glows like a large luminescent watchface. Badly cropped hair sprouts like chopped alfalfa.

A tight grin glints like the cutting edge of a slowly unsheathed knife. . . .

Obviously, overdoing this sort of thing can work like too much hot pepper in the pot. The grub won't be dull, but it won't be edible, either. Work first for clarity, then for an occasional dash of color; figurative language should be used with restraint.

Too, it is possible for an overly picky grammarian to make vigorous prose stiff. One should know the rules, and one should know when to break them *for good reason*. The accomplished impressionist only experiments *after* he is able to paint a classical cow.

The story is told of Winston Churchill, whose lancer's grasp of the English language is evidenced in the many histories he wrote and in speeches that, though often overblown, were filled with powerful phrases like "blood, toil, tears and sweat," "Iron Curtain," and "fighting on the beaches." Churchill well knew how to construct a sentence. One day a speech he sent to the Foreign Office for clearance was returned to him annotated by an overzealous copyeditor. Across this earnest creature's marginal insistence that a sentence shouldn't end with a preposition, Churchill scrawled angrily: *"This is the kind of arrant pedantry with which I will not up with put!"*

When a sentence makes more sense or seems more effective ended with a preposition, go ahead and end it that way. Language is a changing, pliant thing. You might even— with caution— use that most dreaded of English department demons, the Sentence Fragment.

Like this.

Arrangement of detail

Carefully observed detail, we have argued, makes writing real. It can be informational—

> Rescue One driver Jim M.D. Reed ran the infant through the bat-wing emergency entrance doors and designated a Code Blue, the alert call when a life support system stops.

physical—

> The apartment was a spartan single room with a small uncluttered kitchen. A short black baseball bat stood within easy reach at the entry; near the stove was a gallon can of roach killer.

or human—

> Patrolman Ray Hood sat at a typewriter taking down information from a woman about to be photographed for the mug file. Arrested for "theft by unlawful taking," the large-boned lady responded blandly, like a job applicant; when she stood before the big tripoded cable-release Graphic camera with her name around her neck, she mechanically put a hand to her hair.

and for a strong effect the most specific item should be saved for the end.

At the site of the shooting, street kids told a garbled story of a man shot and picked up by another car. "The dude was hurtin'," said one. "He fired four rounds in the air before he cut out." A pile of packing boxes behind the Modern Furniture Co., 513 Madison, disclosed a pool of blood slowly turning pink in the rain.

Sometimes, however, more than the single detail presents itself. A writer must choose with care the order in which each item is set down.

Control is the key; nothing is done well at random.

An impression can be conveyed by juxtaposing selected details. The consequence can be irony—

There is a Bible on the wall shelf of the doctor's Constance Road office, right next to a box of instruction leaflets on how to apply for Blue Cross. A sign by the receptionist's desk reads: "Please, No Credit— Pay Up Old Accounts to Date."

pathos—

The two life squad men are waved to the west complex and wheel in a stretcher. On the ninth floor an old man has become disoriented. His voice is brittle, the result of throat cancer. As he reluctantly agrees to go to the hospital, he insists on taking his cigarettes with him.

or laughter—

The senator drew himself up to his full salmon-suited, sartorially immaculate height and opened his mouth to speak. A sudden gust of wind caught the fine hair he had combed so carefully across the top of his head and lifted it from the bald spot like a lid off a lard can.

In each case the placement of details is crucial to the effect.

When you have a complex subject to describe, the arrangement of detail can be suggested by the shape of the material. Suppose, for example, you are dealing with a skyscraper. Details might be placed in vertical order to emphasize the height of the building. Begin at the base with the floodlit crowd of people looking up, move floor by floor to the high pinnacle of the observation tower, and cap the picture with the topmost thing— an ape swinging at airplanes with a girl in his fist.

Horizontal subjects would suggest a horizontal approach. You might move left to right, from a sleepy midsummer outfielder with a straw in his mouth to second base across the open grass, past the pitcher to the blurred arms of the batsman making mighty contact with the ball. Or you might move right to left, from the startled pianist in a Tucson saloon, to the silent figures one by one along the bar, to the hell-bent honcho standing behind a scattergun at the entry.

You might even provide a moving point of view, ticking off the sensations, rattle and engine roar experienced from the jumpseat of a jeep hurtling flat out over Massachusetts moors.

In any case, you must organize to present an ordered vision. Even apparent chaos can be controlled by *imposing* an arrangement:

> Bespectacled Service Bureau Cdr. Art Heeger bore the look of a scholar literally surrounded by his work. At his left hand was the neutron activator analysis kit which could show whether or not a suspect fired a gun. Before him on the desk were two .22-calibre suicide pistols with bullets attached in plastic evidence envelopes and an aerial photo of the lake from which a shotgun had been recovered in the Gloria Eglian murder case. To his right, propped on a filing cabinet, rested a dual fingerprint blowup marked with seven identifying points of similarlity. Behind him shone the twin eyepieces of a comparison microscope and, in a corner, rose tier on tier of tagged brown paper bags containing hair samples, firebomb bottles and seized narcotics.

This way the reader sees what you see, not a jumbled vision. When you are contrasting two subjects, the organization of detail becomes more complex — and more necessary. To avoid confusing the reader, both subjects should be broken down into manageable parts, and those parts should be approached *in order*. Whatever order you choose, your structure should move from one subject to the other with the logical rhythm of a game of pitch and catch.

Here is an example of organizing the comparison for effect from a 1972 *News Record* editorial. Note the consistent reference to one subject, then the other, straight through to the end for sheer dramatic effect:

> The finest living American writer, never a reluctant witness, roared and waved his arms before the cameras of a talk show. The finest living Russian writer, unused to personal display, sat in his wife's apartment over a glass of berry juice, talking with two

reporters. The medium was the message. Millions of Americans watched Norman Mailer on network television with alternating emotions of boredom and embarrassment; Alexander Solzhenitsyn was overheard by only a handful of Russians, quietly attentive under headsets that picked up the signals from concealed electronic devices in the room.

The contrast is revelatory. Both men had been considered for the Nobel Prize, at worst a literary Oscar, at best some measure of the esteem in which the world held their work, and the achievement of each lay in an evocation of evaluative protest. Mailer had plumbed the psychic pool of American institutions in *Armies of the Night* and *Of a Fire on the Moon;* Solzhenitsyn had cast a cold eye on the Soviet bureaucratic machine in *The First Circle* and *Cancer Ward*. But one man was absolved of his public responsibility because of his success, while the other has been made the victim to it.

Mailer was talking about the onus of his own reputation. Solzhenitsyn was talking about increasing official pressure against him in the Soviet Union. In the first major interview ever granted Western journalists, Solzhenitsyn last week spoke of a slander compaign loose in the USSR to brand him pro-Nazi (he was thrice decorated for bravery as an artilleryman for the Soviets in World War II). This, coupled with calculated harassment of his family and friends by the secret police, could be preliminary to public trial for treason. Every word Solzhenitsyn writes carries implications of arrest — and in Russia this can lead to forced confinement in a mental hospital, all creative forces sapped by "curative" drugs. If the writer's hell is a white cubicle unfurnished with ideas, Solzhenitsyn already finds himself locked in a gray purgatorial anteroom.

Mailer lost the Nobel prize and Solzhenitsyn won it, and one cannot help but reflect the nature of their respective protests had a hand in the results. Despite popular cries of encroaching fascism and the pressures of public opprobrium, it is relatively easy to protest in America, so easy the protestor is often made a flamboyant folk hero *a la* Abbie Hoffman or Bella Abzug, and the issue becomes buried in a cult of personality where personal cool on *Meet the Press* matters more than the answers. Mailer crossed the troop line at the Pentagon march in Washington, spent the night in jail and got a lot of mileage off it in print. When Solzhenitsyn recently turned up at the funeral of a discredited friend and made the sign of the cross at his graveside, he was risking a good deal more; the labor camps of Russia are metaphysical miles from the District cooler.

Protest in America has become easy precisely because it risks so little, and the leaders have become spokesmen for themselves. Solzhenitsyn, a spokesman for nobody, talks little and writes much — and well. Predictably, a scheduled ceremony to award Solzhenitsyn the Nobel Prize was called off— again— in the wake of his interview.

Meanwhile Mailer makes movies starring himself and talks of some natural inheritance of a literary title from Hemingway. It tells as much about the state of art in America as Solzhenitsyn's predicament reveals of what has happened to it in Russia. Mailer wants very badly to be Champ, and Solzhenitsyn wants to be published in his own country.

Here we are beginning to move beyond matters of arrangement of detail to the larger issue of structuring an entire story.

Construction and unity

Before you write a story, you must draw up a design for it that will best suit your intention. Just as each sentence should be crafted with care, and each paragraph, so must the larger whole. Design separates the professional feature writer from the average letter writer who tells a story less effectively as it comes to him.

First cover the assignment as thoroughly as you can. You should ideally come away with *too much* material; this will afford you sufficient incident and detail to choose from. You won't automatically use all of it. You are not trying to prove you did a lot of legwork. Rather you are out to make the essentials of the piece as concrete as possible.

Thin research will make for a thin story. You won't have enough, so you will be driven to include your weakest material, which from a richer store would have been quickly cast aside.

As in description, let the shape of your material suggest the form of the story. This is why it is so important not to preconceive a story— you may wind up insisting on a beach house where a chalet should be. The individual or event or institution you are examining will reveal scenes and themes that will cry out to be emphasized. Like Michaelangelo, who claimed to see his sculpture implicit in the original stone, you are seeking out a pattern in your notes that will give shape to your observations for the reader.

Let's examine the "jinx race" story at the end of chapter one. I went to the track to do a jockey story. But at the end of the evening, when Bright Blend broke her leg in the sixth race, I knew that had to be the key incident of the piece. It had drama and pathos, where the rest of the material had only color.

I had been getting all the information I could that night, which is how I knew details like the names of the officials and how many volts go through an electric starting gate. I watched races from trackside at the finish line to be as close as I could to the sensations of horse racing. I stuck equally close to jockey Jim McKnight, short of getting on a horse with him.

I noted times and movements — I had some vague idea that if McKnight won a race I could focus on that, which meant *every* race had to be carefully logged in.

When Bright Blend went down I headed upfield with the trainer. I talked to the jockey who rode her and drove out to where the horse's body had been abandoned.

All this went down in my notebook.

Now notice what came out of it. I didn't want to ignore McKnight— he'd won the next race. So I used his success as a contrast to the fate of the animal. Using a chronological time order from just before the sixth race to just after it, I alternated my attention very deliberately between the two subjects, like this:

Set-up First graph: the contrast.

Second graph: McKnight before race.

Third graph: Bright Blend before race.

Graphs 4-7: McKnight's earlier prophecy— *irony.*

Graph 8: McKnight & Bright Blend on way to race.

Graph 9: McKnight & Bright Blend mounted.

Graphs 10, 11: the track— *more irony.*

Key scene Graphs 12-16: the race up to the disaster.

Outcome Graph 17: Bright Blend fallen, McKnight at finish.

Graphs 18-23: the injured horse.

Graph 24: the victorious jockey.

Graph 25: McKnight's "luck"—*final irony.*

Graph 26: Bright Blend's "luck."
Graph 27: delight of McKnight.
Graphs 28, 29: regret of Bright Blend's trainer.

The result is a unified piece with a distinct beginning, middle and end. The events determined the emphasis for me. I simply perceived the pattern in what happened and imposed it on the page.

Graphs four through seven, ten and 11 are what novelist-reporter Robert Ruark termed "nosepickers," digressions that add information and vary the rhythm of the piece.

There are as many forms as there are stories. The material will always tell the writer which one to pick. I was once assigned a feature story on what graveyard-shift working people were up to after midnight while the rest of us slept. I spent several nights cruising the city, looking for lights to tell me who was up, and that eventually revealed the form to me.

I began the story with the sun going down and the city starting to light up like a circuit board as people drove home from work over the Brent Spence and Clay Wade Bailey bridges that span the Ohio River. Then, from the score of interviews I made, I selected one job for each hour from midnight to eight a.m. — security guards, firehouse dispatchers, truckers, coffee shop waitresses, cops. I began each section with the identifying beacon each one worked by — a neon sign above a doughnut dinette, the white glow from a control tower, running lights on a ferryboat.

I included nosepickers like this:

Coffee is the eventide adhesive of the night people. It glues them inextricably to their work and each other, and their instinctive gesture to the stranger is to share a cup of it, including him in that quiet insomniac fraternity that sleeps the day shift and never quite gains the rest sunsiders do. In the main they like it black, and anybody who mentions Sanka marks himself an outsider for sure.

I finished the piece with a disc jockey watching the sun come up on the same bridges as day folk drove to work past the now homeward-bound night people.

This unifying device of coming full circle is the same organizational method J.Y. Smith employed in his ambulance article at the end of chapter two. He begins in action in the middle of a run. The rescue squad team is dealing with "Edward," a "regular" who they immediately recommend should be taken to a detoxification center for alcoholics to dry out. The story then moves to a second incident concerning a man the team feels should go to the same place. The end returns us again to Edward, gone at last to his inevitable destination. Smith is not forcing a unity on his story that doesn't exist. Rather his form makes explicit his message, which occurs as a nosepicker after the second rescue run:

> Service on the 11 ambulances operated by the D.C. fire department is generally unpopular. Battalion Chief Joseph R. Shelton, 42, says it is necessary to "draft" men to do the work. So most firemen have to put in one year on the vehicles during their first five years on the department. Many who are doing it now can tell you the exact day when their year will be up.
>
> Part of the problem, said Shelton, is the number of "taxi runs" the men have to make. So far this year, the fire department ambulances have responded to more than 70,000 calls. By one city estimate that some fire officials think is conservative, 60 per cent of them have been "taxi runs."

The core of the story is the preponderance of Washington misuse of its fire department service, so Smith emphasizes that in his structure.

Smith provides evidence first, however, and only then offers an interpretation of it. Have a point; save the sermon. Each article should have a clear direction, but as we indicated earlier the reader does not like to be patronized, nor does he want to be preached at. The congregation tends to nod during the long prayer. So engage your audience first; then, when they're caught by the concrete substance of the story, flash the Tablets and get straight back to the action.

The feature writer attempts to tell truths which, like most curative medicine, are unpleasant to the taste, so he surrounds those truths with formal coatings of good writing and dramatic content that get the pill down where it can do its work. To properly instruct one must first amuse.

Style

"I've always believed," said political cartoonist Bill Mauldin, "screw style. Make the best picture you can."

Beginning writers worry about finding their own individual voices. The way to start is to work through someone else's. "Play the sedulous ape," Robert Louis Stevenson counseled; study the masters and imitate them. But remember, at length you must break with your influences. Otherwise you will always be second-rate, standing forever in the shadow of the writer's work you most admire.

True style is functional. If you filmed an Olympic runner's stride and ran the sequence back at slow motion, you would discover no excess movement, no unnecessary gesture that does not contribute to the graceful forward motion. Achieving an individual voice is more a paring away of spare parts than adding fancy mannerisms. Compare these lines:

> *Oh, wow. What is life? What is death? Heavy thoughts, henchfolk.*
> *Mindsnap: I'm mulling it over.*

with these:

> *To be or not to be. That is the question.*

Style is too often equated with literary flamboyance. In truth, the essence of good style is clarity.

Overembroidery for the sake of decoration comes off like so many doilies in a display window. Only an amateur resorts to self-conscious elegance. "The artist," observed Robert Frost, "has to grow up and coarsen a little before he looks on texture not as an end in itself."

The story should come first.

I remember sitting over a typewriter in the city room one day just before deadline, my face a mile long. Metropolitan editor Jerry Samuelson looked up from her desk.

"What's wrong?" she asked me.

"This story." I shook my head. "I'm not good enough for the material. The stuff is dynamite. I don't know how to write it."

"Just start at the beginning and tell it as plainly as you can," she said.

I cranked in copy paper and concentrated on saying the thing as simply as I could, no rhetoric, no frills, no reaching.

It made front page.

Keeping the "I" out

In every one of his films, Alfred Hitchcock shows up briefly. The director will be off in the background boarding a bus, or waiting by a phone booth, or hailing a cab.

He does not stand dead square in front of the camera for the whole picture.

The same should be true of a writer. Some egocentric scribes just can't seem to prevent themselves from popping in and out of their copy like "Tennis, anyone?" types in old midcentury melodramas. They interpose themselves between the reader and the subject, setting up a picket fence of I's across their page.

Stay out of the story unless you affect it in some crucial way. Keep your eye on the material, not the mirror.

Let's look for a moment at some famous examples of stories in which the reporter was legitimately inextricable from his material.

Henry Morton Stanley was sent by the *New York Herald* in 1869 to find David Livingstone, a Scottish explorer-missionary who had disappeared three years before on an African expedition in search of the source of the Nile. Stanley went from Zanzibar deep into the Dark Continent. After many long months of ruthless effort and jungle fever, Stanley found the doctor among the natives of Ujiji to produce one of the most famous encounters in journalism:

> There is a group of the most respectable Arabs, and as I come nearer I see the white face of an old man among them. He has a cap with a gold band around it, his dress is a short jacket of red blanket cloth, and his pants— well, I didn't observe. I am shaking hands with him. We raise our hats, and I say:
> "Dr. Livingstone, I presume?"
> And he says, "Yes."

The story concerns Stanley's search— he belongs in it.

Louis "Lepke" Buchalter was a mob war lord in the 1930s who terrorized New York businesses and exterminated 60 to 80 men with the highly efficient criminal machine called "Murder, Inc." At length he was arrested for fur industry racketeering. Instantly freed on bond by a crooked judge, Buchalter jumped bail.

A massive statewide manhunt ensued. Fifty thousand dollars in reward money from city officials and the FBI rode on his capture. Matters grew warmer than somewhat for "Little Louis," and he decided to surrender— but he didn't want to go out like Dillinger, who had retired under a hail of federal bullets five years before. He contacted famed newsman Walter Winchell, who was to arrange things with J. Edgar Hoover himself. At one point in the negotiations Hoover blew up. Wrote Winchell in the *New York Daily Mirror,* August 26, 1939:

> "This is a lot of bunk, Walter. You are being made a fool of and so are we. If you contact those people again, tell them the time limit is up! I will instruct my agents to shoot Lepke on sight."

But Winchell picked up the short fat killer and delivered him safely, a reportorial coup and a public service. Buchalter went to the chair and Winchell to the annals of journalistic notoriety. The point is that the story had to center on Winchell's maneuverings. The drama would be missing without his personal presence. So he wrote himself in, successfully.

But William Howard Russell, reporting the Battle of Bull Run for the London *Times,* sticks himself in at the outset to the detriment of his yarn:

> July 22, 1861 — I sit down to give an account— not of the action yesterday, but of what I saw with my own eyes, hitherto not often deceived, and of what I heard with my own ears, which in this country are not so much to be trusted. Let me, however, express an opinion as to the affair of yesterday. In the first place, the repulse of the Federalists, decided as it was, might have had no serious effects whatever beyond the mere failure— which politically was of greater consequence than it was in a military sense — but for the disgraceful conduct of the troops. The retreat on their lines at Centerville seems to have ended in a cowardly rout— a miserable, causeless, panic. Such scandalous behavior on the part of soldiers I should have considered impossible, as with some experience of camps and armies I have never even in alarms among camp followers seen the like of it.

Russell was a courageous man who got himself in a lot of trouble for telling the truth about martial matters in an era when that wasn't fashionable. Still the excess in his stuff is instructive. The story is not Russell "sitting down to give an account" but the mad retreat of the Union forces. He offers us the conclusions of his "undeceived eyes" immediately instead of looking through them for us first. The story would have been better cut to begin with a later graph that reveals it all without Russell's bluff presence:

"Turn back! Retreat!" shouted the men from the front, "we're whipped, we're whipped!" They cursed and tugged at the horses' heads and struggled with frenzy to get past. . . .

Writers who recount events sometimes need reminding that they are historians, not autobiographers.

An examination of a dying gunfighter seems an unlikely occasion for authorial intrusion, but the following piece shows what can happen when a writer insists on his own presence where it doesn't belong:

I went to Tombstone looking for a man, but I really didn't expect to find him there. After all, he'd been dead for 83 years. What I did expect to find was something of the substance of him, some ghost-memory separable from legend and attainable through a kind of triangulation in time. For I was convinced that the psychic key to Doc Holliday was key as well to the thing that was the matter with America. He was a clue: in his violent doomed sense of dignity and stubborn self-destruction, Holliday approached archetype.

The town was holding back. It seemed hardly large enough to hold its own history. When "Red Ed" Shieffelin struck silver there in 1877 Tombstone exploded into existence; by 1881 there were 10,000 people in it, and the daily output of ore exceeded $50,000 a day. A apir of boots went for better than $30; overalls were only five. The golden bar and sideboards in the Oriental Saloon and Gambling Hall had been shipped out all the way from San Francisco. The business district boasted of real gas lighting instead of oil. Copies of the great masters hung in Tom Corrigan's Alhambra card parlor. It hadn't lasted.

In 1970 the false fronts had been painted up and nailed together a bit, and yes, one had to pay to get into every one of them, but too many of the markers were in the wrong places. The wooden crosses on Boot Hill were metal now. There was an ice cream stand where the Wells-Fargo office had been, and the Bird Cage Theater — were vaudevillian Eddie Foy had once dodged bullets onstage — now sold souvenirs and cactus candy. Pastelled and prettied up, Tombstone was an aging whore come unwisely out of retirement.

The clincher was the O.K. Corral. The story had it that this was where the Earps and Holliday shot it out with the Clanton gang one warm October morning in 1881. It was nothing more than an open lot, boarded over on all sides like everything else so one had to pay to take a look. Life-size dummies had been set up as surrogate gunfighters, but the dummies were falling apart; one of Holliday's hands was missing. Irony invested itself in that.

For if there had been anything beautiful about Holliday at all, it lay in his hands. They were the nexus between his high-born eastern past and the western outlawry later. He had been good with them as a boy on the plantation, better later at dental school in Baltimore. Those who knew him said they had a life of their own: they were the hands of a surgeon, a musician. Later they would be what Holliday had to fall back on, and they became the hands of a card sharp and killer. The tools were the same; the skills were not.

The change had to do with the war, that aborted, botched amalgam of ideals and venality. Holliday had watched Atlanta burn from the steps of his house, but it was not the demolition of an era alone that drove him off; the unbalanced starvation diets of the southern young during the war years and after left him, along with many others, victim to advanced tuberculosis. He'd already opened a practice when they told him he had a year to live; that had been when he was twenty-one, and he learned quickly the market was slim for a coughing dentist. He went west for his health.

Holliday's vocabulary and manner remained impeccable. There were occasions when he discouraged editors from printing reports of shootings done in establishments of his choosing on the grounds that he was opposed to sensational literature. He once chivalrously prevented complaints about the food at Nellie Cushman's boarding house by blazing away under the table. But there was bitterness beneath the panache. His hands had given him a trade: dealing on the gambler's circuit was a system of outcheating the other and outshooting him after, and be certain the doctor did both. His first killing seems to have taken place during a racial encounter at a swimming hole in Georgia; after that altercations over the cards came often. They were encouraged. For if Bat Masterson attested "he was afraid of nothing on earth," yet there remained a dread elsewhere: every time the cough doubled him over, Holliday saw Death laughing up at him from out of his handkerchief. There were easier ways to die.

Liquor, quarts of it, held him together; that and the climate took him past his diagnosed time and carried him on more than a decade longer. Incursions into the underworld led to the strange friendship with another gambler named Wyatt Earp who, in the company of his brothers, ran a gang around Tombstone and environs. Earp was a sometime constable who owned the land on which Dutch Annie built her house of prostitution. Brother Virgil, as deputy marshal, had the major responsibility of inspecting the town brothels. The others assisted with enough enthusiasm to earn them local fame as "The Fighting Pimps."

None of this was evident in the plasterboard Tombstone of 1970. Mined out, with dead shafts sealed away under the town, there was still money to be made there. Holliday burned white-hot in a self-consuming flame of whiskey and TB until he became history at the O.K. Corral behind the barrels of a shotgun. Research suggests the battle was less gunfight than execution; the autopsy revealed wounds on the Clantons had been taken under the arms with the hands in the air. But once a year during Helldorado days, the city historians live another version — four men in frock coats moving down Front Street, mock holy war to the whine of blanks and movie cameras.

No, Holliday was not to be found there, and what is left of him hides among the pages of old books and forgotten records. He was in and out of clinics in his last years. Wyatt and the dancing girl Earp deserted his second wife for visited him in a sanatorium in Denver once; it would be interesting to read an account of that meeting, but none exists. Holliday later wound up in Glenville Springs, Colorado, lured by an advertised "sulfur vapor" cure that finally finished him. There is an account of his passing, and one wonders if Holliday wasn't possessed of some prescience of his place in future folklore. When he came out of the coma for the last time he asked for straight whiskey and tossed it back. He handed back the glass; "This is funny," he said, and died. He was 35.

The man remains an enigma, the lapsed existential aristocrat who went down the drain on his own terms. But the enigma widens. He once claimed conscience was something he had coughed up with his lungs; yet the evidence is that Holliday maintained steady contact with a single correspondent through all the desert years that passed between Baltimore and Glenwood Springs. That correspondent was a Sister of Charity in an Atlanta convent, and the letters have been lost.

This story would have been improved had the writer cut the first paragraph altogether, eliminating the references to himself and his symbolic ambitions. If a story has any symbolic significance, it will be manifest in the material; calling attention to it is an expression of insecurity, like the canned laugh track in a comedy.

Avoiding the ego trip of inserting yourself in the story may not only improve the impact, it may even carry the point. In the fall of 1974 the corpse of a murdered woman was found beyond the floodwall on the Kentucky side of the Ohio River. Gloria Eglian had been a lively woman who liked to shoot pool and take her children to amusement parks; lately she had been separated from her husband. I located Douglas Eglian and found him strangely effusive; at length he even agreed to include me on a hunt for his wife's killer. The crime had been a particularly cold-blooded one. Mrs. Eglian had been hit at point-blank range by four blasts from a shotgun; the x-rays the coroner showed me made her chest look like a cheese grater. Douglas Eglian was the prime suspect. The hunt was a charade, of course, and I knew it; he was using me as a mirror to put him in a favorable light. I wrote the story in such a way as to put the reader in my place — the idea was to reveal the hollowness of the whole business without commenting on it.

The official investigation of the shotgun murder of Gloria Eglian was on hold Friday, but an unofficial one continued.

Covington Detective Lieutenant Robert Robertson, in charge of the case, was off duty, and his partner, Detective Paul Herzog of the commonwealth attorney's office, was home sick.

"They haven't got one damned clue," said Douglas Eglian, 3827 Autumn Lane, Elsmere, estranged husband of the murdered woman. "I've been doing some looking around of my own."

It was 11 o'clock Friday night. Eglian sat at home waiting for his niece, Bonnie Floyd, 18, to arrive back from her duties as a nightshift nurse's aide for the St. Charles Nursing Home at Kyles Lane and Sanitorium Road, Covington. In her absence he was looking after his two children, Barbara Ann, 11, and Douglas Lester Jr., 8, and Miss Floyd's daughter Rachel, 1. When Miss Floyd returned Eglian would leave on his private midnight search for the killer.

"I got one friend out hunting around right now," Eglian said. "His name is Tommy. He's a crook. He's not a rough crook, not a robber or anything, but he knows his way around. He knows the area where Gloria was killed."

Eglian indicated "Tommy" made money hauling untaxed whiskey across state lines.

"He's been hanging around the Was Riverview, listening. He says somebody's been down there telling some lies about me. I plan to meet him down there tonight and do some listening myself."

The Was Riverview Cafe, 802 W. 2nd St., Covington, had been frequented by Gloria Eglian before her death. Her body had been found only a hundred yards from there, under a powerline tower behind the floodwall across the street.

As John Wayne in a jeep rode after a rhino on the television, Barbara Ann labored over long division at the kitchen table. Douglas Lester Jr., who said he wanted to be a writer, was getting his start beside her practicing the cursive alphabet. Little Rachel sat on the floor ripping the bottom out of a cornflakes box.

"Bonnie made a mistake a couple of years ago," Eglian said. "For a long time Gloria thought I was Rachel's father. I wasn't. Bonnie wouldn't tell me who he was, because she was afraid I'd go after him and get him to marry her.

"I was giving Bonnie a lot of attention. She needed it. She's been going through hell. Gloria resented that.

"Gloria gave me the cold shoulder for years. We didn't sleep together. She'd sleep on the couch with one of the kids.

"So now I'm the number-one suspect. Well, I want the one that killed Gloria caught. I want the cops off my back."

Eglian said that he had been up all hours lately looking at the case from every angle, sifting his memory.

"I'm waiting for that autopsy report to come back," Eglian said. "If Gloria was sexually assaulted, that's going to give us some answers right there."

(Col. Jesse Sanders, chief of detectives, indicated that the autopsy report was still not in the hands of the Detective Bureau. Nor was the Kettering Lab report on the results of a police sweep of Eglian's car.)

"Detective Robertson is all right, he's just doing his job. But I don't like Mousey, never did."

Eglian was referring to Detective Paul Herzog, whom he had known for some years.

"And he don't like me, either," Eglian said. "We used to fight all the time. I won some and I lost some."

Eglian, 43, a stocky man, stood up and stretched. He wore a tee shirt which exposed a tattoo of a knife on his left forearm and the same tattoo on the right, dripping blood.

"I'm going to change my appearance so they won't recognize me down at that bar," he said, and left to clean up.

Barbara Ann recalled a phone call her mother had received before her death. The caller had been a man. Mrs. Eglian had told Barbara Ann not to mention the call to her father.

The children were rounded up for bed. Eglian kissed Barbara Ann goodnight and gave Douglas Lester Jr. his 10 handshakes. Rachel, who would not sleep until her mother returned, pulled toys from a box by the TV. When Eglian returned his face shone from a fresh shave and he wore a brown $50 sport coat and an open-necked shirt.

"This ought to do it," he said. He ate part of a stick of butter to coat his stomach against the beer he would be buying later.

Miss Floyd, a slim, red-haired woman, returned with a friend to keep her company in Eglian's absence. Eglian reminded them to answer only his code knock. He drove out in his red four-door 1970 Chevrolet Impala, the same car earlier impounded by police. A pocket watch hung from the rear-view mirror like a ticking pendulum.

"I always start out with the lights off," Eglian said. "Since all this happened I don't want anyone to know where I'm headed."

Eglian explained his reluctance to take a lie-detector test sprang from a fear that his past and some of his associations might be probed. "I know too much," he said. "I've wheeled and dealed some — had to, to support my family. I just don't want to talk about it."

Eglian indicated that he might be willing to accept such a test if he were guaranteed police questions would be restricted to matters concerning his wife's murder.

The car wound down Western Avenue. At length Eglian parked it one door down from the Was Riverview, squared his houlders and went in.

Tammy Wynette sang "Your Good Girl's Gonna Be Bad" on the juke box. Behind the bar a television played an old Marine movie. A thick-necked, blunt-featured Aldo Ray stared out from the screen like a younger version of Eglian.

Tommy was long gone. He had left earlier when the crowd had thinned to attend a bowling tournament.

Eglian ordered a Hudepohl and looked around. At twelve-fifteen the Was Riverview contained only a few customers, most of them playing pool in an adjoining room.

Eglian got up and looked in there. Three tee-shirted men bent over their sticks where his wife had once played the same game.

"I heard a girl was killed around here," Eglian said to the bartender.

"Not here. Across the street."

He asked a few more questions, then went back to his stool and chain-smoked Kools until closing. There was nothing for him there.

He left at once. "Take care of her, Mr. Eglian," the bartender said as he went through the door.

"He knew me," Eglian sighed. "Well, that was a dead run. Nothing."

He drove part way down the dark twin-rutted road behind the floodwall to the powerline tower where his wife was found. Brush scraped the car and it creaked on the uneven ground. Eglian got out and stared up at the tower disappearing skyward in the black a.m.

The air was loud with crickets and sounds of the river below. Far away a moving necklace of lights marked traffic on the I-75 bridge.

"I'll have to try another angle," Eglian said. "Besides Tommy, I've got two other guys out looking around. They're professionals."

The tower stretched up from the weeds like a vast grave marker.

"I'm not done yet," Eglian said.

The irony is there— John Wayne in a jeep, Aldo Ray in a soldier suit, the awareness of the bartender— but I am not. I was watching him, all right; I maneuvered him down to the scene of the crime because I wanted to see if he would let slip on which side of the powerline tower the body had been dumped, because only the police knew that and I hadn't printed it. The flesh crept for sure. I was playing with trouble. Eglian, an old con, had been sent up for armed robbery and was watching me as carefully as I was watching him this moonless midnight. But *I* wasn't the story — the game he played was. So I dealt the reader in.

They found the shotgun in the lake where he dumped it and Bonnie Floyd finally blew the whistle on him. It took the jury only 50 minutes to convict.

Three for the Emergency Room
by William Ruehlmann

[I picked a night of the full-phase "leaper's moon" to cover the workings of an emergency room on the theory that it would be busy. It was. A single incident would not have expressed the extraordinary variety of the experience. More than three would have been too many to sustain focus.

The attempt was to reveal through scene without comment.]

Part one·
pathos—   At 10:20 p.m. the kid who lost his legs in Vietnam came into the William Booth Hospital Emergency Ward, 323 E. 2nd St., Covington.

He was crying.

"Help me," he said. "I need some help. Look at me."

"You've been shooting," LPN Ann Crowel told him.

"Yeah," he moaned. "Heroin."

Proximity—   His face was pale as paper under a black dust of two-day beard. His eyes might have been two stuffed olives, the lids heavy and half-closed. His jaw hung slack; desperate sounds were coming out of it.

Dialog for
drama—   A girl friend and a brother were with him.

"He's addicted to downs," the girl friend said. "He took nine Valium and eight reds."

"Sleeping pills?" RN Mary Lou Eilers asked her.

"Yes."

"Seconal?"

"Yes."

"He's been in here before," Mrs. Crowell said as he signed the treatment release. He was using everything he had to do it, spelling the name out loud letter by letter. "At least once for an overdose. He got hooked in the hospital overseas when his legs were amputated."

Single
sentence
graf for
emphasis— He still wore his metal service tag chained around the neck
outside his shirt.

They wheeled him into Minor Surgery for examination. His
story was that he'd been off the stuff four days trying to shake
the habit. His stomach tied itself into knots and his head began
to hurt. His friends strapped him down to a bed. He snapped
and shot up again— twice; the tracks showed up on the insides
of his arms like angry red ants.

"I tried to cut my wrists tonight," he murmured, "but they
wouldn't let me."

"How much do you use?" Miss Eilers asked him.

"Every day, four or five shots a day," he said.

"How can you afford that?"

"I'm a veteran. I got a pension."

Dr. Felicisimo Rodriguez checked his eyes for pupil dilation.

"Doc. You going to lock me up?"

"Nobody's going to lock you up."

The kid handed over his wallet; the name of his doctor was in
there, but he was in no shape to find it himself. A plastic accordion of cards unfolded. There was the usual array of iden-
Irony—tification, pictures of girls, and something else— a photograph
of a confident-looking Marine taken at the end of boot camp.
The kid was and was not the same soldier.

"Veterans' Hospital (in Cincinnati) says they know him,"
Rodriguez said. "He's been in and out several times. They
won't come and get him, but if he wants to go over there they'll
take him."

There was nothing to be done for him at Booth. He would
either kick the habit or he wouldn't. Mary Lou Eilers encouraged him to admit himself to Veterans'.

"I don't want to go there," the kid cried. "They lock you up
in a strait jacket and put you in a padded room and make you
go cold turkey."

"They don't do that any more," Miss Eilers said. "That's
out. You've got to go; it's the best thing."

(Officials at Veterans' denied any presence of strait jackets
and padded cells there.)

The nineteen-year-old ex-Marine put his hands across his
chest and rocked.

"I can't accept my legs," he said brokenly.
He went to Veteran's. Miss Eilers paid the cab fare for the others.

*

Part two:
humor— It was midnight and another shift. Al Angelini and Jim Shelton of the Covington Life Squad arrived with a regular.
"It's John," groaned Angelini, and pushed his hat ruefully forward on his head.
Behind him a fat man in his 60s moved down the corridor from wall to wall like a tacking sailboat.
"Hello, John," greeted RN Donna Boeckley. "How are you doing?"
"I got the whooping cough again," he grinned.
"You can't get whooping cough at your age," Mrs. Boeckley pointed out.
"How about a free drink at Jack's Lounge?" he invited hopefully, and his breath filled the hallway like mustard gas over no man's land.
Mrs. Boeckley put him to bed in the Observation Room. As he struggled with his trousers, John's hand groped in the hip pocket and emerged with a screwdriver.
Dialog— "Look what I got in with!" he noted delightedly.
"You'd better give that to me before you sit down and have another injury," Mrs. Boeckley said.
"I didn't take no bath this morning," John observed.
"I know," said Mrs. Boeckley.
At the nurses' station Jim Shelton helped himself to a lollipop from the "Dum-Dum Tree" on the refrigerator and shook his head.
"We always get a call from him about this same time," Shelton said. "He's always at the same bar, sitting on the same stool. And," he added, "we always have to wait for him to finish his beer before we go."
"Put that on your tongue," Mrs. Boeckley said, handing John a thermometer.
"But I already got a cough drop," he replied.
LPN Patty Miller watched him with affectionate dismay.
"Rodriguez is going to have a fit," she said.

Angelini and Shelton saluted her in friendly farewell and strolled off arm in arm, like the scarecrow and the tin woodman on their way to Oz.

Rodriguez arrived.

"I got a cough," John told him defensively.

Rodriguez had a fit.

"How come you always come to the emergency room, but never talk to your doctor?"

John gave him a dark look.

"I just want the Lord to take me away from this Communist country," he said.

"I told you the last time you were in here," the doctor said. "If you're going to get nasty, I'm not going to look at you. The hell with it."

Compassion
shown, not
told—

He walked out.

Then he sighed and walked in again. The prescription was for cough medicine.

"John is lonely," Donna Boeckley said. "He's old. He gets his pleasure by going to the beer joint and then coming here to get us to feel sorry for him.

"We make a fuss over him and let him go. You can't turn him away," she pointed out. "One day he'll come in and it will be the real thing."

*

rt three:
ofessionalism—

Covington police officer Thomas Schoenecker arrived at 1:30 a.m. with a girl who had been beaten.

Nurses Miller and Boeckley took her immediately to the trauma room, removed her coat and laid her on the examina-

Saved
last
detail—

tion table. Her face and blouse were blood-spattered. Her upper lip was laid cleanly open to the nose line.

"What did that?" Mrs. Boeckley asked.

"A fist," the girl said. "I tried to break up a fight my brother was having and he hit me."

"The guy that was worse off wouldn't come in," Schoenecker said. "He was hit with a tire iron."

Dr. Felicisimo Rodriguez pulled on vinyl gloves as Patty Miller collected the instruments for suturing. All the equipment in Minor Surgery is at eye view for easy access. After injecting a local anesthetic, the doctor began stitching with sterile

A touch
of
metaphor— thread like fishline, about 10-pound test.
There was a weightless quality about his hands, which moved with the grace of birds in tandem. His were the hands of a mime or a gambler, strong, precise, quick without the appearance of haste. They moved over the wound and it was closed.

Officer Shoenecker waited to drive the girl home himself, working patiently on an orange dum-dum in the hall. He would return later with free coke and coffee for the staff.

Dr. Rodriguez started wearily down the hall to the elevator and his fourth-floor room. He'd been on since 5:30 the afternoon before, and would remain until 7:30 in the morning. Mrs. Boeckley put her arm around him.

"Coming with me?" he joked.

"You're too tired," she smiled back.

When Hunters Become the Hunted
by Craig Waters

[Like geometry's noncollapsible triangle, the three-incident story is structurally sound. Craig Waters uses case histories as counterpoint to his commentary in this tough assessment of an outdoor "sport." Each carefully crafted part moves the whole to its inevitable, bitter finish.]

Example
one— *November 15 was a clear, cold day in northern Michigan. The sun was bright, the air tinged with ice. It was a perfect day for football, or for hunting. Tom Gruenberg rubbed his hands together as though they were stiff. He was starting a fire; slowly, a bit of warmth came back to his hands. He thought about the hand warmer he had left back in camp — a lot of good it was doing him there.*

His father had already killed a deer, and now Tom was waiting for his. He sat in an aluminum lawn chair, in a deer blind on the back side of a gove of trees. He was less than 30 feet from the deer trail, but completely hidden by a heavy undergrowth of oak and evergreens. He cupped his hands and blew into them; the hot, moist air seeped between his fingers like steam escaping from a manhole. As the steam departed, the cold returned.

There was a faint scuffle of sound behind him and, as Tom

turned, a shot. The bullet struck Tom Gruenberg in the back, 9 inches above the bottom of his jacket; it exited from his gut.

The 1976-77 hunting season has begun. Some 22 million hunters are expected to invade the forests of Maine, the fields of Kansas, and the mountain chapparal of California, escaping the warm domesticity of their homes. During their day in the field, they will lay waste to worlds of deer and duck, to generations of quail and rabbit and bear.

Single sentence graf for emphasis—

And they will kill hundreds of men, women and children.

During the hunting season of 1974-75 (the most recent season for which figures are available), hunting accidents took the lives of at least 700 people, according to the National Safety Council. (State figures, notoriously incomplete, count 337 fatalities.) All indications are that the number of accidents, and the number of victims, increased the following season. It is not, by contemporary standards, a major or even a significant bloodletting. It does not compare to the mass annihilation of war, or to the gross carnage ground out by the automobile. In 1974, more than 46,000 Americans died on the nation's highways; 1,687 were killed in airplane crashes, and another 1,-579 perished in boating accidents. Hunting is significantly safer than skiing.

But each death is a tragedy nonetheless. A tragedy because, in the vast majority of cases, the victim is shot by a relative or close friend. A father kills his son; one brother takes the life of another. It is a tradition as old as Cain and Abel. And a tragedy because, in all except a handful of instances, the accident could have been avoided.

Man has hunted since the dawn of time. He knows what circumstances and practices precipitate accidents and has learned how to avoid them. The National Rifle Association, state game commissions, hunting organizations and others have developed comprehensive hunter safety courses; the NRA curriculum covers every aspect of hunting from ethics to fundamentals of shooting to wilderness survival. All of the courses bespeak a passion for safety; if the practices they preach are followed, it is virtually impossible for one hunter to shoot another. Since Utah instituted its mandatory Hunter Education Program in 1957, the number of accidents has plummetted from 126 to 14 (in 1975), and only five of the 14 were fatal. This despite the fact that the number of licensed hunters nearly doubled during the same period of time.

Despite the efficacy of such programs, hunters continue to be killed. The roll call of victims continues to grow for a number of reasons: the vast majority of hunters are not hunter safety certified. Only 21 states—Colorado, Delaware, Illinois, Iowa, Kansas, Kentucky, Maine, Massachusetts, Minnesota, Montana, New Jersey, New Mexico, Nebraska, North Carolina, North Dakota, Oklahoma, South Carolina, Tennessee, Utah, Wisconsin and Wyoming—currently require such training. And even they hedge with their legislation: most mandate courses only for hunters who are taking out their first license; those who have hunted in the past, or are from out of state, are exempt.

Of the 10 states which recorded the most hunting fatalities during the 1974-75 season, eight—Arizona, Florida, Georgia, Idaho, Michigan, New York, Texas and Virginia—had no instruction requirements at all.

Hunters, whether trained or not, frequently disregard recommended procedures while in the field. There is little need to observe them: it is impossible for game officers to patrol thousands of acres of wilderness; and, even when accidents do occur, penalties are light or nonexistent. The largest fine exacted in one recent year was $229; the hunter had shot and killed two children who were riding bicycles on a public highway.

Periodically, there are rumors of *premeditated* accidents. If, in fact, a person has murder in mind, he's well advised to invite his victim hunting; not even Barnaby Jones will find out.

Until there are strong laws and strict enforcement, ignorance, carelessness and arrogant bravado will continue to byline tragedies, and an occasional black comedy, in the nation's newspapers:

Specifics— •"At least six hunters, two of them 15 years old, were shot to death during the first 48 hours of the deer hunting season. . . ." UPI

• "FAYETTEVILLE — A 16-year-old Wilmington boy, wearing a squirrel-skin cap, was shot to death Saturday morning on a hunting trip with his cousin. Cumberland County

Coroner Alph Clark said Archie Lee Butler III was killed when struck in the head by a bullet fired by his cousin, Willie Butler, 16. . . ." *Raleigh (N.C.) Times*

• "Officials said Fredrich's 17-year-old son, Michael, fired three shots at a deer which had doubled back while members of the party were making a drive. One of the shots struck Fredrich in the right hip. He was dead on arrival at a Rhinelander hospital." *Capital Times* (Madison, Wis.)

• "KALISPELL, Mont., Nov. 23 — An 18-year-old Kalispell deer hunter has been shot to death only 10 days after his father died in a hunting accident." AP

Example two—
The sun had set more than half an hour before, but Frank Madera and Bob Anthony were reluctant to leave. Color had already fled the hills outside of Guerneville, California, the earth, the brush and the sky were light and dark masses of gray, but still the two men pushed through the thick chaparral, lusting for a deer.

Madera's wife, Laura, waited impatiently a short distance away.

The men, co-workers at Pacific Gas & Electric, had decided to spend their day off together. Though there was an 18-year difference in their ages — Madera was 33 and Anthony 51 — the two men enjoyed each other's company, and both loved to hunt. These hills, 60 miles north of San Francisco and just 10 miles west of their Healdsburg homes, was one of their favorite spots.

It was mid-August, and the day was hot, but pleasant; a light breeze curled up off the Pacific five miles away. Together, Madera and Anthony combed the landscape for game, zigzagging their way up and down the overgrown grades. In his feathered cap and camouflaged hunting suit, Madera resembled a latter-day Robin Hood. The trek was tiring, but the two men stopped only for an occasional breather, and once to have a few drinks. Then the hunt resumed.

It was still on at 8:15. The sky was waxing black, and Laura, who had come along for the pleasure of her husband's company, was anxious to start home. The men knew that it was too dark to be shooting, but harbored a faint hope that luck would strike; they were about to abandon it when, suddenly, Anthony

spotted the rack of a four-point buck above a thicket of brush.
With a grace perfected by 35 years' practice, he raised his 30-
06 Winchester, aimed, and, with a prayer of thanks, fired. A
feathered cap flew into the air. Behind the brush, something fell
to the ground, groaned once, and was still.
"My god," Anthony moaned. He charged into the brush,
and, coming out on the opposite side, found a scene far worse
than he had feared. The shell had struck his friend on the left
side of the head just below the eyes and had exited by the right
ear. The mushroom-shaped lump of lead had torn away the
front and top of the head, and had blown away its contents.
Bits of bone and brain matter speckled the earth and trees.
Frank Madera, 33, of Healdsburg, California, was dead.
And all Anthony could do was tell his friend's waiting wife.

Though the principal beneficiaries of safe hunting laws, hunters violently resist such legislation. Committed, in theory, to safety at any cost, they are vehemently opposed, in practice, to anything which restricts their activities. It is not unlike being *for* safe highways, but *against* the testing of drivers; as a symbol of the American Way, the automobile takes a back seat to guns.

The National Shooting Sports Foundation preaches that "The rewards of hunting are physical, emotional and in many cases spiritual," and professional hunter Charles Askins, possibly taking his cue from Marx, writes that: "Hunting is a glorious sort of vice working its narcotic with all of the efficacy of the ubiquitous poppy." Which may explain the strange behavior of some hunters.

Evidence— An estimated 22 million persons — or approximately one American in 10 — are hunters; we have more *hunters* than Mormons, or Jews, or Southern Baptists, or Episcopalians. The National Rifle Association, with a membership of one million plus, is larger than all but three of the country's labor unions. It has a staff of over 250 full-time employees, an annual budget of about $10 million and assets totaling more than $24 million. Grass-roots membership and grass-roots resources make the NRA a spectacularly effective special interest agent. Whenever government threatens to curtail hunters' rugged individualism, the organization launches an expensive and, invariably, successful lobbying campaign. "The lobby's ability to elicit letters from its constituency is phenomenal," Massachusetts Representative Michael Harrington notes. The NRA's goals are shared by manufacturers who have never hesitated to buy some consideration via generous contributions to political campaigns. Hunting, after all, is big business: last year hunters shelled out more than $1.25 billion for the pleasure and approximately 35 percent of that was spent on equipment.

It is not surprising, then, that less than half of the 50 states require *any* hunter safety training, or the use of hunter orange, or mandatory marksmanship tests. Not even property rights take precedence over the hunter's— in many states, hunters are free to hunt on private land unless No Hunting or No Trespassing signs are posted every 50 feet; and, even then, the signs may serve no purpose other than target practice.

Specifics—   The consequences are predictable but nonetheless frightening: in California, a 28-year-old welder attempts to quick-draw a pistol but shoots himself in the thigh and hits an artery; he bleeds to death within three minutes. In Texas, a youngster who tries the same trick blows off his right kneecap. A duck hunter who accidently fires at another hunter's decoys is promptly blasted by the owner. A Columbia County, Wis., sheriff reports that overzealous hunters are climbing fences, tearing down No Trespassing signs and shooting at houses; he notes, "One owner called in madder then heck saying a carload of hunters had spotted a pheasant in the middle of his cattle. They jumped out and took a shot at it without a care about the cows. Luckily, none of the cows was hit." In New York, a city

Dialog for drama—   slicker *bags* a cow and takes it to a weigh-in station.

Carol Koury, the head of the Massachusetts office of Fund For Animals, walks with her parents up the dirt road to the summer home and finds a hunter plunking shots into the door of their barn. Her father is incensed: "What do you think you're doing?" he demands. "Get the hell out of here!"

The hunter squeezes off two more shots, then turns and faces Fred Koury. "Who's got the gun here, friend?" he asks. Slowly, he bends, picks up the dead rabbit lying at his feet, and swings it over his shoulder, flecking the air with its blood; then, when he is ready, he leaves.

A few states, and most other countries, take a somewhat more limited view of the freedom to hunt; they regard it not as each citizen's birthright, but rather as a privilege to be earned. In Wyoming, hunters must obtain the owner's written permission before they hunt on private property. Norway requires its big game hunters to pass an exacting marksmanship test. In West Germany, the price of a license is a rigorous year-long course, plus high marks on the final exam; and a "concession," which permits a hunter to shoot on private lands, may cost $3,-000 to $40,000.

Such requirements restrict the number and activities of hunters, while upgrading their qualifications. West Germany's 250,000 licensed hunters represent only .4 percent of the country's 62 million residents, which contrasts sharply with a 10 percent figure for the United States. A German forester observes: "There are occasional attempts to insist on the right to hunt for every citizen, but they never get anywhere." For the time being, hunters short of deutschmarks must be invited to hunt by concessionaries who are friends or who need help controlling the deer population. The result is that your average German hunter is a safer and more proficient hunter than our typical Dan'l Boone: less than half a dozen die in hunting accidents each year. During the 1974-75 season, American hunters shot and wounded more than 2,500 people according to state figures. The National Safety Council reports a more realistic figure of 5,500.

Example three—

Blam! As easy as that.

Alvin Brown savored the moment, indulging the anticipation.

It was November 15, the first day of Missouri's deer hunting season, and Callaway County, halfway between St. Louis and Kansas City, was an ideal spot to be. The skies were clear, the air unseasonably warm, and the deer fat and anxious to die.

Brown, his father and three of their friends had spent the first hours of the day wandering among the wooded hills of his father's property, and now their path and good fortune's had crossed. Alvin Brown squinted down the length of the barrel at the buck.

So easy.
He pulled the trigger at the same moment his target moved. Instead of striking the heart or lungs, the shell exploded to the rear of the animal's body. The deer took off, maneuvering awkwardly, and disappeared among the trees.

Brown, George Harrington, an employee of the Wellsville Fire Brick Co., and Paul Medley, the manager of Kingdom of Callaway Estates, a nearby campground, began to follow the bloody trail; the other members of the party went off to find a deer of their own.

As the three men tracked the wounded animal, the cool restraint of the hunt was replaced by the abandon of the chase; they began to race through the woods. They were breathing heavily, and their faces were slick with sweat when they broke into the clearing. Harrington saw the buck first: It lay on its side not 30 feet away.

The buck lifted its head and saw the men. With a lowing grunt and a crippled snap of the neck, it attempted to wedge its front legs beneath its body. The men sprinted across the clearing. Harrington raised his Marlin 30-30 carbine and clubbed the animal down.

The blow splintered the gunstock and the rifle fired. The shot passed over Harrington's shoulder, struck Brown in the chest, and showered out of his back. Alvin Brown, 28, of Readville, Mo., was dead on arrival at the Callaway County Hospital.

Irony— *That afternoon, they brought in his deer.*

As the number of hunters continues to grow, higher standards and stricter controls become virtually essential. In 1965, there were 13 million hunters in the United States; by 1969, the number had soared to 20 million, and now, seven years later, there are two million more. Before, it was like playing kick-the-can on a one-lane dirt road; now it's a game of blind-man's-bluff set on the Van Neys Expressway.

"There are 700-800,000 hunters in the field on the first day of Pennsylvania's deer hunting season and 950,000 on the first day of the general season," says Hunter Education Coordinator John Behel, "and they concentrate in certain areas of the state. Even if they used baseball bats, there would be some accidents."

For most of these men and boys, hunting is not a way of life. They have not grown up in forest and field, patiently learning nature's ways. These hunters— attorneys, welders, high school students, accountants — have no need for the game they kill and little respect for its source. Hunting is a divertissement, a different way to spend one's weekend; it is a brutal game which people other than pro athletes can play.

For all too many, hunting has become a perverse symbol of their mastery over life. The pleasure of being outdoors, the pride engendered by skill matter less than the fact that they can
Specifics— kill. In Lenox, Mass., hunters shoot two fallow deer in pens at a private zoo. In Amagansett, N.Y., a truckload of hunters slows as it passes a house in order to shoot the family's collie puppy: It is Christmas Eve.

"They've never had a chance to be in the wilderness," observes Carol Koury. "They live in cities, and in the suburbs of cities, and two or three times a year they load their gun, pick up a couple of six-packs, and raise some hell in the woods. It's impossible for them to behave naturally in what, for them, is such an unnatural setting."

A columnist for the Madison, Wisconsin, *State Journal* reached an equally disturbing conclusion after taking a short drive last November. James Selk told his readers: "On a 40-mile stretch between Mauston and Pittsville, I saw a traffic jam of cars and trucks and campers crowded onto shoulders and pulloffs.

"I saw hundreds of orange-clad hunters stalking their prey in large groups a few hundred yards off the highway. I saw a wounded deer limping across the road and several others, panicked, chased across the road by men and small boys blazing away with their guns. I saw huge blotches of blood and gore at close intervals on the highway.

"At one . . . spot, I saw a bloody carcass, split in two, half on one side of the road, half on the other. . . .

"I took a different route back and found much the same thing. . . . Crowds of hunters among cars and trucks, apparently discussing their next forays into the brush; panicked deer, blood, cars with gutted deer lashed to bloody bumpers. . . .

"Maybe all the slob hunters were on those small stretches of road last weekend, but I doubt it. I think that they represented a pretty fair cross section of the entire breed."

Return to example one: unity of closure—

Tom Gruenberg was 15, a ninth grade student at Flushing High School in Flushing, Mich. His 17-year-old sister, Julie, whose birthday he shared, was a student at the same school. His father, Paul, was a supervisor with General Motors' parts division in Flushing; his mother, Marilyn, was ill with cancer. Like his father, Tom Gruenberg loved the outdoors and horses. He owned a half-Arab mare named Ginger and intended to become a horse breeder. He was a tall, blond boy with handsome features; his parents had invested $3,000 in orthodontics. He was a good student, played varsity basketball and sang with the State Junior Honors Choir. On the morning of November 15, 1975, he went hunting with his father; he was shot in the back by a stranger.

He is dead.

Saved final devastating detail—

"Even if he wasn't my son, I would have liked him," his father said, "but he was my son . . . and I loved him. And my heart aches every day since I lost him. . . . I feel bad that he's not here to share hunting with me any more."

4. Ideas

Awareness and news sense

I was traveling across a stretch of Arizona desert once in a battered pickup with a man who hunted all of the meat for his family's table. We were rocketing at 40 miles an hour past the dry washes and the open spaces with their even, distant ranks of saguaro cacti when, quite suddenly, he brought the truck to a shuddering, sand-grinding halt.

"What is it?" I asked him.

"Rabbit," he said, backing down the narrow one-vehicle silt track.

I didn't see any rabbit. My laconic friend was tamping a ball down the barrel of his muzzle-loader rifle.

"Where?"

"Under that tree," he said.

After a minute, I saw the tree. Barely. It was a sad, scraggly thing about a hundred yards away. I didn't see any rabbit.

"I don't see any rabbit," I said.

He stepped down from the cab with that long jeaned outdoorsman's ease and put the rifle to his shoulder. It barked once, and he set off across the intervening distance with the confidence of a man who never wasted bullets he had to make himself.

I still didn't see any rabbit.

When he walked back he had one, though. A big jack. As was his custom, he had shot it through the head, so as not to spoil the meat.

"How the devil did you spot him?" I asked, utterly at a loss.

"I watched for the wink of the sun off his eyes," he told me.

He wasn't kidding.

He knew the desert as a scholar knows a reference library. He knew what to watch for. Jackrabbits freeze in place to blend with the landscape when they sense danger, but the marble-glint of their eyes points out their position to those who know where to look for it.

A writer should know his territory the way my friend knew the outdoors. Finding stories is like hunting rabbits; you've got to know where to look for them, how to spot them where the untrained eye passes blithely over.

Curiosity is the other side of wonder. It is the child's incessant, nagging need to know, and all good reporters are possessed by it. They are forever trying to get to the bottom of things.

If a reporter sees four antique Duesenbergs parked at a truck stop, he's going to pull over and find out why they're there. If there's a pumpkin festival upstate, he'll be at it, relentlessly poking about. If police are diving for a night suicide at a stocked fishing lake, he'll want to interview the frogman.

He is insatiable, as you should be. You should walk the streets with the expectation always of finding something remarkable. You will, too; the readiness is all.

A picket line of priests stalk back and forth one morning in front of Theo's Boom-Boom Room. Why? A woman in black shows up at the graveside of an old screen idol on the 50th anniversary of his death. Who is she? The mayor suddenly has city police escorting his twin girls to grammar school. What for?

A reporter's beat is a rich store of stories. He knows it as well as the yard he played in as a kid, every country club and corner bar. He acquaints himself with the people who live there and encourages them to contact him. Today's piece may be a lever on tomorrow's; the bandleader at the fireman's ball may be the brother-in-law of a man raising a promising Derby entry. The health faddist who is pulling a barge downstream with his teeth as a birthday stunt may be the same guy who played Superman 30 years earlier in some forgotten movie serial. The golf pro who built his own three-masted schooner may know when a famous entertainer is expected to play in a Saturday foursome. While working on the present story, a reporter has one eye out for the next.

The fabled "nose for news" is nothing more than a logical sense of what material is promising and therefore worth pursuing. A strong story will have one or more of the following qualities (if it has them all, it's dynamite—like the Patty Hearst kidnap case):

1) *Currency.* Yesterday's news is ancient history. The thing you write

about should be happening *now*. A retrospective on Orson Welles might be amusing enough, but the exciting—and uncirculated—information will involve what he is up to at the present moment. A possible release date for his mysterious new *magnum opus*? A television role as Nero Wolfe? What has the caped Svengali of the camera got up *today's* sleeve?

2) *Celebrity*. If the President of the United States is stopping in your town to shell peas and set a spell, that's news. Conway Hogbody down the road can total his '56 Chevy without much down-home stir, but let Richard Burton get a ticket for overtime parking and readers are interested. Newspapers and magazines have built entire circulations on the often insignificant doings of notables; witness *People* and the *National Enquirer*.

3) *Proximity*. Local angles interest local readers. If the lad who crossed the Atlantic on the rice paper raft comes from your town, the folks there are going to want to hear about it. Area fires and bank robberies are of endless interest. The wranglings of city committees and civic associations carry little influence elsewhere, but they have important implications for the municipalities they serve. If the governor proposes to build his next state prison in one of *your* public parks, that's news.

4) *Impact*. If a situation or event directly affects your readership, your story about it will receive plenty of attention. The record-breaking cold spell has depleted natural gas reserves, and homes are going without fuel: news. A nylon-stocking strangler has killed seven suburban housewives and remains on the loose: news. The river is up, and fault lines are showing up on the floodwall: news.

5) *Oddity*. The unusual always captures our imagination, and it is everywhere. A charter member of the local WCTU becomes inebriated from giving a drunk mouth-to-mouth resuscitation, then rampages a Christmas party. A county sheriff is trapped for 24 hours in a car wash. A pet duck at a 4-H fair swallows somebody's $30,000 diamond ring. Most people are under the impression that life is generally humdrum, but any reporter with access to a teletype knows that the incredible is a constant in this crazy world. As I write the radio reports a successful young television star sitting among friends last night quietly put a gun to his head and shot himself. He was 22. Bad news, tragic news—but news all the same.

The feature writer is alert for the newsworthy subject. If he has particular interests of his own, he will examine them for story possibilities.

Are you a coin collector? Perhaps a downtown dealer has a curious tale to tell about a recent acquisition. Are you a film buff? Get a color story on location with the camera crew for the latest disaster epic. Do you fish? There's an article in the comparative piscine merits of area lakes and streams. Even the art of tying flies has real potential.

Read everything. Observe everything. Become earth's well-traveled eavesdropper. The stories aren't scarce—they're too plentiful.

Inspiration vs. hard work

Inspiration is like an inconstant friend: nice to have around, but not to be counted on.

Robert Louis Stevenson claimed the whole of *The Strange Case of Dr. Jekyll and Mr. Hyde* came to him in a dream. Charles Dickens said mysterious voices guided his writing. Rod Serling was accused of eating exotic foods just before turning in to induce a plot-producing sleep.

But these fine professionals also wrote regularly without benefit of sudden bonuses from the imagination. It was their routine use of everything available that led them to employ even their unconscious—not the reverse. They didn't wait for inspiration, but they took advantage of it when it came around.

The more one writes, the more accessible one's material becomes. The engine started daily runs the most reliably.

You have been encouraged to keep a notebook both as a means of making observation a habit and as an idea mine. You should be making entries every day. Your experience will begin to suggest stories, angles, possible sources for information. Beginning writers always say they have nothing to write about, and they are right; you can't draw water from an empty well. But once they start venturing abroad and using their eyes, a thousand possibilities present themselves.

It is a commonplace that hard writing and rewriting improve prose. James Dickey, who has been known to take his poems through perhaps 150 drafts, has said: "It's worked over to get the work-on quality out of it." But it is also true that such constant literary wrestling brings a second victory: While you're beating the present assignment, the next one will suggest itself.

A writer must also read. Voraciously. The things others have done will serve as points of departure for his own work. He must read the classics and the daily newspaper, slick magazines and old yellowing pulps, handbills passed out by street partisans, the backs of cereal boxes. He should look on all of his reading as not only entertainment but important research. The work of the masters should be examined for style and form; the casual printed matter that presents itself at every turn should be scrutinized as a possible source for stories.

That is to say, from now on you are never off duty. Your mind never runs on automatic pilot. In everything you see and read, you are subtly digging.

The morning newspaper provides scores of story possibilities, which is why reporters read their own papers with care—and those of the competition. There has been a bomb scare at the local courthouse; is there a possible follow-up on increased security measures? The *Press* has a piece on subway line shutdowns because of heavy snow; can the *News* do a more ambitious one on the efforts of the transit authority to dig out? A local leader's name keeps cropping up in connection with racial tensions in area secondary schools; he may merit an in-depth profile. These documents should be scanned by writers with the concentration of archaeologists going over so many scrolls for clues.

Even the classified section should be read with care. Every now and then items like this appear:

FOR SALE: ONE BENGAL TIGER, two desert pigs and a white-faced Hereford. Call Lou after 5, 846-4554.

There should be a story in that. Or this:

WANTED, TWO NUBIAN SLAVES to serve flaming dinner, carry emperor's carriage at Order of Mystic Mullahs annual banquet. Regalia provided, good pay. 723-5810, ext. 114.

Or this:

HAVE GUN, WILL TRAVEL. Mercenary for hire. Will fight any cause anywhere for a fee. Adept in Ken-Do, karate, all weapons. Crack bodyguard. Ben, 922-7420.

Each of these ads is not more outlandish than many routine listings that can be found in any metropolitan daily, and each is a sure-fire feature possibility.

Two other regular story sources in newspapers are the Action Line columns and the Letters to the Editor. The Action Line attempts to provide a conduit for consumer complaints, and much of it has to do with getting traffic lights fixed and neighbors to fence in dogs. But what about something like this?

Last week the utility company shut off our heat. We are in our 80s and on public assistance and simply can't pay the $18.50 past due. Our thermostat reads 38 degrees as I write this. What can we do? We are freezing to death.

Or this:

The book club computer won't believe we stopped our membership a year ago. In spite of our continued letters to that effect, the bills keep coming in, printed in red now with a lot of marginal aspersions on our integrity. According to the latest card, we owe the book club $38,464.83!

Both of these interesting communications bear investigation. The Letters to the Editor section of the paper also is a rich mix of the sad and serious, wild and worrisome. Many of these missives are intelligent debate, many more are unreasoning diatribe, and some are simple statements of insanity. But once in a while a letter like this finds its way into print:

Much has been said and written about the relationship of violence on television to the behavior of young people. I want you to know that in our community there is a gang of boys seven to ten years old who are conducting dawn raids on suburban homes after the exact fashion of the hooligans on *Hell's Robin Hoods,* so popular this season on Channel Seven.

The little monkeys are material.

Ideas do not come to brooding types sitting fist-on-chin in their windowless cloisters. They come as the consequence of hard work and the constant heads-up attention of those who miss nothing in their research on reality.

Getting out of the office

There is a certain big-city newspaper encased in bullet-proof glass that has a reputation for weakness in street reporting. One day I passed the windowed office of a columnist there and saw him sitting inside, interviewing two men. It was symbolic of what was wrong with the paper; the reporters were bringing pieces of the world into the city room by appointment instead of venturing beyond their plastic hive to meet it on its own terms.

Columnist Bob Greene recalled an experience he had at the Columbus *Citizen-Journal* where he was working summers away from college. He was sitting blankly at his desk when the city editor asked him why he wasn't working on anything. "Nothing to write about now," Greene shrugged. The editor hit the ceiling. *"Nothing to write about? There are people out there!"*

Indeed there are — fascinating, strange, remarkable people, but you won't meet them at your desk. They're *out there,* and you should be among them. Every individual — every one — is a story full of passion, laughter, love, sadness and sorrow; this is what is called, for want of poetry, "human interest." The gregarious reporter can dig it out, in casual conversation, over coffee.

Cab drivers know things. So do cops and cocktail waitresses, receptionists and elevator operators. Brace them. Get acquainted. Leave your card.

When you find yourself absolutely without ideas, washed up on the desert island of a slow news day, one certain source for stories is the courthouse. Make friends with the court clerk — that individual will be useful for the proper spelling of names on the docket, charges and arresting officers. Having done that, sit in court.

You'll have to take voluminous notes. As each separate case is called, you must treat it as a potential sure feature — that means getting names, quotes, the works. Frequently the case will offer nothing of interest; but at least once a session, often more than once, a case will come up that captures an intensely human moment.

Police court on any random day might offer a take or two about an "angel" who packs a wallop:

> When a man snatched her coat at the corner of Pike and Washington Streets Saturday night, Marie Angel, 24, was not one to stand helpless.
>
> She ran right after him and grabbed the coat back.
>
> "I hit him up the side of the head with my purse," said Miss Angel, a bookkeeper for the Bode-Finn Co. in Cincinnati. "I had a lot of stuff in it, too."
>
> Charged with the criminal attempt of robbery in the second degree was Aubrey Harmon, 62, appearing in Covington Police Court Tuesday for a preliminary hearing.

Aubrey stood silent while Miss Angel, of 727 Main St., identified him as the man who approached her after she left her car at 7:30 p.m. for a walk in the unseasonably warm evening.

"I didn't know what he was trying to grab," Miss Angel testified.

She was carrying the $40 coat draped over her arms in front of her with her purse.

"He ran away with my coat," she continued. "I chased after him and took it back."

Using the shoulder strap as a roundhouse version of David's sling, Miss Angel brained the man soundly with her bag.

The man responded with a threat.

"He said, 'Hit me again and I'll kill you,'" Miss Angel stated.

She summoned the police from a phone at Joyce's Cocktail Lounge, 104 Pike St. Officer Jim Rieskamp responded to the call and took down her description of a man in "a long gray overcoat." Rieskamp went in search of the man and arrested Harmon, who was wearing a coat similar to the one in Miss Angel's statement, on the 700 block of Main Street.

"He had been drinking," Rieskamp testified, "but he wasn't staggering. He had a bottle of wine on him." Harmon told Rieskamp he hadn't been doing anything.

Police court judge William B. O'Neal bound Harmon over to the grand jury.

"I just figured I had to protect myself," Miss Angel said later, "because nobody else was going to."

Five-foot eight and game, the bespectacled Miss Angel expressed only one regret over her staunch self-defense.

"It ripped the dickens out of my purse," she sighed.

Or traffic court might provide a vignette about cats and star-crossed lovers:

A black cat meant bad luck for Danny Zornes in Kenton County Court Wednesday.

Charged with failing to stop for a stop sign at Route 17 and Nicholson Road late Feb. 17, Zornes, 16, of 142 McCullum Rd., Independence, firmly placed the blame on a fell feline named "Kitkak."

Zornes had been returning home in his white 1964 Chevrolet Impala from an evening at the movies with his girl friend, Brenda Corbin, 17. After he left Miss Corbin at her home at 308 Walton-Nicholson Rd., Zornes headed for his own house alone—or so he thought.

"I was slowing down for the intersection," Zornes explained in court, "when Brenda's cat jumped up on the seat from in back."

Zornes, unnerved by the sudden appearance of this furry stowaway, sailed on past the stop sign.

"That," admitted Judge William E. Wehrman Jr., "is a new one."

But Zornes' tribulations were not over. When Officer Paul Eckler of the Kenton County Police pulled him over down the road, Zornes opened his door to talk— and the cat escaped.

"He lost Kitkak!" protested a miffed Miss Corbin. "And he's going to have to get me another cat."

Thus Zornes in the space of a few seconds found himself in dutch with the law and his girlfriend both.

But the story has a better ending than that. Zornes received a minimum fine of court costs, and when he and Miss Corbin returned home after trial Kitkak was there waiting for them.

"Mr. Nie brought him back," reported Zornes.

Bill Nie, 70, owner of Nie's Pharmacy, 5653 Madison Pk., Independence, had discovered the offending feline prowling the area around his store.

Home safe after causing all the trouble, the cat buried his face in a food dish with no evidence of apology.

Courtrooms are occasions for manufactured minidramas with all the ingredients: conflict, dialog, sudden emotion and final resolution. The trick is to listen attentively and pursue the principals into the corridor during recess. The novice always fears no one will want to talk to him; actually, most people are so forthcoming it is hard to get all their comments down.

Courtroom situations sometimes can lead to larger stories beyond the dock. Bob Woodward and Carl Bernstein's explosive political investigation recounted in *All the President's Men* began as a routine police court story. The following piece simply pursues a defendant after sentencing out into a situation past his control:

Carl White, a transient arrested on a drunk charge, politely asked Covington Police Court Judge William O'Neal for 30 days in jail.

"I can't stay out there," he explained, gesturing toward the chill winter world beyond the courthouse.

Judge O'Neal granted the request, which was not an unusual one.

"We get a lot of people like that," confided Court Clerk Mary Ann Woltenberg, "and most of them don't even live around here. They wander in and out of the state."

She shook her head.

"They're put in jail by the police because they're cold and need something to eat," she said. "They just have no place else to go."

George Kraut, another transient called before the bench on the same docket, found himself in a similar situation.

Officer Charles Vallendingham discovered him at 11 o'clock Saturday morning leaning against a building on 8th Street.

He fell down.

Kraut picked himself up, walked a block to 7th and Scott and fell down again. Vallandingham brought him in for sefekeeping.

Police court convened Monday at nine and Kraut was fined $10 and costs on a drunk charge. The fine and costs were probated on the condition that he not appear in court again. But when Police Court Prosecutor Ed Henry left the courtroom later, he discovered Kraut sitting forlornly on a bench outside.

"You can't let a fellow like that just wander the streets," Ed Henry said. "He'd freeze to death out there."

Kraut was wearing a seamsplit summer coat and a thin cotton shirt. He had no socks, and his feet flapped loosely in worn laceless shoes.

Prosecutor Henry put him back in a cell to stay warm. But on Tuesday morning when he appeared before the judge again, there was no charge against him and no justification for holding him longer.

"Where is your home?" Judge O'Neal asked him.

Kraut's face was empty.

"The red, white and blue," he said.

O'Neal referred him to the Kenton County Welfare office. There Jeanette Andrews admitted her organization was not equipped to help him.

"I'll personally pay a week's rent and buy him some clothes," she said, "but there is nothing we as an agency can do."

Kraut could not remember his birth date nor his most recent address. He carried no identification. He had forgotten his social security number and all the details of his past history.

"I was born on a farm," he noted, attempting to be helpful. He did not recall where.

Kraut was referred again, this time to the 4th Street Community Center. Director Doug Thiele came to the courthouse to walk the shivering man to the center office a block away.

"We're a Community Chest agency," said Thiele. "Our philosophy is that certain areas are public responsibility, not ours — like this kind of community assistance.

"But at present there is no comprehensive public program in this area for people in need of shelter. There's no private facility, either."

Police officers learned later that Kraut had been released from 30 days in jail on a drunk charge just prior to the time Vallandingham picked him up.

"We're in desperate need of a resource where people in crisis can come," Thiele said.

The 4th St. Center would not be sending George Kraut back out into the cold. But as he sat sipping Thiele's coffee alone and without expression in his eyes, it was clear there was very little room for him in Covington.

Stories do not come to the writer. He must go out and meet them, and when he encounters one he must fasten himself to it like a fat man on a free lunch.

The slant: a sideways look

Your story on the Rotary Club picnic should distinguish itself from every other story on the same subject. When the circus comes to town, when the mayor throws a costume ball or when the world's largest hardware store holds its grand opening, you can be sure there will be a lot of other feature writers hanging around with their teeth all sharpened up for a good meal. The story you get has got to be better than theirs. You've got to beat them, and you have to use your head to do it.

A lot of stories have been written to the effect that veterans are forgotten figures in times of peace. It's true; most true things have been said more than once. When Ernest Hemingway set about making the same point for the *Toronto Star Weekly* December 8, 1923, he made sure he had an angle. His problem was how to show in some concrete fashion that the heroisms of war were of small regard after the armistice; his solution was to make the rounds of city pawnshops in search of the sale price for soldiers' medals.

The woman in charge brought them out from the cash till.
They were a 1914-15 star, a general service medal and a victory medal. All three were fresh and bright in the boxes they had arrived in. All bore the same name and number. They had belonged to a gunner in a Canadian battery.
The reporter examined them.
"How much are they?" he asked.
"I only sell the whole lot," said the woman, defensively.
"What do you want for the lot?"
"Three dollars."

Hemingway's unsentimental 750-word story outshines whole volumes on the subject.
When the National Restaurant Show came to Chicago, Bob Greene of the *Sun-Times* made sure his coverage of it would be distinct. Instead of a flat color story on pretzel booths and pie exhibits, Greene delivered a fast, funny account of what happened when he turned a junk food freak loose on the premises. Copyboy Bill Cunniff proceeded to chew his way through seas of fruit punch and salad oil, crags of chopped steak and fried clams, white cake and canned tuna.

And as this was happening, Cunniff was becoming a star. Word of his presence at the show spread. The regular delegates, who know enough to steer clear of all the food, began to gather and observe Cunniff. They began to take bets on when he would drop. A businessman asked him how he felt. "I feel wired," Cunniff said with a grin.

The presence of the indefatigable Cunniff was the difference between Greene's arresting piece and the predictable ones of others.
Managing Editor Tom Marquardt of the *Ypsilanti Press* wanted his paper's story warning against the consequences of drinking and driving

on New Year's Eve to be particularly forceful. So he assigned reporter Anne Gold to get drunk—under the sober scrutiny of officials from the Washtenaw County Alcoholic Abuse Center. She consumed 14 ounces of alcohol in three and one-half hours, during which time she failed a maze test, her handwriting became illegible, and her ability to light a cigarette markedly diminished. The story scored.

Make it yours. When press legions and politicos flocked to the Carter inauguration in January of 1977, Jimmy Breslin hung back to watch members of the Queens County Democratic organization board the noon train for Washington, all of them brandishing crisp resumes. Breslin saw in their grasping job-seeking the real story and wrote it up.

The trick, then, is to take a step away from the pack — or set a squeaking mouse loose among it.

What is not news

On July 22, 1975, using a motor-driven camera, *Boston Herald American* photographer Stanley Forman took pictures of a 19-year-old woman and her goddaughter, 2, trapped on a Back Bay fire escape as a firefighter beside them beckoned for a ladder. When he grabbed it, the fire escape collapsed— and Forman developed a horrifying triptych of the woman and child falling, the woman to her death.

The photographs, prominently displayed in papers across the country, drew vociferous criticism from some who said they were shocking and exploitative.

Well, they were shocking. But they were not exploitative; they show-ed something that happened. Unpleasant, tragic, certainly. And Forman won the Pulitzer Prize.

During the 1968 Tet offensive, Associated Press photographer Eddie Adams photographed the chief of the South Vietnamese police, Brigadier General Nguyen Ngoc Loan, calmly shooting a suspected North Vietnamese sympathizer through the head. Also unpleasant. And Adams won the Pulitzer Prize.

It is not the reporter's job to protect his audience from reality in the name of good taste. He is not to present a sanitized picture of the world; he is to present a truthful one. That may involve terrible revelations. The world can be a terrible place.

Still, there are matters that should give even the tough-minded reporter pause. Overplay of trivial misery can be vicious, like this story sent out over the United Press International (UPI) wire:

LONDON (UPI) — Actress Rita Hayworth, Hollywood's red-haired "love goddess" of the 1940s, was half-carried off a transatlantic jet disheveled, distressed and waving her arms in protest, airline employees said yesterday.

The story went on at length to recount— second-hand, by the testimony of unspecified "witnesses" — her "rowdy behavior." This was accompanied by photographs which were taken, the piece noted gleefully, in spite of "an unsuccessful attempt to decoy waiting cameramen."

This kind of coverage is in the best tradition of the *New York Mirror,* which reprinted a front-page blowup of one of Lana Turner's love letters to Johnny Stompanato after her daughter knifed the man to death.

Such riffling about the dirty-sock drawer should be left to those best suited for it. There is other material. One need not be associated with the kind of story indicated by the following memo sent over the UPI wire December 30, 1976:

To: Grant Dillman, Washington [news editor].

Out in Tracy, Minnesota, we have a couple who lost both legs in the blizzard of the century two years ago and we are planning some kind of anniversary story—grisly as it may be.

Is there a department in Washington—health, surgeon general—that could tell us whether four lost legs in one married couple is a record? And happy new year.

Dibble, Minneapolis [bureau].

This kind of thing is on a par with the mobile microphone thrust into the face of a survivor of a family disaster. There is a line between being a witness and being a voyeur; it cannot be taught, but it is the difference between Stanley Forman and record-keeping in Minnesota.

Just as the judicious feature writer avoids licking his lips over human sorrow, so should he avoid smacking his hands together over the specious ploys of public relations. Don't be taken in. Politicians, corporate interests, even charitable organizations are always out to draw as much favorable attention to themselves as possible. The consequence is that many of their actions are directed toward creating an appearance of excellence rather than achieving it.

For example: Senator William Proxmire (D., Wis.) works for a day as a pea picker in his home state. Getting a feel for the folks? Staying in touch with the soil? Maybe. But he arranges to have his picture taken and issues a press release—interesting feature material if you want to be his flack.

The President of the United States carries his own luggage, a garment bag slung over his shoulder. Does he do it to spare the servants—or insure a wirephoto image of a man without pretensions? Evel Knievel asserts publicly that he is going over the Snake River Canyon on a rocket-powered motorcycle. Lavish publicity insures the event will make him millions, and he ends up skiing down the side of the rockface in an elaborate tin can.

The rule: Suit your coverage, in quality and tone, to the news value of your subject.

All News is Good News for Enquirer
by Robert Cross

[The National Enquirer *is at once American journalism's most striking success and least distinguished failure. The largest circulation newspaper in the United States, the* Enquirer *has been known to offer a reporter $22,500 to start; at the same time, its content remains aimed stone single-mindedly at the support-stocking grocery store set, featuring front-page photos of aging screen stars squiring about agate-eyed nymphets and big poster graphics of Gary Gilmore seated in front of a firing squad.*

Still, it is never dull. . . .

Chicago Tribune *writer Robert Cross does a fine job of looking into the tabloid's abrasive banner-head business. Notice his insistence on interviewing the principals as well as seeing the operation first-hand.]*

LANTANA, FLA.— Harried men and women barked into telephones and pounded typewriters. Intense editors scribbled instructions on reams of copy. Somewhere, presses roared and circulation trucks sped for distant points with fresh news and headlines from the *National Enquirer.*

"Jean Dixon Predicts the Next President," "Baby Girl Falls 20 Floors—And Lives," "Black Belt Karate Expert—At 8," "Barbra Streisand's [never before revealed] Unloved Childhood," "Andy Williams Croons: I'm in Love with a Wonderful Girl. . . ."

Oh, oh. As bad luck would have it, Andy Williams crooned his devotion to girlfriend Laurie Wright on the *Enquirer's* copyrighted front page during the very week that Williams' ex-wife allegedly shot her boyfriend. Well, that's the sort of embarrassment a weekly "good news" publication risks when it works several days ahead of time to put 64 pages of gossip and "human interest" into virtually all of the nation's supermarket checkout newsstands.

Oddity— The *National Enquirer* isn't an ordinary newspaper. While metropolitan dailies are covering crime, wars, government scandals, presidential primaries and such, the newshawks here in Lantana are tracking down stories that fit into their paper's rigid, "reader-oriented" tabloid format. The *Enquirer* insists on looking at the brighter side of things—from a movie star's latest romance to the latest "cure" for cancer.

"We have different categories than the dailies, but we feel they're the types of things people like," says the *Enquirer*'s 49-year-old publisher and sole owner Generosa Pope Jr. "Unless a story has an upbeat ending, I won't run it."

News p Pope's positive attitude is supported by the *Enquirer*'s circulation figures. In January, when psychic Jean Dixon's predictions for the year were front-paged, the nation's best-selling periodical hit an all-time high sale of 5,300,000 copies for a single week. Even in ordinary weeks, circulation regularly tops 4,500,000 and some members of the staff wear "6 [million] in '76" buttons when they go out to cover their stories on UFO sightings, flagpole sitters and sculptors of pinheads. Ultimately, Pope hopes for 20 million weekly circulation and widespread foreign distribution.

He bought the *Enquirer* for $75,000 in 1952 when it was little more than a New York City tout sheet. A former Central Intelligence Agency agent and son of a prosperous sand and gravel contractor, Pope got a smattering of publishing experience when he worked on his father's Italian-language newspaper, *Il Progresso*. Experimenting with his own paper, he soon hit upon a formula to build circulation: gore.

Pope has denied rumors that mobster Frank Costello, a friend of the family, got him over the lean years with cash loans. Anyway, soon after the *Enquirer* launched its bloody decade on the mayhem beat ["Madman Cut Up His Date and Put Her Body in His Freezer," screamed a typical headline of the early 60s], the publisher became financially independent. "We ran a lot of gore purely because I noticed that people used to congregate around accident scenes," Pope says. "That's not something we're proud of."

When circulation got stuck at one million and corner news-stands were closing at an alarming rate, Pope began hiring what is now a field force of 172 full-time and 700 part-time "salesmen, checkers, and job-rocking guys" with supermarket experience. These aggressive men and women put the *Enquirer* near the check-out counters of every major grocery chain and most independents.

Pope realized that supermarkets prefer to confine butchery to their meat counters, and so in 1968 the *Enquirer* swept out the gore and became wholesome. The current melange of exposes [government waste is a favorite theme], celebrity gossip, psychic phenomena, inspirational messages and bizarre adventure is put together by a staff of 180 which is liberally sprinkled with ex-perimental tabloid hands from the United Kingdom and Australia.

"To me, this is a carbon copy of the Fleet Street papers, a hodgepodge," one *Enquirer* employee said. "But we do have the best soccer team in the area."

A slant on slants—

"We look for angles all the time, which is, perhaps, British tabloid journalism," said executive editor Iain Calder, a native of Slemannan, Scotland, "but it's also American tabloid jour-nalism. The *New York Daily News* always looks for angles."

Although all of the 50 reporters and writers are American, the executive level is thick with British accents. High salaries [as much as $44,000 a year for the equivalent of an assistant city editor] do tend to attract top talent from Britain, where journalism is considered more of a craft than a noble profession.

"Pope runs this place with an iron fist," one editor said. "People are always going around with the fear that they'll not deliver what the boss wants."

Pope spends freely on his product—$14,000,000 a year for the editorial department alone—and thinks nothing of sending a reporter around the world in search of Paradise or up the side of Mt. Everest looking for the Abominable Snowman.

Then, likely as not, the story might be killed for lack of an angle, an upbeat ending, proper documentation, or simply because Pope doesn't feel good about it. He recently spent $150,000 for serial rights to the book being written by Judith Campbell Exner, who claims that she was an intimate friend of President Kennedy.

"It will either be a bomb or the greatest thing that ever happened," Pope shrugged. "If Jackie ever writes her book, I don't care what we spend to get it," Pope said, grinning. "Kennedy stories invariably boost circulation," he said, "any one of them, it doesn't matter which one."

As frivolous as much of the *Enquirer*'s content seems to be, Pope and his staff insist that all stories must be thoroughly documented. Reporter Frank Zahour was sent to Rio early this year to inspect a statue of Christ that reputedly bled and performed miracles.

Street emphasis— "An Associated Press guy down there was amazed at all the leg work I had to do," Zahour said. "I tracked down the guy who diagnosed the blood and got a signed statement. I even went through medical records."

Finally, Zahour and his editors were convinced that the "Bleeding Christ" was legitimate, and the *Enquirer* published a story about the alleged phenomenon.

Yet when reporter Mike Wallace of CBS's "60 Minutes" recently confronted Calder with a doctored front page photographs of Raquel Welch and Freddie Prinze, Calder readily admitted that separate photos of Welch and Prinze had been blended together. Calder claimed the gaffe was unprecedented and wouldn't happen again.

But another staff member inadvertently indicated that the *Enquirer*'s passion for accuracy might not always rule out its thirst for sensation. Julies d'Hemecourt, a former articles editor now working in the executive suite, was marveling about the *Enquirer*'s lavish photo coverage of Aristotle Onassis' funeral. Someone had caught Jackie Onassis with a smile on her face.

Culminating point: lapse in taste— "It was a terrific photographic coup," d'Hemecourt said. "I couldn't believe it. I thought it was gimmicked when I first saw the front page."

City's 4 Toughest Film Critics
by Carol Oppenheim

[Well, if the city has a "film review board," what does it do? How is it run? Who's on it?
Carol Oppenheim allows herself a look under a small rock and finds all manner of interesting things crawling about beneath.]

Moses, played by Burt Lancaster, was wandering through the desert. Beatrice McGill was resting her eyes, as old folks say.

Oddity—   It was 10:30 a.m., and the Film Review Board, the city-appointed watchdog of the morality of Chicago movie goers under age 18, was at work.

News
peg—   The board's task, set by municipal ordinance, is to preview all motion pictures shown in Chicago theaters—except adult-only X-rated ones—to determine if any film, as a whole, is obscene when viewed by children.

The ordinance covers both American and foreign films, with and without English subtitles. It ignores the fact the movie industry issues its own ratings.

Angle—   Currently, the smut-hunt falls under the purview of four genteel, aging women with apparent political connections.

There's Mrs. McGill, the deacon with 25 years' service. Her husband was an attorney and the first black appointed to the Library Board. Among her friends was the late Congressman William Dawson.

Next in line is Ilene Frymire, one-time West Side Democratic precinct captain who keeps a "Howlett for Governor" button pinned under her coat lapel. She's been on the board 20 years.

Jennie Drakos has 17 years of tenure. She represents the Greek-American community.

The newest member—6½ years—is Irene O'Connor, widow of the former police commissioner, Timothy O'Connor.

Besides viewing movies—the records say the women saw 38 last month—the board issues permits to each theater showing films that pass their critical eye.

In March, 155 permits were granted and the board took in $1,961.

Evidence— The salaries for four reviewers and two projectionists is $6,429 a month. If you add the police officers and one typist assigned to the board, the monthly payroll comes to $12,275. The total budget appropriation for this year is $148,814. Sgt. John Orbon, who's been shepherding the board for eight years, says he likes the job. There's no night work, and he's off weekends. And there's the fringe benefit of inviting his family and friends to private screening. "We had *All the President's Men* for a day and a night," he said. "I ran it special for myself and my wife and some others."

Orbon and the board members say movies aren't what they used to be. Mrs. McGill admits that looking at films does get "boring." Mrs. Drakos quickly added, "But it is our work."

Each morning, the ladies meet in their private screening room in the Traffic Court Building and settle down in their high backed chairs behind a judicial looking desk to see what movies have arrived for screening.

Though the new law doesn't require them to view X-rated films, these sometimes are submitted to the board. "Then, we have to sit through them," Mrs. O'Connor said.

Single
sentence graph
for emphasis— Their object is to hunt for obscenity.

"We reject movies on how we feel about them," explained Mrs. Frymire, who makes copious notes on each scene of each reel. "No," corrected Mrs. Drakos, who was taking no notes, "how we see them."

The board puts an "Adults Only" stamp on an average of less than two movies a month.

Violence cannot affect the board's ruling. But Mayor Daley wants to change that. Last week, he introduced an ordinance keeping children away from films with violence, including "cutting, stabbings, floggings, eye gouging, brutal kicking, and dismemberment."

In recent years, the board has attempted to ban minors from *The Owl and the Pussycat* — they thought teens would be upset to see Barbra Streisand play a prostitute — *Georgy Girl* and *Diary of a Mad Housewife* which have been on TV, *Carnal Knowledge* and *Boys in the Band.*

They won on *Carnal Knowledge,* according to the Corporation Counsel's office.

Whenever they reject a movie, their decision automatically is appealed to the Motion Picture Appeal Board, another city appointed group which acts as reviewer of the reviewers.

Daniel Pascale, assistant corporation counsel, said the board viewed five movies last year and reversed the women's decision on all of them.

The angle re-emphasized— Oh yes, there's one other thing: the city ordinance says the lower board must consist of "not less than six members." Which means there are at least two vacancies. Judging from the present membership, only politically connected widows need apply.

5. Grabs

Action!

It was on a bitterly cold and frosty morning during the winter of '97 that I was wakened by a tugging at my shoulder. It was Holmes. The candle in his hand shone upon his eager, stooping face, and told me at a glance that something was amiss.

"Come, Watson, come!" he cried. "The game is afoot. Not a word! Into your clothes and come!"

Still reading?

Of course you are. The beginning of Arthur Conan Doyle's "Adventure of the Abbey Grange" grabs you by the lapels, shakes you and pushes you forward into the story. Like Watson, you are startled into wakefulness. Something is "amiss," and who wouldn't want to follow the world's greatest detective out into the London fog on a promise of high adventure?

Doyle knew that a good story wouldn't get read unless it captured the reader's imagination immediately. If the beginning of a tale is dull, the reader has every right to expect that the rest of the thing will be, too — and, quite sensibly, he'll go on to something else. It was true in Doyle's day and still is: The only unforgivable thing a writer can do to a reader is bore him.

So there ought to be at least some minor firework going off at the outset of a story, especially in nonfiction. Who wants to read about humdrum?

There are lots of ways to do it. One way is to jazz up the opening with a few literary pyrotechnics, like Mike Winerip does in this fast start for a *Louisville Courier-Journal* feature:

Louisville is home for Ralph W. Ray, leading dustpan magnate of the free world.

In less than three seconds his dustpan factory, J.V. Reed & Co., produces a dustpan. *(Thump-a-blimp.)* More than 20 a minute. *(Thump-a-blimp, thump-a-blimp.)* More than 1,300 an hour. *(Thump-a-blimp, thump-a-blimp, thump-a-blimp.)* More than six million every year. *(THUMP-A-BLIMP!)* Twenty per cent of the dustpans for the non-Communist world.

Winerip makes his material interesting by amusing us with it — dustpans have never been so fascinating. Or you can begin with a twist on the reader's expectation, as *Washington Post* reporter Bart Barnes illustrates:

Sometime in June, 18-year-old Terry Gingell of Fairfax County's Thomas A. Edison High School will travel to Cincinnati for a national championship involving highly developed skills of form and precision.

He won't be hitting a ball or taking a written test filled with arcane questions designed for young geniuses. Instead, Gingell, the reigning Virginia welding champion, will be trying to form the perfect T-joint while torching hunks of aluminum and iron.

He's caught us out. Just when we expected another dull contest story, he rings in an angle. Or you might start by sending in your heavy hitter right at the top of the order, as Donnie Radcliffe, also of the *Washington Post,* does so brilliantly:

The object, said the President of the United States, was to roll the egg — not push it.

"Somebody roll an egg," he said with all the authority of the Commander-in-Chief.

With stainless steel spoon in hand Amy Carter, 9, obeyed, beginning the eight-yard-long feat by pushing a blue egg down lane No. 2 to the finish line of the annual White House Easter Egg Roll yesterday.

Eggs may not grab the reader, but the President will. In each of these examples, the subjects are not intrinsically exciting—but the writers have made them so, and *immediately* at that.

Another stunt the feature writer can borrow from literature is the action opening or "narrative hook," a scene that places the reader smack in the center of a dramatic situation. The notion goes back some distance: *The Iliad* begins that way, as does *Paradise Lost,* pursuant to Horace's edict that the epic poet should start *"in medias res,"* in the middle of things. Homer and Milton knew how to stage a story; steal from them. If it's a fire story, try this:

When 36-year-old Penny Singleton woke at a quarter to one in the morning, she had no idea the house was in flames only a wall away.

She heard someone yelling downstairs, but the nuisance of late noise in that building was not unusual. She turned over with annoyance and drew the covers close.

That was when she saw the smoke.

If it's an occasional piece, try this:

Santa Claus stuck his head out of the window of the station wagon.

"Merry Christmas!" he roared.

The man in the pork pie hat seated in the Chevy at the stoplight did a take and rubbed the fog from his windshield. His jaw dropped. A black youth at the crosswalk took it in stride.

"What's happenin', Santa?" he said.

Or if it's a courtroom yarn, this:

"He told us not to come any closer or he'd shoot," Officer Jim Hammons said grimly in Covington Police Court Tuesday.

He indicated lanky wide-shouldered Ester Young, a contractor charged with wanton endangerment in the second degree.

"That's the weapon," Hammons affirmed, pointing to a shotgun entered into evidence by Prosecutor Ed Henry.

The idea is to push some of the drama to the top and tease an audience's attention with it. Like the material that precedes the credits on a TV show or a movie, your opening lines exist to sell what follows.

Start off, then, with a sock. Mike Barnicle of the *Boston Globe* did it literally:

Just at 7:15 p.m., after the last light had faded from Beacon Hill, after all the young stockbrokers and lawyers and middle management people had settled in for the evening, after the traffic on Charles Street had thinned and the noise had softened, the old woman turned the corner onto Pinckney Street and got hit right in the face with the right hand of the young man who stood in the shadows waiting for an easy mark. She reeled back, stunned, and fell down just at the edge of the sidewalk.

Your lead paragraph shouldn't ask for attention, it should demand it. Catch the reader with the first paragraph and you'll have an easier time of it hauling him through the rest.

Beginning specificity

One way of insuring a strong opening is to display something specific — an item, an illustration, an incident — that not only rivets the attention but also manages to embody in some symbolic way your subject.

This is a species of the same method of selection you were encouraged to employ in describing people and places. Here you present an arrested moment as a kind of emblem of what is to come, like a fortune teller's tarot card. *Boston Globe* reporter Ken Hartnett, writing about his city's power structure, starts with the literal seat of power:

Twenty-four red leather chairs ring the mahogany table in the properly paneled and softly carpeted board room in the upper reaches of the John Hancock Mutual Life Insurance Company building.
All the chairs are equal—but one is more equal than the others. It is the 24th chair, the one at the center of the table facing the door.
The back of this chair is taller than the backs of all the others. This is the one reserved for the chairman of the board.

A piece on Bill Veeck for *TV Guide* by William Barry Furlong stresses the baseball innovator's unconventionality by beginning the story in the same unlikely place that Veeck begins his day:

It is before dawn and already his bathroom is cluttered. He needs a telephone at hand. He has note paper and pencils to jot down some of his more spontaneous and outrageous ideas. He gathers books to read. And if he thinks of it, he'll bring in the five-gallon cannister of popcorn that's on the living-room floor. He won't often eat breakfast, but he'll nibble on the popcorn all day.

For about 90 minutes every morning, Bill Veeck settles into his bathtub to start the day's mental work. . . .

And *Esquire* columnist Nora Ephron includes the following opening on an unsuccessful feminist in her second book *Crazy Salad,* emphasising some otherwise plain duds that, in their poor fit and seeming incongruity, sum up the whole story to come:

> Somewhere in the back of Bernice Geva's closet, along with her face mask and chest protector and simple spiked shoes, is a plain blue man's suit hanging in a plastic bag. The suit cost $29 off the rack, plus a few dollars for shortening the sleeves and pants legs, but if you ask Bernice Geva a question about that suit— where she bought it, for example, or whether she ever takes it out and looks it over— her eyes widen and then blink, hard, and she explains, very slowly so that you will not fail to understand, that she prefers not to think about the suit, or the shoes, or the shirt and tie she wore with it one summer night last year, when she umpired what was her first and last professional baseball game, a seven-inning event in Geneva, New York, in the New York-Pennsylvania Class A League.

When done as well as these writers have done it, the single item can have the same quickening effect on a reader that showing a single bauble from a brimming cache to a buccaneer would: He'll want the rest of it.

The use of a small detailed situation serving as an example of a larger problem goes back to Biblical times and earlier. Introductory vignettes can have the force of parables if they are well chosen. One should be wary of this device, since it can result in mere digression when it is not properly precise; and digression at the beginning of a story is as dangerous to its success as a third eye on a prom queen. But pros like Nelson Algren make the hard thing look easy, as this intriguing lead-in indicates:

> A female elephant named Raji escaped from a circus near Lansing, Michigan, several years ago. She attacked nobody. Raji simply walked off the circus grounds and began wandering the outskirts of town. Four thousand men, women and children turned out with squirrel guns, World War II bayonets, rakes, barrel-staves, bows and arrows, BB guns, baseball bats and housebricks for The

Great Elephant Hunt.

They pelted, hacked, slashed, stoned and tore the defenseless brute all around Lansing, until someone had the simple decency to shoot her through the head.

The lynching of Raji was scarcely more degrading to the people of Lansing than the defamation the people of Dallas worked on the bodies of Bonnie Parker and Clyde Barrow on their own killing-ground. . . .

Here Algren is in absolute control. Never allowing rage to fray itself out into rant, his aim as measured and implacable as a range hand's shooting diseased cattle. He gets us mad and prepares to make us madder.

The symbolic scene either occurs before the reporter or it doesn't, but if it does an alert feature writer will seize on it. If, in the course of researching a story, you are witness to a moment that captures the essential spirit of the thing in one compressed human action, try leading with it. *New York Times* reporter Gerald Eskenazi began a piece on football running wonder O.J. Simpson brilliantly in scene:

In a darkened room, the football coaches huddle aroung a 16-millimeter projector and stare at the wall.

Click.

The film begins. O.J. Simpson receives the ball and heads for a hole. Suddenly, the hole is clogged. He pirouettes and finds another opening.

Click.

The shot is replayed again. And again. Each time the coaches shake their heads.

"We had him," one coach says. "We cut off his routes. But the guy's so good, he can find a secondary opening, just like that. No wasted motion."

That is one reason why O.J. Simpson is the most productive runner in the history of the National Football League. . . .

Or watch Rex Reed, celebrity interviewer *par excellence,* catch an ailing literary lion's mannered insecurity in the comments he chooses to begin with and the lush style he employs to describe the man:

"Baby, I've been sick." Tennessee Williams sits under a chandelier sporting a rosy suntan and a freshly thatched beard, having dinner at Antoine's. He is eating Oysters Rockefeller and sipping cold white wine and talking about life. If a swamp alligator could talk, he would sound like Tennessee Williams. His tongue seems coated with rum and molasses as it darts in and out of his mouth, licking at his moustache like a pink lizard. His voice wavers unsteadily like old gray cigar smoke in a room with no ventiliation, rising to a mad cackle like a wounded macaw, settling finally in a cross somewhere between Tallulah Bankhead and Everett Dirksen. His hands flutter like dying birds in an abandoned aviary. Tragic flamboyance mocks tortured sensitivity. At the age of 60 the world's most famous playwright stands precariously on the ledge of vulnerability, fighting like a jaguar and talking like a poet. "The carrion birds have tried to peck out my eyes and my mind, but they've never been able to get at my heart."

Or, for sheer riveting surmise, try this crisp first line from a story by Glenn Esterly written for *Rolling Stone:*

> In preparation for tonight's poetry reading, Charles Bukowski is out in the parking lot, vomiting.

Remember: Writing an effective story is like facing a mean drunk twice your size. You'd better get in the first punch, and it had better be a damned good one, or he'll chew you up. And he won't even remember in the morning.

The single effect finish

Now let's talk about the other end of the story.

Just as there should be a jab at the start of your piece, there should be a roundhouse at the finish. Your first line says: "Read on." Your last line says: "Aren't you sorry it's over?" The most important detail of a description, we have argued, comes last, like the ink that powers the point of a pen. So too the most powerful material must explode at the end of the larger structure, a shaped charge at the end of the narrative's burning fuse.

Edgar Allan Poe was a romantic by inclination but a realist by profession. His "dreams" were the consequences of craft, not the unconscious. Poe, for all his solitary voyages out on alcohol and drugs, was openly contemptuous of artists who operated on "ecstatic intuition" alone. One did not exorcise demons by giving them their heads;

one contained them by laying down the strict margins of the pentagram, by exerting the architect will on the urchin chaos. With this result: each of his works moved forward "step by step to its completion with the precision and rigid consequence of a mathematical problem."

He argued in "The Philosophy of Composition" that a narrative should be constructed *from the ending backward,* not the reverse. "Nothing is more clear," he wrote, "than that every plot worth the name must be elaborated to its *denouement* before anything be attempted with the pen."

> It is only with the *denouement* constantly in view that we can give a plot its indispensable air of consequence or causation by making the incidents, and especially the tone at all points, tend to the development of the intention.

The *denouement*—or finish—for Poe had to be conceived at the outset, so the story could work toward it inevitably. The idea was to produce with that finish a single effect which, in the concentrated economy of its achievement, would afford the work unity.

Poe's advice can be well applied to feature writing. Consider this story of a modern-day Midas by Gerald Strine of the *Washington Post*:

> Who hasn't dreamed the implausible dream? To make off with $1,000,000, tax-free, and fly away forever to a cozy little island in the Caribbean where the sun is warm and the living is easy.
>
> Oh, to leave behind family obligations, along with the money problems and the day-to-day drudgery of having to work. Take only your two favorite dogs and an attractive young thing willing to help make the nights as enjoyable as the days.
>
> This is the stuff of which pulp fiction is made.
>
> But I saw a man last week who had done just that, in Grenada, the West Indies. His name is now "John Clancy." He was Eugene Zeek until January, 1974. As the year changed, so did Zeek's name. For good reason. He had just perpetrated one of the great cons in the history of American horse racing—a $1.1 million ripoff.
>
> From Dec. 14 to Dec. 30, 1973, Zeek stuck Liberty Bell with 26 checks worth $616,200; Penn National with 29 checks worth $407,600; and Laurel with six worth $74,500. Left holding the empty bag is the Bank of West Jersey, Delvan, N.J., owned by the Fidelity Banking Corp. of Newark.

Zeek was a good trainer of thoroughbreds, grossing $200,000 a year with a stable of 30 to 40 horses campaigned in Pennsylvania, New Jersey and Maryland.

Executives at the two Pennsylvania tracks apparently adored him. Zeek had been at Liberty Bell when that Philadelphia oval opened to thoroughbred racing in 1969, before Keystone was built. When Penn National began operations at Grantville, near Harrisburg, in 1972, Zeek was one of the best-known trainers and gamblers on the grounds.

Before long he was cashing three personal checks a day for a total of $20,000. By May, 1973, his own version of a "triple" had grown to $30,000; by July, $35,000; by October, $40,000; by November, $42,000.

From time to time Zeek's checks would bounce but, always, he quickly would make them good. His credit rating at the tracks was excellent. At the bank he was in like Flynn.

Zeek switched his personal account from a bank in Shoemakersville, Pa., to the Bank of West Jersey's Mt. Laurel branch in the summer of 1973. When a friendly bank officer was transferred from Mt. Laurel to the Riverside, N.J., branch, Zeek's account made the same move.

The bank officer had been royally wined and dined by Zeek, and treated to more than a few winning bets at the tracks. The officer trusted the trainer, so much so that when Zeek asked him to occasionally hold a check or two until he could cover them, the banker did. And Zeek, for months, was as good as his word to the bank official. He made the checks good. There were days, seemingly, when he used his private plane primarily as a money carrier for making bank deposits.

Zeek was not a professional con man. It would be unrealistic to say he planned his million-dollar swindle years in advance. But once he saw how easy it had been to create a "trusted" relationship with the tracks and the bank, he began to plan for a fantastic New Year's Day celebration.

Between mid-December, 1973, and the end of that month he made his play. Sixty-one checks were cashed at the three tracks. The bank held the early ones, as it often had, without notifying track officials Zeek's account was overdrawn. His friend at the bank believed Zeek was in Ohio, buying a breeding farm. Zeek's lady friend, "Julie Zeek," even went so far as to reassure the bank officer on New Year's Eve that she and Zeek would be at the bank early on Jan. 2 to cover the checks that already had accumulated. But Zeek and Julie and his regular jockey, Karl Korte, left by plane from Philadelphia on Dec. 31. The trainer took along his two favorite Rottweiler dogs and left two others in a kennel. He also left behind his real wife and three children.

Zeek went straight to Grenada, arriving approximately one month before that island gained its independence from Great Britain. For two years his whereabouts were unknown until, early last month, the FBI announced the missing man had been located in Grenada. There is no extradition treaty covering his crime.

Only once during this period is Zeek known to have contacted anyone connected with the case. Last fall, through an intermediary, he sent word he wanted to speak with an attorney for the bank. They met. Zeek inquired as to the possibility of returning to the states, if the money came along. He received little encouragement.

Several stories appeared last month updating Zeek's zigging and zagging. His "cover" having been broken, it seemed to be a good time to visit the homesick horseman.

Grenada is the southernmost of the Windward Islands, 90 miles north of Trinidad and 70 miles south of St. Vincent, not far off the coast of South America.

Grand Anse Beach is one of the world's finest; the temperature averages 83 degrees; the sailfish are plentiful and the sailing throughout the Grenadines is so good that champions Stormvogel, Sorcery and La Forza Del Destino regularly pay their respects to the Cavenge, the beautiful harbor at St. George's, Grenada's capital.

There is no horse racing in Grenada. Still, Zeek seemed to be reasonably happy during the short time we observed him at the yacht-building company he is associated with. We tried to strike up a conversation only to find him shy and uncommunicative. Julie is still with him, as reportedly is Korte, as "Paul Clancy," John's younger brother.

Few of Grenada's 110,000 inhabitants know who "Clancy" really is. One who does commented: "He has the IRS off his back down here. I think they were getting bothersome. What worries him the most, I believe, is the possibility a new government might be elected next year, or that some Mafia types he once bet with in the States might pay him a visit. They wouldn't be coming in on any of the big cruise ships, either."

Zeek is 45. At 6-feet-2, 250 pounds, he has always stood out in a crowd.

He is a man who has made off with more than $1 million. The Caribbean sun shines virtually every day. He owns a yacht. The fishing's great. So's the sailing. No longer does he have to take care of his horses. He never has to worry about his checks bouncing.

Yet he wants to come home. . . .

Strine's finish is the payoff; it provides an astringent irony that sets off the rest of the story. Like the heady billions of Howard Hughes, Zeek's wealth has imprisoned him rather than set him free.

If you want to maximize the force of your piece, the knockout must come at the end. The one-minute scrap with the hour-long wrap-up to fill dead air is simply anti-climatic. Go for the long brawl and the killing blow.

When I wrote the following account of the youngest old man I ever met, I attempted to sum him up overwhelmingly at the end, to express his values in a final symbolic way. I *aimed* the story at its ending:

"I'm not a bit backward about asking questions," college student James K. Caldwell confessed.

But the persistent quality of his curiosity is not the only unusual side to this inquisitive Northern Kentucky State College sophomore.

Because James K. Caldwell is 70 years old.

"At my age you're ready for the theory after living through the practice," Caldwell observed. "The more experience you get, you find there is more to life than just fighting it out from day to day."

And James K. Caldwell has done his share of struggling. Fifty years ago he was a college freshman, but economics interfered with his education.

"I was an orphan boy," he recalled, "and my own family needed my money."

The Depression provided him no alternative, and Caldwell worked as a conductor at Cincinnati's Union Terminal for 30 years. His belief in education continued, however; he put each of his six children through school. One became a doctor of veterinary medicine, while each of the others earned Master's degrees. His deceased wife, Thelma, one of the first special education teachers in Boone County, amassed more than 200 credit hours at various area colleges. Meanwhile Caldwell's own inquiring mind was a constant.

"I'm the nosiest guy on earth," he grinned.

Seated in the library of his sprawling home on US 25 in Richwood sending out locomotive gouts of black smoke from a black briar, James K. Caldwell was at his greatest ease— in the company of his books. Ranks of bright bindings ringed the room: a complete set of Dickens, the Oxford English Dictionary, Will and Ariel Durant's ten-volume *Story of Civilization*, collected works of Nobel Prize winners.

"I like to caress the covers," Caldwell confided. "I may not have it all in my own mind, but I know where to find it."

With his broad rugged features and turned-up military mustache, Caldwell looks less like a scholar or conductor than he does a World War I German flying ace, his eyes cinder-sharp. He pushed tobacco down in the bowl of his pipe with a thumb and spoke of the curriculum, which includes for Caldwell biology, Biblical lit, psychology, sociology and finite math. And—above all—political science.

"I've got to know what's going on," Caldwell said. "I've always been an avid news fan, and I enjoy getting underneath the facts. Technical matters are of less interest to me—I'm getting too old to remember all those long names in the sciences."

His views are staunchly liberal. Caldwell's first Presidential vote was cast in 1928, for a Democrat. That has been his pattern ever since.

"There are two exceptions," Caldwell recalled. "I voted for Republican Flem Sampson—he was for free textbooks and the creation of national parks. And I supported Sherman Cooper for senator. I like the man's vision."

Vision is something James K. Caldwell values. When a pacemaker was installed in his heart recently, it enabled him to continue looking at the world with the habitual wonder he holds for it. Caldwell is up at 5:30 each morning to observe the sunrise; at dusk he is the willing watcher for each sunset. College is only an extension of Caldwell's personal investigation of the universe.

"I had 460 African violets I was cultivating," he noted. "But I had to give those up for my studies."

Caldwell subscribes to *Soviet Life*, a magazine imported from Russia, "just to get the other side." He traveled widely with his wife and has seen every major city in the continental United States.

"Except Seattle," he sighed. "We didn't quite get around to that one."

The result of his learning and life has been a large-hearted tolerance.

"You can't deny there's other people in the world," Caldwell insisted. "I'd like to see us do business with Cuba, for example. We don't have to crawl in bed with Castro, but it would be a friendlier situation if we could share with him."

There is supposed to be a communication gap between the young and the old, but Caldwell finds none with his fellow students. Nor with contemporary ideas: One of his favorite writers is James Baldwin, who, he notes, "lays it on the line." He admires the tough-mindedness of Hemingway and points out that that kind of strength through informed suffering may be the only quality which will enable America to survive its current difficulties.

"When I was young we were pressurized from having too little," he commented. "Now we're pressurized from having too much. But you can't keep a dog in the house all its life and expect it to survive in the pack later."

Caldwell, who used to stand at the draw bar of the Presidential train at Union Terminal to listen to Harry Truman talk, admires candor because above all else he is fascinated with the truth.

"For a while there I thought Gerald Ford was going to be another straight-talker like Truman," the studious septugenarian said. He puffed reflectively on his pipe. "But I have since changed my mind."

The temptation in the presence of a man of Caldwell's perspective and years is to ask him what advice he has for the young. James K. Caldwell does not like to give out advice; it is the habit of the arrogant. But pressed he offers this suggestion, which does not restrict itself to any age group:

"Don't miss a chance," he said. "Never turn down an opportunity. The first day you say no, you begin to level off."

James K. Caldwell, whose prime satisfaction is associating himself with books, has not leveled off. As he passed from the library to the living room where he does his studies, the reporter felt the warmth of a wood fire and a similar warmth from an oil painting just over the mantle above it.

The painting is of Caldwell's wife as a young woman, and there is a diploma in her lap.

Everything depends upon the last two graphs—and that was the intention.

In a story for *New Times* titled "Murder on the Bayou," Associated Press reporter Wayne Slater investigated a bad-temper redneck union war going on at the Jupiter Chemical Company ammonia plant in swampland Louisiana. What he found was "a strange alliance, a power structure made up of construction union thugs, select contractors, local politicians, moneymen and law enforcement officials, and everybody is working to preserve the status quo. Everybody wants to keep the insiders on top and the outsiders out." In a dawn raid on a construction site, an independent union man named Joe Hooper got in the way of a .9-caliber round nobody remembers firing. Slater's conveyed impression is one of outlaws holding absolute sway over the bewildered majority of the AFL-CIO. So he ends his story in a personal confrontation with one of the thugs, who smilingly shows him the watermain mouth of a .44 Magnum from the cab of a Chevy pickup:

"Look, you've been around here long enough. It's time you went back to wherever you're from. Got it? This ain't your kind of town." Big Grin sort of laughs at that line, and then he raises the gun barrel straight at the reporter's head. "You've been asking all the wrong questions. Things are going fine here and everything will be okay as long as you just mind your own business.

"This ain't New York," he says. "This here is Louisiana." And suddenly it's all so clear. The men who planned the Jupiter assault are an elite guard, protectors of the status quo, of the oligarchy, of the comfortable insiders. They are the gunsels of *L'Alliance*.

"You've got five minutes," says Big Grin. "And I'm not kidding. If I see your ass again, you're a dead man."

What more immediate way of conveying the company town We/They perception of reality could there be than to show the journalist, that quintessential outsider, being forcefully invited to leave? The leveled gun aims itself at us, and Slater's angry helplessness becomes our own.

The snapper

"Frankly, my dear, I don't give a damn."

Rhett Butler's famed parting shot to Scarlett O'Hara in the film version of *Gone With the Wind* expresses at once his impatience with a particular woman and his final break with the moral world she represents. A great last line, one that drives home a writer's point with a quick departing fillip of the verbal whip, is called a *snapper*.

Snappers sew matters up, offer emphasis, provide the parting shot. Just as the jest in the following news bright has a fast finish, so does the story around it:

In his shop, Boone Aire Country Club pro Gordon Waldespuhl has an enormous outsized golf ball with a spigot that dispenses to member players on wintry days the secret ingredient of "Gordon's Special Coffee"—booze.

It is a clue to his puckish side. Be warned: If you're playing against him, you'd better be more than skillful. You'd better be clever, too.

"I was playing recently with a member who was beating me with his handicap," Waldespuhl recalled, smiling innocently. "On the par four hole I made him a little proposition.

"I told him I would give him one stroke for the hole and tee off with a six iron if I could throw the ball once.

"He thought that over and jumped at it.

"As the hole progressed, he kept asking me when I was going to throw the ball. Finally I did.

"I threw his. In the water hazard."

The opposition took a penalty stroke to get it out and — what else?—Gordon Waldespuhl won.

Waldespuhl does not linger over his joke, nor does the writer over his story.

A snapper can indicate mood, as does this one from a color story on the last days of George McGovern's unsuccessful 1972 quest for the Presidency:

The crowd applauded again and he was gone, moving in the middle of a flying wedge of federal agents, shaking hands as he went. Outside the Secret Service trotted with the limousine, three on a side, like professional pallbearers rushing through an overtime funeral. A girl in a straw campaign hat turned to her boyfriend in the mob that massed after him. "At last I've actually seen a real live breathing politician," she said. She put her hands in her pockets and sighed.

"Who's going to lose."

Or the snapper might be ironic, as is the following from a piece on the frustrations of policemen trying to serve an unappreciative public:

The shift pays itself out slowly like anchor line until the radio crackles with a trouble call on Fisk Street.

"That's where that woman got cut last night," says Lt. Al Meyer, and heads across town at speed.

Sgt. Don Plageman is already at the scene when Meyer arrives. A heavy-set man in a tee shirt is standing on the sidewalk with a gun in one hand and a blackjack in the other.

"He smashed in the back window of my car," the heavy man raves. "This is the third time."

Plageman tells him to put the weapons away.

A boy who saw someone running from the car offers his assistance.

"You can't miss him," he says. "He's tall."

Or the snapper might move to summation of the subject, as does this one at the end of a story on the breakneck campaign style of a Kentucky senatorial candidate:

While Wendell Ford shaved in the car in preparation for his next-scheduled television appearance, there was time to reflect that his favorite phrase, now overquoted to the status of dead metaphor, gave clues to what he admired. "If you can't stand the heat, get out of the kitchen," Ford said and said again that day, doffing the elocutionary hat to an earlier midstates Democrat.

"What we need is a 1974 Harry Truman," he asserted, and the evidence was that Truman was the man he emulated. In spite of the expected political laying on of hands and salesman's handshake, in spite of the news photographs that placed him clowning behind the plow, Ford seemed to be running a campaign based on his responsiveness to the people as a plain man speaking plainly.

The pace of the day afforded him no time at all for any real dialog with his constituents. But if he wasn't really talking to the people, he was at least saying hello.

These endings are intended to resonate backward through the story and forward as our last memory of it, conveying an impression in keeping with the tone, be it sad, serious or silly. Call it ham on wry.

The following story sits tidily on the snapper like a top on its spinning end:

The night the Russians took over the town their artillery began a bombardment that woke young Mike Weiland and his father.

The boy felt a large hand on his shoulder.

"Mike," his father said softly. "We've got to go down to the bunker again."

It was a ritual that had been enacted several times daily in the Hungarian town of Dvecser with the advance and retreat of the Germans. But the boy Mike was more accustomed to lying in the grass unmoving of a morning, watching in silence the air battles of Americans and English against the other side as another child might have watched quarrelsome birds.

"We went down the street and around the houses," recalled a grown Mike Weiland half a world away. "Suddenly there were Russian soldiers coming toward us, ten in a line. One of them yelled, '*Stop!*' "

His father started to run, Mike followed suit, and the Russians opened up on them with automatic weapons.

"The sparks from their bullets hitting the stone wall in front and behind us lit it up like daylight," Weiland recalled.

They took shelter safely in separate houses, and that night the boy and his father each bore the certainty the other was dead.

Disconsolate, young Mike walked home the next day to find a crowd of men at his father's door.

"They killed my son!" said someone from the midst of it.

The voice was his father's, and their reunion was an emotional one.

That was in 1945. The boy had been 11. Now the man is 41, lean and graying with close-cropped hair and pale green eyes. Today

Weiland is under evaluation at Goodwill Industries Rehabilitation Center, 227 Court St., Covington, after sustaining a back injury that incapacitated him.

Seated at a shop bench laden with stopped clocks and small appliances, he does not look like a man who has survived a war and a bloody revolution. The eyes are gentle, the arms unflexed. But they are the eyes and arms of a man who does not need to advertise himself.

It had been Weiland at 22 who marched with his friends through Veszprem on the first day of the 1956 Hungarian revolt, armed only with a flag. And it had been Weiland and 27 others who, days later, took the high ground where the city buildings were.

This time they were armed.

With small 72-round machine guns they sniped from the windows at an army under a three-day rain.

"You had to get back fast when you shot from a window," Weiland said. "They had cannon, and in the next minute the window would be gone."

He and a 13-year-old friend dragged a wheeled water-cooled gun to the top of a firewatch tower and used it for half a day until the Russians trained tanks on it.

"We lost 10 men over there," he added quietly. "We had no medical help at all. If someone was hit, he had to bleed to death."

The third night 17 escaped.

"They would not confront us outside the city," he said, "but once in a while they gave us a showdown."

Weiland remembered an old man gunned down in the streets by the Russians "just to show us they were there."

The revolt failed and Weiland fled. One abortive escape attempt put him within crawling distance of three Communist border guards 200 yards from Austria.

"The ground was frozen like bones," he said.

Later, with the help of an old man hauling firewood in a wagon, Weiland made it across the ditch dug around his country to freedom.

For 19 years he has worked in America at various tasks from carpentry to hard labor on the killing room floor of a packing house.

Now, with a wife, Rosemary, 34, sons Mike, 10, and Joe, 5, and daughters Marie, 13, and Kati, 12, Weiland considers himself lucky in spite of his slipped-disc disability. "People do not know how good they have it here," he said. "There is no match to the United States. Anywhere." Though he is seeking work for a man with a bad back, Weiland's strength remains somewhere beyond his body. Even his address has an earned quality about it. Mike Weiland now resides in a Kentucky town called Independence.

Save something for the end. The snapper can be mournful, arch, mild, wild or witty, but it should never be lame or lacking in freshness. Old tag lines will work if a new context renders them striking, as in the case of this acid use of a Hallmark Cards slogan by James S. Kunen at the end of his *New Times* examination of nuclear testing:

> Testing new weapons makes nuclear war more likely. Right now, peace is maintained by mutual deterrence. Both the U.S. and Russia know that a first strike by either could not destroy the other's ability to retaliate. But if we develop delivery systems which could destroy Russia's weapons before they are launched, or if our testing leads the Russians to *fear* that we have such a capability, Russia's only defense would be to launch an offensive strike.
>
> All of our testing just hastens the day of reckoning. When the missiles fly, at least we'll know we cared enough to send the very best.

The plant

Related to the snapper is the "plant," an item that either carries symbolic weight at the end of the story or emphasizes its point. Symbolic items at the beginning of a story fasten the reader's attention on it; such items at the end enforce a specific impression. They are "plants" because the writer positions them deliberately to fulfill his purpose. In itself a plant has no particular meaning; the artist invests it with one.

A story about the endless minutiae of crime lab work, for example, might end this way:

> Now lab man Gary Linn leaned over the enlarger as he worked on photographs of the scene of a drugstore shooting.

"The pictures sometimes reveal things you missed during the actual investigation," Lynn explained. "Look at this."

He hung the shot from clips on a string above him. The store aisles were a mess, magazine racks violently askew; a pool of black blood crept the length of one of them. Linn's finger pointed to a corner of the pool, a dark spot perhaps a thirty-second of an inch square.

It was the toe end of a footprint, which was exactly the sort of small detail the Service Bureau specialized in.

The item carries the effect.

Plants are more powerful when they are alluded to earlier in the story as a kind of preparation for the stress they will receive later. Frank Norris opened his turn-of-the-century novel *McTeague*, concerning a well-meaning man driven by forces utterly beyond his control, with a scene in the protagonist's San Francisco office. Among the things that furnish the place is a singing canary in a gilt cage. Now the book is about "the destruction of an innocent," to use scholar Carvel Collins' precise phrase; so at length McTeague will find himself, through the toils of fortune and feckless friends, fighting for his life over a sack of money in the desert. But here's the clincher: Norris has dragged that canary over long miles of barren ground and 300 pages of manuscript to make a single symbolic point.

> McTeague did not know how he killed his enemy, but all at once Marcus grew still beneath his blows. Then there was a sudden last return of energy. McTeague's right wrist was caught, something clicked upon it, then the struggling body fell limp and motionless with a long breath.
>
> As McTeague rose to his feet, he felt a pull at his right wrist; something held it fast. Looking down, he saw that Marcus in that last struggle had found strength to handcuff their wrists together. Marcus was dead now; McTeague was locked to the body. All about him, vast, interminable, stretched the measureless leagues of Death Valley.
>
> McTeague remained stupidly looking around him, now at the distant horizon, now at the ground, now at the half-dead canary chittering feebly in its little gilt prison.

The canary's predicament is also McTeague's. Both are terminally trapped by circumstances quite beyond themselves, caged helplessly in a world they never made. Feature writers are not allowed the luxury of inventing plants, but they can use them to good effect when reality offers them up. Here is a true story about a modern good Samaritan whose name was changed to protect him from possible reprisals for being one, even after he moved away from what he saw:

Mickey O'D. heard the yelling in front of his South Boston house on 5th Street. He saw a kid in an Afro and a white jacket running up Farragut Road near Carson Beach. Another dark-haired boy ran behind him.

At their heels were 40 youths ranging in age from nine to 20, some of them on bicycles.

"Get the niggahs!" somebody screamed. "Kill the niggahs!"

Mickey saw that this was coming from the mouth of a little girl.

He had been outside on a warm Memorial Day afternoon doing some work on his eight-year-old Volkswagen. Mickey is a spare-looking middleweight who was born in South Boston and later helped build the base at Subic Bay when he was in the Seabees. He did not like what he saw.

And he did not like the next thing, either. A large Puerto Rican woman was crossing the street distractedly. She seemed to have some connection with the boys being chased. A white youth in his twenties came out of one of the houses and punched her in the face.

"I could hear the smack," Mickey notes with anger. "He was one of those guys who probably never won a fight in his life."

He won this one. The woman went down, and Mickey went to help her, his tool bag in his hand.

The plant— She had been holding a large plastic bucket with clams in it. They now lay in a clutter on the sidewalk.

Mickey helped her up as her husband came to her side. The man did not weigh much more than a hundred pounds. He had a hand over his right eye, which had been punched.

Mickey cannot forget the looks on their faces.

"I could just see the picture in Treblinka right before they went to the gas chambers," he says. "That's what they looked like."

Somehow, using fragments of what little he knew in Italian and Spanish, he got them back to his house with instructions to hide in the hallway. They told him they were a family that had come from New Jersey for the holiday weekend, the husband, the wife, their son and a nephew. They took the subway from downtown and walked to the beach to collect some clams.

They didn't know there was anything wrong with that.

They didn't even know how far Mickey was sticking his neck out just keeping them inside his house.

Meanwhile they were bleeding and they didn't know where their kids were.

Mickey's Volkswagen was out of kilter, so he went to a friend—"a big stocky Irish fellow straight out of Damon Runyon"—who came over in his station wagon.

"They were standing on the porch when we got back," Mickey says sadly. "I'm sure they were afraid to stay inside. They probably thought I was coming back with the others to beat them up some more."

They wanted to go looking for the boys, but Mickey's friend explained that he did not think that would be wise. The thing to do would be to go down to Station Six at D and Broadway and come back in a patrol car.

They were glimpsed by a gang on the corner at P and 5th who later told Mickey's friend they thought they saw him with some blacks in his car. The gang had been worried that he had been kidnapped by the blacks.

The husband and wife were out of their minds with concern for their kids. Mickey and his friend dropped them off at the station house but did not leave their names.

"There are people who will break your windows, slash your tires for doing something like that," Mickey explains.

The two Puerto Rican boys had made it all the way down to the white fuel depot at the industrial park, where another South Boston man got them in his car and got out of there to safety.

"I was sick," Mickey says.

The next day he noticed the white plastic bucket with the clams still strewn across the sidewalk. He did not think the

Puerto Rican family would be back for it.

The empty clam bucket seems to express the sad, pointless, futile waste of everything that comes before it. The irrational anti-busing racism that the Puerto Rican family fell into is magnified by their innocence. Vulnerable, harmless, the plastic bucket seems to indict by those very qualities the thugs who caused it to be spilled and left behind.

The frame story

A long, ambitious piece can be unified by containing it within the cohering mortar of a continuing narrative, like a lecture wedged between the installments of a serial. The beginning and ending of one yarn frames the text of another. Geoffrey Chaucer used the "frame story" to good effect in *The Canterbury Tales*; connecting the disjunct subjects of each pilgrim's interest is the larger plot of their spring progress to the shrine of St. Thomas.

Look back to Craig Waters' story "When Hunters Become the Hunted" at the end of chapter three. The piece begins—in the midst of things—with a father and son hunting deer. The son is killed. The end of the piece emphasizes the tragedy of the boy's death and the father's evident failure to comprehend its significance. Between these narrative bookends comes the rest of the article, carried forward by other specific disasters. The device leaves us not only with the disturbing drama of a powerful start and finish, but with a formal sense of inevitable closure as well.

Turn forward to the Appendix. "The Deep Six Connection" by Howard Kohn and Clark Norton, written for *Rolling Stone*, is a brilliant example of the successful use of the frame story as a unifying device. The story is at once intensely interesting and valuably informative—your dual goal. Read it.

Now look at the story's structure. Kohn and Norton sought a specific incident that would illustrate immediately their account of modern piracy. The example was not the whole story; it was the device that would make vivid an extended and pervasive problem. With attention to the frame story and what it contains, we can outline "The Deep Six Connection" like this:

1. The sailboat *Kamalii*, moored in Honolulu, is boarded and captured, then set on course for Thailand to collect a cargo of drugs.

138 *Stalking the Feature Story*

Frame story of specific incident, 1-5.

A. The sudden phenomenon of missing modern pleasure boats is examined.

2. The crew of the *Kamalii* is put over the side in the open sea.

B. Yachtjacking for purposes of drug smuggling is shown to be widespread in recent years.

Detailed examination of larger subject, A-D.

3. The members of the *Kamalii* crew are rescued as their boat sails on with pirates aboard.

C. A formal probe of modern piracy reveals only unconcern and alibis from federal investigative agencies.

4. The *Kamalii* is pursued and seized by the Coast Guard.

D. Dread lingers among the yachting community.

5. The *Kamalii* captain expresses continuing wariness.

As the outline shows, "Connection" is exceedingly well-crafted; each pause in the frame story comes as a cliffhanger that carries us through the rest of the material to the next installment of the frame story. The ending is at once a symbolic moment and a snapper driving home the frightened vulnerability of the survivors. Although the story is a long one, it *seems short* because it is behind us so fast — a consequence of fine writing and careful construction.

He's Leading Light of the Charge Brigade
by David Larsen

[Here's something fast and flossy by Los Angeles Times *reporter David Larsen. He presents us with a fancy first line, an equally fancy last one, and a ripping toboggan ride of a story in between.]*

SANTA CLARA — You've got to give Walter Cavanagh credit.

Everybody else does.

News peg— Cavanagh has the world's largest collection of credit cards —788 of them—all different. Mr. Plastic Fantastic.

"It started four years ago when a pal and I made a bet as to who could get the most in three months," he said. "I got 40 and I won."

Cavanagh saw no reason to stop, and now his life can be summed up on the T-shirt his friend Nancy gave him: "Charge!"

Actually, he makes use of only a handful of the cards in his collection. Cavanagh, a pharmacy manager, is quick to point out that if he used them all he would be hard pressed to afford the interest.

He keeps no cards that charge a monthly fee.

The pharmacist, who is mentioned in the Guinness Book of World Records, keeps most of his collection in a safe-deposit box, in foldout wallet windows. They would stretch to the ground from the top of a tall building.

"The tiresome part is filling out the applications," he said. "The most I've ever done at one sitting was 16. I just couldn't take it any more."

Cavanagh, 32, can charge gas at 49 different brands of stations. One oil company was a little curious as to why he wanted their card, since their closest station was 2,000 miles away, but they sent one anyway.

Cavanagh has been in only about 3% of the establishments in his aggregation, which includes cards from England, Canada and Mexico.

"I've only scratched the surface, though," he said. "More than 10,000 credit cards have been issued in the United States alone."

Hardly a day goes by without the awed mailman bringing some new cards, but the collector is still waiting for one from Newberry's.

"Saks Fifth Avenue, Neiman-Marcus, you name it. I have them all," he said. "But the Newberry people wrote me that I had too much credit outstanding."

Little do they know that if he wanted to, he could get up to $750,000 in merchandise and cash elsewhere.

Snapper— The loan arranger rides again.

The Frozen Dream of Tony Williams
by Bob Greene

[Everything moves inevitably toward the last line in this tightly woven story by Chicago Sun-Times *columnist Bob Greene. It's a quiet throwaway line, and quietly it takes off the top of your head.]*

You've seen them before, a thousand times. The playground hotshots, the young black kids who are going to fight their way out of the West Side hell with a basketball and a pair of Converse All-Star sneakers. Tony Williams was one of the best

The point— of them, and he knew the rules: if you're going to make it out of this misery, you'd better have the moves.

"They called me pretty good," Tony said one Monday afternoon. He speaks softly and with an absence of comfort. "I could shoot, and I could handle the ball. I was hoping to go to college, and then make it to the pros. I used to play every day."

He knew that basketball was his only hope. There was no money at home. In the afternoons he would deliver a paper route and then go to a schoolyard near Jackson and Albany

Dramatic and play in his pickup games. Two years ago this month—late
impetus— in the afternoon March 27, 1973—he practiced his basketball and started to walk home for dinner. Tony was 15 years old, and it was the last time he would ever step on a court under his own power.

"Someone shot me," he said, no emotion in his voice. "I was walking down Jackson. No one knows why. The police said that someone must have taken a shot from a window, for fun or something. The probably weren't even aiming for me.

"At first I thought I had been hit with a rock or something. Then I hit the ground, and that's when I knew that I must be shot. When the feeling in my legs went away, it felt like I was dying. The feeling went away real slow-like."

A bullet was lodged in Tony's spine, and he was paralyzed from the chest down. He was treated at Garfield Park Community Hospital, and then Presbyterian-St. Luke's, and then
Single the Rehabilitation Institute of Chicago. The doctors determin-
sentence ed that Tony's paralysis was permanent.
graph for
emphasis— "Yeah, they told me no more basketball," Tony said.

It took the life out of him. According to a Rehabilitation Institute nurse, Tony's depression was far deeper than that of the other patients. "He didn't get involved in any of the activities," the nurse said. "He would just sit in his wheelchair holding a basketball on his lap and not say anything. We tried to cheer him up — we told him that maybe he could learn to be a sports writer or a broadcaster — but he knew that he could never hope to be a basketball player again."

In June of 1973, Tony was released from the Rehabilitation Institute. He now lives with his mother, Mrs. Mattie Handy, at

3531 W. Monroe. At first he attended Spalding High School, which has facilities for physically handicapped children. But Tony and his mother live by themselves on the second floor of their apartment building, and it became impossible for his mother to carry Tony and his heavy wheelchair down to the street. The building is not equipped with elevators or ramps, and Tony's mother, who is on public aid, could not find another place ot live. Because of this, Tony is unable to go to school any more.

"Can't nobody carry me downstairs every day," Tony said. "My mother's not strong enough, and most of the neighbors are old. So I don't get outside the apartment much. I haven't been outside in a month."

Tony is 17 now. Most days he spends in front of the television set. He doesn't see his old friends from the basketball courts often. "That's OK," he said. "I was a basketball freak, too, and I know what it means to spend all of your time playing the game." He watches every Chicago Bulls game that is televised. "It's playoff time," he said. "We're hoping to win."

He has two idols in this world: Bob Love and Norm Van Lier, who are players for the Bulls. Tony's one small dream is that he could get a chance to meet the two men. One of the nurses at the Rehabilitation Institute, without telling Tony, wrote to the Bulls last year and told them how much Tony would love to meet Love and Van Lier, but she never received a response.

e point
emphasized—
Whatever bitterness Tony may feel about what has happened to him, he masks in conversation. He realizes that he lives in a world where there are very few chances for a better life, and that the one chance he had has been taken away. The fact that his chance was stolen from him in a random, awful way does not mean that he will cry. He does not even own a basketball any more.

"That's all I do, watch TV," Tony said. "I heard about something called wheelchair basketball, and I was thinking that maybe if I could exercise and make my arms stronger, I could play some. But we have that problem with getting me and my wheelchair down the stairs, so I probably couldn't get a chance to play, anyway." Tony paused for a moment, and then he asked a question:

Snapper— "Has it started to get warm outside yet?"

6. People

The necessary news peg

You don't learn anything when you're doing the talking.

At the time that Harpo, the silent Marx brother, was invited to dine regularly with the members of the celebrated Algonquin "Round Table" in New York, some of his friends expressed complete astonishment. The famed wits of the Round Table — among them Dorothy Parker, Robert Benchley, George S. Kaufman and Alexander Woollcott — were well known for their reputations as raconteurs. Meals at the Algonquin Hotel were choreographed occasions for wry comment and acerbic riposte. What possible legitimate interest could these mordantly loquacious creatures have in the usually taciturn Harpo?

His explanation was characteristically to the point: "They needed," Harpo said, "somebody to listen."

Fundamental to getting stories out of people is the development of an attentive ear. In general, folks are so used to having to compete constantly with a harvest of other talkers to get any kind of attention, they just naturally open right up in the presence of receptive mutes.

Half the battle of getting strangers to talk to you is won when you indicate an interest in what they have to say. That's flattering. How many people asked you for *your* views today? The rest is a matter of encouraging individuals to keep it up, easily accomplished by judicial nods and responsive grunts.

The amateur usually makes one of two mistakes. He may be so impressed with his subject that he tries to appear more impressive himself— the error of the admirer who wants to be loved more than he wants the story. That's vanity. Or he may find himself in such awe of his subject that he conducts himself with the passive acceptance of a vegetable in the presence of a threshing machine.

One should be neither slavish nor intimidated. Celebrities and other individuals pushed to the fore by human events differ from other mortals only in the fact that they have become temporarily newsworthy. They have to change their socks and evacuate regularly just like the rest of us. They are frightened by unexpected loud noises and gratified by honest approval. Even kings have these things in common. Minding that they are thus heirs to all the frailties of the flesh to which the species is accustomed, you should be able to approach them with the simple respect you would accord any ordinary person.

But it isn't just the amateur who resorts to posturing at the expense of his project. Watch any televised Presidential news conference. There you will witness grown men and women, the veterans of collective centuries of journalistic experience, reduced to pompous, quacking incoherence in the presence of their peers and the network cameras. Instead of asking pointed questions and shutting up for the answers, certain members of the fourth estate take the floor like filibusterers, declaiming two-minute interrogatories nobody could possibly keep track of and generally seeking center stage instead of the proper role of prompter. The hell with them. The reporter makes his reputation by the stories he writes, not the figure he cuts.

In seeking out a subject, the writer must keep in mind that the present moment governs the feature game. It is not sufficient to select a Notable and do a story on that person. He or she must be *currently engaged* in something that makes them newsworthy even as the piece goes to press. Your audience— and, consequently, your editor— wants to know what's happening *now.* Thus George Burns, an unfailingly interesting and gifted man with a performing career extending back to vaudeville, is not terribly newsworthy in 1974. But in 1975 he's a hit at 80 in a film called *The Sunshine Boys,* and in 1976 he's the winner of an Academy Award, and in 1977 he publishes his memoirs— each event is an occasion for a story.

This present endeavor or angle is called a "news peg," and it is the pretext for any personality story. Though the writer need not confine his story to the news peg — it can be an opportunity for all kinds of offshoots and digressions — still the news peg must be addressed, preferably early in the story. An actor is in town to plug a new film. A politician is engaged in controversial legislation. An author undergoes an obscenity suit. Each of these matters is a news peg that can lead to an investigation of the more engaging question of what the individual is like. The news peg informs the reader about why the personality is worthy of attention; from it is hung differing garments of various sizes, depending upon the tastes of the authorial tailor.

Once you have chosen a subject with the requisite news peg, you have to arrange a meeting. Arrange it directly. Avoid if possible going through secretaries, public relations representatives or other generally wary minions who dart protectively about the principal like symbiotic birds cleaning the mouth of a croc.

Public relations people are not, as is widely believed, present to make their clients accessible to the media. Quite the reverse. Their purpose is not to foster news but *good* news. They are of course the natural enemies of the journalist, who simply wants the facts; the PR person wants to ration out only the more antiseptic ones. So PR people are as suspicious of reporters as pie vendors at a fat farm; one never knows what the heavies will carry away.

Thus PR people dole out interviews like special dispensation to the pious. The faithful are served first. Access is granted in direct proportion to the harmlessness of the interviewer and the influence of the publication he represents. But even when an arrangement is agreed upon, PR people sometimes neglect to inform the principal. Or neglect to inform the interviewer of cancellations. Or confidently send the both of them to lunch at separate restaurants on either side of town.

Go to the source. See your subject directly — at his home, office, health club or holding cell. It's harder to hang up on you when you appear in person. If that isn't possible, try the telephone. When that doesn't work, then and only then resort to the PR route. In each case, identify yourself. Ask for an hour at a specific place and time; less is superficial, more is presumptuous. You can get what you need in an hour, which should be extended only on the invitation of the principal.

If the PR person insists on being present at the interview, suffer him. He will be in particular evidence with movie stars for two reasons: 1) to prevent the star from embarrassing the studio; 2) to prevent the star from embarrassing himself. The PR person can be expected to steer the conversation safely leeward of negativity, dutifully filling in any dead air should the actor be inarticulate unaccompanied by a script. He is the supportive side man who laughs loudest when the audience isn't.

Research the subject. PR bios are predictably unreliable, right down to the birthdate. Use the library, the newspaper clip file and the special knowledge of experts. Learn everything you can about your subject. It is insulting to be interviewed by someone who hasn't indicated enough interest in the occasion to prepare for it, and the best questions come from those who have been briefed.

Oriana Fallaci, whose global beat includes international notables and heads of state, prepares herself emotionally as well. Neither awed nor intimidated by her material, she advances on it as an adversary. "I'm tense," she has admitted. "I'm worried because it's a boxing match."

Oh ho! I'm climbing, I'm going into the ring. I'm nervous. My God, who's going to win? But no inferiority complex, no fear of the person. When someone starts acting superior, then I become dangerous, then I become nasty.

An interviewer should be on edge the way an athlete is before an especially interesting contest. It is not fear but anticipation that sets the backs of the hand pricking.

Formulate a list of questions from the information you have gathered. The list is to give you something to fall back on during conversational doldrums. It should be regarded as a security blanket, not an iron maiden. The interview should not be conducted rigidly from one formulated phrase to the next; rather the subject should be allowed to digress, to lead in new directions, and the interviewer should follow encouragingly, returning to his list in rangy circles like a pilgrim hawk to the jesses of a falconer.

The questions should be ordered from the casual to the most probing. Leave any tough ones for the end. That way, should you be thrown out for asking them, you will leave with enough other material for a story. Ask the toughies first and you may come up empty.

What follows is a quickie with a news peg and evidence of having done the homework:

The idea was to have him make friends with the bears. So they handed him a fistful of marshmallows and shoved him into a cage with ten of them.

"The bears had only been in captivity for a couple of weeks," sighed Patrick Wayne. "The marshmallows didn't last very long."

Wayne was in town to promote his new film *The Bears and I,* a

Walt Disney production opening here November 6th. He plays a Vietnam war veteran who finds post-war direction among the Indians in Canada.

"The bears are totem to the tribe," he explained. "It took us quite a while to establish rapport. I felt pretty silly talking to them, I can tell you that."

Wayne's smile is easy, a match to his manner. He has the look of a varsity athlete grown older, boyish but at home off the playing fields. His is a strong face, full of planes and angles; it would require jowls and a few beatings to resemble that of his famous father, John.

Or the seamed and sun-cracked countenance of his co-star in *Bears*, Chief Dan George. Wayne remembered the deep impression the Indian's presence made on him at their first meeting.

"Of course I expected a stoic. There were all these things going on in his eyes, but nothing coming out of his mouth. I half expected him to instruct the Great Spirit to call down rain upon the land, that sort of thing.

"Then my eye caught this beautifully crafted turquoise wristband he was wearing. I asked him what religious significance it had.

" 'I can get you all you want at 25 bucks apiece,' he told me, and we both laughed. He's really a big city boy."

Wayne started acting 23 years ago in his father's films during summer vacations. Summer was his only contact with John Wayne, who had been divorced from his mother when Patrick was four. Some of those films have become classics, like *Rio Grande* (1950), *The Quiet Man* (1951), and *The Searchers* (1955). His older brother Michael became a kind of father substitute, and he still thinks the best director he ever worked with was his godfather — John Ford. When Patrick was college age, he wasn't sure he liked working in film because of the nature of the medium or because of the proximity it gave him to his father; only after he studied biology at Loyola University and served in the Coast Guard did he discover the movies were indeed for him.

Since then he has worked with the best in the business, both on the screen and on television. Patrick Wayne's comments about his colleagues are always kind and display real admiration. Richard Boone is "a real wild man, completely loose, open, out front."

Maureen O'Hara is "a big girl with a big heart." And movie heavy Jack Elam is "a very unheavy man— a gentle sweetheart of a guy, in fact." Wayne seems to have a fondness for his profession and fellow performers alike.

But film acting is an uncomfortable business. "The actor has no control," Wayne pointed out. "He has no control over his performance because of the confinement of the camera, the intrusion of the director and the disjunct sequence of shooting scenes. You're forced to develop a character from the middle forward and back, not from start to finish as you can in a stage production.

"And the actor has no control over his career, either. So much depends upon the subjective decisions of other people— producers, casting directors, sponsors. There is no security in the acting profession."

Which may be in part why Wayne has organized his own production company, called Cinatrope. "There you're packaging a product out of your own intentions and ideas— without deletion or interference. There you have control."

It is the kind of control Wayne exerts in the choreographed saloon brawls he fights on film. "Every move is planned out, every frame. And since the medium is two-dimensional, you can swing wide as you want as long as the guy goes down when he's supposed to."

Which brings us back to the bears of *The Bears and I,* who would not be choreographed. "There was a buzzer that meant food to them. We used that to get them to move."

Wayne shrugged and smiled again.

"But they couldn't read the script, so we just shot what they did and worked around it."

Wayne hasn't forgotten his estranged youth. He keeps his own family with him on location as much as he can. And his son is named not John, but Michael.

The idea is to capture a prose photograph of somebody that should seem unposed. Remember the sideways look; keep an eye out for the other side of the obvious.

Surfaces

It is the electronic age, and interviewing like any other 20th century pursuit has acquired certain technological accouterments. A word on them.

A disarming way of accomplishing an interview is to conduct it cold turkey, with nothing but a memory as disciplined and retentive as a chess master's to record the proceedings. When necessary, it can be done. *Washington Post* reporters Bob Woodward and Carl Bernstein related that they never used notebooks in the presence of the skittish employees of the Committee to Re-Elect the President; the tentative assertions and sudden expressions of frustration they pulled from these people were set down later on little scraps of paper that would eventually pile up and wall off an entire administration.

To be capable of this one must call upon complete concentration, making the mind a sound camera that records gestures, the contents of a room and whole exchanges of dialog exactly as it is spoken. This kind of a mind can be developed through practice. Truman Capote did it in preparation for *In Cold Blood;* he had friends read to him for long stretches, then sat down afterwards and wrote what he remembered. This went on until he achieved the eye and ear evident in that book. You can do it. The process may be a brain-fraying experience, like a power surge through an overloaded circuit, but you *can* do it.

When Jack Anderson was investigating the influence of International Telephone and Telegraph on the Justice Department under John Mitchell, he sent his assistant Brit Hume (now with ABC) to interview Dita Beard, an ITT employee who had purportedly written a memo implicating the company. Mrs. Beard was upset when he spoke with her, so Hume thought it impolitic to produce a notebook. The conversation lasted more than an hour; Hume drove home and typed up what he had.

His notes appear in *The Anderson Papers* by Jack Anderson and George Clifford. Hume remembered Mrs. Beard chainsmoked Chesterfields and wore a chartreuse sweatshirt and yellow cotton slacks. He remembered they sat on wooden slat stools and he noted the time and each of three people to whom he was introduced in the course of the conversation. He remembered she had five children and had been married twice, once to a man she described as an alcoholic. And he remembered four detailed pages of admissions by Mrs. Beard, including her assertion that Mitchell told her Nixon had called him with instructions to "lay off ITT."

All in a day's work.

The important thing in a no-notes encounter is to write down what happened as soon as possible afterward. Retention diminishes in direct proportion to elapsed time. Some reporters have found pretexts to escape momentarily from such situations for some fast jotting in privacy. Gail Sheehy recalled an interview she conducted with a pimp in a penthouse: "Every 15 minutes," she wrote, "I had to excuse myself and dash for the bathroom to make notes with an eyebrow pencil on the back of a checkbook." The old weak-kidney dodge.

But cold turkey interviews are carried on that way only because they can't be carried out any other way. Either the subject is shy and shuts up when there is a notebook in evidence, or the subject is hostile and figures you can't be getting it all down without one. You are, though— every incriminating word.

Another way of pursuing an interview is to use any of a startling variety of tape recorders. It is unethical to tape anyone without telling them about it in advance. You can't be sued for it, but the practice is bad faith at best and, as sources in San Clemente will attest, it can lead to trouble. There are wire recorders with mikes that can be hidden in sleeves; recorders that can be made to look like packs of cigarettes; even recorders with mikes shaped like fish hooks that can be cast from fly rods through open windows. They're all strictly over-the-transom stuff. You might want one when you sneak into some mob initiation or the local illegal cockfight, but remember these people will do interesting things to your person if they find it on you.

With permission, recorders can be useful from one point of view. They provide the reporter with a greater opportunity to concentrate on the subject, the questions and the surroundings without that endless intermittent fastening of the face to one's notes. They offer an auditory record when the subject comes back after the story's out claiming he was misquoted. They make it easier to capture the extended quote exactly.

But here's the rub. They're machines, and machines break down. They squeak, run out of tape, stop, fall apart when they're dropped. Tape recorders are whirring electronic crutches the complete reporter shouldn't have to call upon.

For one thing, recorders can intimidate people in a way notebooks don't. Television cameras have been barred from courtrooms because witnesses tend to clown around or clam up in their presence; just watch what happens to the members of an otherwise rational TV audience whenever the lens is faced toward them. The same is true of recorders. Those turning spindles tell the subject *every word he utters will be frozen in time.* An unnerving thought. That microphone pushed in his face— or circumspectly situated on the table at his elbow— becomes an accusing silver finger.

Leave the damned thing at home and get it the right way. Why should you, a feature writer working against a deadline, fool around transcribing a tape when you could be writing the story? In effect, you're playing the interview back to get what you should have gotten the first time you heard it. Just as a reporter trusts nobody, he trusts no devices either.

If you're going to use one, test it out before the interview. If it gums up anyway, don't say I didn't warn you.

The best way to do the job is with a pen and a notebook. There are reporter's pads available that are about half the width of a stenographer's tablet; the advantage to them is that they fit easily in a pocket, so you're less likely to leave them around or be readily identifiable as a scribe in any crowd because you're the one with the sheaf of paper. Any ballpoint pen will do, but you should have two in case one runs out of ink. Avoid felt-tips; if you're covering a story in the rain, or your hands are sweating in the heat, the notes will melt right off the page.

The notebook should not be brandished. It should seem almost an afterthought. When the subject drops a bomb— i.e., an admission he murdered his mother or he has a direct line on the Argentine location of missing members of the Third Reich— the reporter is encouraged not to bend over his pad and write like hell. Furious scribbling tends to put the subject on guard. If you want to take it all down in full, lob off a softball— an easily answered, negligably newsworthy question— and continue writing on the bomb while the subject drones innocuously on.

Make sure you get it right. A reputation for carelessness or inaccuracy will make future interviews justifiably harder to get. Even the most fastidious reporter, however, can expect to be accused of misquotation, especially when the material is damaging.

Stand on your integrity and let 'em scream.

The art of the interview

Arrive a full five minutes early. Any earlier and you'll feel foolish sitting around paging through back issues of the *Farm Journal* or staring gravely off into the broadloom, especially if you're surprised by the subject. Any later and you'll risk arriving breathless or tardy, which isn't done. Rag-thief or angel, the subject has granted you a piece of his life *gratis,* and you should be respectful enough not to waste it.

Incidentally, it jolly well should have been granted *gratis;* don't pay for information. Checkbook journalism, occasionally practiced shamefacedly by certain networks and news organizations, goes against the goal of the game, which is to pass the truth on to the public. Every time you buy the truth you reinforce the notion of some that it should be sold to the highest bidder. Reinforce that notion long enough and ultimately only the rich will be able to afford the truth. Besides, people who get paid for what they tell tend to tell what they think will earn them the most, which is not necessarily straight talk. If the subject wants money, talk him out of it or get the goods somewhere else.

Conduct yourself with unfailing courtesy, especially at the beginning of the interview. The mythical Wally "Scoop" Ballew with the press card in the hat and the cigar wouldn't have been able to get his mother to talk to him, let alone anybody more distant. Reflect: The occasion of an interview is an impossibly artificial situation. Two complete strangers are supposed to sit down and talk to each other as if they had some mutual interest. They don't. So the subject is going to be at least a little uneasy, even if he's hardboiled and has done it a thousand times. The best way to relax the subject is to prove you possess some of the refinements of civilization; shake hands, speak softly and don't pick your nose in public. Cast about for an icebreaker: If there's a crew team trophy on the desk, inquire about it; if it's storming outside, commiserate; if the subject has a grizzly chained in the corner, go on about that. This lets the subject know you're OK. If you don't let him know you're OK, he'll be guarded as a hippie at a Young Republicans rally.

You're aggressive, or you wouldn't have gotten the interview. But you don't have to keep proving how tough you are or how smart. In fact, it is better to appear more mild than wily. Joan Didion, *Esquire* columnist and author of *Slouching Toward Bethlehem,* presents an unprepossessing appearance that she claims accounts for her success.

My only advantage as a reporter is that I am so physically small, so temperamentally unobtrusive, and so neurotically inarticulate that people tend to forget that my presence runs counter to their best interests. And it always does. . . .

This unintimidating air is especially useful if you can attach yourself to an individual for a period of time; at length your presence will invariably be forgotten, and like a fly on a wall you will have the opportunity to see the subject as he is, not as he wishes to appear.

Interviews over lunch can work well, but don't order the cracked crab. In fact, don't order anything at all elaborate; you didn't come to eat, you came to get a story, and you can't take notes if you're having to busy yourself with steak knives and snail tongs. Order a salad and ignore it except for stage business; get the story and you can eat yourself into a coma at home.

And no more than one drink, either. There have been reporters who have had sensational times with their subjects only to discover later their notes are illegible and they have only a vague memory of what went on after the third martini. Let the subject get loaded; you sip your sherry.

Be aware immediately of the circumstances under which you find the subject. Offices express personality; so does the choice of a restaurant. Use your descriptive sense to provide something more than a mere record of what is said. Look for those details you now value so highly: the fine scars on the backs of an ex-pug's hands; the complete set of Zane Grey on a football coach's bureau; the gold-plated housefly pinned to the *hausfrau's* hat. Watch Rex Reed display actress Ava Gardner at the center of her hotel suite like a soft statue in an ersatz pastel cell:

> She stands there, without benefit of a filter lens, against a room melting under the heat of lemony sofas and lavender walls and cream-and-peppermint-striped movie-star chairs, lost in the middle of that gilt-edge birthday-cake hotel of cupids and cupolas called the Regency. There is no script. No Minelli to adjust the CinemaScope lens. Ice-blue rain beats against the windows and peppers Park Avenue below as Ava Gardner stalks her pink malted-milk cage like an elegant cheetah. She wears a baby-blue cashmere turtleneck sweater pushed up to her Ava elbows and a little plaid mini-skirt and enormous black horn-rimmed glasses and she is gloriously, divinely barefoot.

Even before Gardner speaks in the story, Reed has made a statement about her. There is a certain artificiality about the scene and a certain impatience in the woman at the center of it that have real bearing on the portrait Reed is preparing to paint.

Your job is not simply to record what the subject says and does. You must in the course of doing that capture a piece of his soul. Of course no one can expect to know anybody else intimately within the short space of an hour; some people live together for years without much understanding of each other. But you should be able, by dint of picking up on a few clues, to reveal something of the personality of the individual you've been talking with. The clues are there: a consistent topic the subject keeps returning to, like money or women or the fear of death; a mannerism, such as a tendency to pose or an inability to sit still; or an attitude, be it defensive, patronizing or forceful.

In *All the President's Men, Washington Post* reporter Bob Woodward interviews a friend of Watergate burglar Howard Hunt over lunch at the Hay-Adams Hotel. He pumps him for information, but in the process Woodward also reveals something of the quality of the man. The fellow makes a production of his tastes, selecting at length braised lamb and broccoli with Hollandaise sauce. "The lamb arrived," Woodward deadpans, "and was pronounced adequate." But the Hollandaise isn't fresh, and Hunt's associate petulantly throws down his fork. Later he orders a custard pie for dessert and knocks over the water glass with his menu. "He glared at the waiter as if it were his fault and told him what the Hay-Adams could do with its Hollandaise," Woodward reports. The man has become a living being for us, if an unattractive one.

John Bowers' interview with pop singer Janis Joplin included in his collection *The Golden Bowers* reveals one salient trait about her: a wounded vulnerability that has translated itself into self-destruction. Though he wrote the piece long before her tragic death by drug overdose, the inevitability of a self-induced early demise weaves itself through the story like the pattern in a hand-stitched counterpane. Bowers recounts a particularly telling exchange between them concerning the Texas town in which Joplin was born and raised:

"You asked what I think of Port Arthur," she said, after a couple of drinks. "Here's what I think of Port Arthur." And then, on yellow note paper, she drew a heart and a kind of scrollwork that is found on current psychedelic posters. The lettering read: JANIS LOVES (TEE-HEE) PORT ARTHUR AS MUCH AS PORT ARTHUR LOVES HER.

"They hurt me back there, man. They made me miserable. And I wanted them so much to love me."

"How did they hurt you? Why were you so miserable?"

She thought awhile. "I didn't have any tits at 14."

Something of the anguish of every bright, nonconforming but not particularly attractive teenager lingers in those unhappy lines.

Oriana Fallaci goaded the then-Secretary of State Henry Kissinger into making quite a different kind of an admission as he attempted to account for his popularity:

"The main point arises from the fact that I've always acted alone. Americans like that immensely. Americans like the cowboy who leads the wagon train by riding ahead alone on his horse, the cowboy who rides all alone into the town, the village, with his horse and nothing else. Maybe even without a pistol, since he doesn't shoot. He acts, that's all, by being in the right place at the right time. In short, a western."

It was a perhaps distressing vision for an international diplomat to encourage; under Gerald Ford there were those who said Kissinger was left entirely too much alone, and America had a questionable record during that era of shooting more than once from the hip. But the comment caught the essential Kissinger; it said things about him.

The following short interview makes use of ambience and admission to demonstrate the terrible isolation of an old man who became the unfortunate victim of both a predatory flim-flam team and his solitary situation.

The man who conned 82-year-old Walter Murphy out of almost $4,000 gave him back ten to tide him over.

"He was a real fella," Murphy sighed. "You would've liked him."

Murphy, winter clad in a leather all-weather cap and flannel shirt buttoned to the collar, sat back on a worn sofa in the six-room cyclone-fenced brick house that has been his home for 40 years. A retired foreman for the Southern Railroad System, Murphy lived alone with his routine until the phone calls started.

"He said his name was Harris," Murphy recalled. "He was checking on the computer at the bank and he wanted to know about my deposits."

Murphy cashes his monthly $250 railroad retirement checks at the First National Bank and Trust Co., 6th and Madison, Covington. No man named Harris works there; the calls established that Walter Murphy's balance was worth stealing.

Then the men in the London Fog raincoats showed up at his home.

"Why do they always go after the guy that's got nothin'?" complained Murphy. "They don't go after the guy that's got a lot."

There were two of them. One introduced himself as "Lt. Kelly of the CIA" and flashed a badge. "Kelly" would do all the talking. His assistants, who changed in a succession of visits, kept contact with someone outside on a walkie-talkie.

"They didn't want to sit in here," Murphy said, gesturing at his tidy living room with its ancient upright radio that still received signals from steamships. "You can see in from the street."

He showed where they sat with him in the small kitchen, carefully drawing the shade. In a skillet on the stove four lean strips of bacon awaited Murphy's lunch.

"Kelly claimed I'd been passing counterfeit twenties," Murphy continued, across again from his 24-year-old Spartan television set. "They wanted to examine any money I had in the house."

Murphy had $1,680. He had lived through a Depression in which banks had not always been the best places for savings.

"I had an aunt that lost $26,000 when a bank failed in St. Louis," Murphy explained. "That was one reason for me keeping extra money in the house."

Kelly examined the money and pronounced it bogus. He sealed it in two envelopes and told Murphy to keep them until the arrival of a Federal Reserve man on Friday.

As Murphy was to learn later, the envelopes he was left with were not the ones containing his cash.

"That was on Wednesday," Murphy said. "Before he left he asked me if I needed any of the money until then. I said ten would last me, and he handed it over."

At the gate outside the man who called himself Kelly turned and doffed his hat in farewell.

Thursday Murphy got a phone call from him.

"He said they had a camera hidden in the bank and someone

there was passing the counterfeit money."

Murphy ran a hand over his jaw, rough now with a sugar-sift of white stubble.

"They wanted me to withdraw $2,000 to help catch him."

He was to go in a cab. Curiously, the driver turned out to have the same kind of expensive velveteen hat sported by Kelly and his associates — and contrary to the cab driver custom, he did not open the door for his fare.

When Murphy returned home his money was again examined, again found wanting, and again sealed in an envelope pending the arrival of a Federal Reserve officer Friday.

Who of course didn't show. And the envelopes, again surreptitiously switched, now held not greenbacks but sheaves of something far less valuable.

"Some people think I'm a sap," Murphy said, staring out past the porch swing into a gray noon rain. "But others say I done right. They came for money and they were going to get it.

"If I had gotten tough, I might have gotten the worst of it."

Although police are working on a lead Murphy could not discuss, he admitted he did not expect to see his money again.

"Why worry about it?" he asked without bitterness. "I don't owe anybody or anything. All my good friends that I used to go around with, every one of them passed away."

His eyes rose to the photograph of his deceased wife Edna on the mantle. There were artificial flowers on either side of it, and above a row of porcelain swans and perching birds.

Surviving his social circle, Murphy passes the solitary hours with a timeworn radio, television or bestseller — like William Vogt's *Road to Survival,* a 1949 Book of the Month Club selection.

"And I like to fool around in the garden." He shook his white head. "Since I been in the hospital I ain't any good at all."

Murphy is under treatment for uremia and high blood pressure. He adjusted a napless carpet with care to cover a little household dust.

"I expect others will be coming around now."

Walter Murphy, whose only recent guests turned out to be grifters, laughed a mirthless laugh.

"But they ain't going to find much," he said.

Murphy's home of 40 years has become a hiding place where even his reading matter is out of date. Having outlived his work, his wife, his peers, and even his health, the man has become a casualty of the self-reliant culture, too trusting to identify his enemies and too frail to fight them.

The questions you have prepared should be specific. If any one of them elicits a mere "Yes" or "No", the next words out of your mouth should be: "Why do you feel that way?" Don't be afraid of asking a dumb question; the "dumb" question may elicit a definitive response. Should you avoid it, you may walk away with a hole in your story. The genuinely dumb question is the unasked one. Children are great interrogators. They are relentlessly inquisitive, and they ask things because they really want to know the answers, not because they want to impress anybody with the questions. When the astronauts were gathered before the press on the day of the first moon launch, they were peppered with questions about rocketry — matters of fuel, thrust and trajectory. The only solid question was put to them by Oriana Fallaci, who chose one she thought her youngest sister might have asked, and it cut through all the plastic pomp and computer jargon with just three small words: *"Are you scared?"*

Strive to keep your questions fresh. Don't forget if you are dealing with a notable, chances are he's done this many times before. So he quite naturally gets deathly sick of the same old obvious questions. So do the readers. Edwin Newman's *Strictly Speaking,* a wry book about the steady impoverishment of coherent English in the mass media, includes a typically cliche-ridden sports interview in which familiar cues elicit familiar responses:

> The sports writer is named Buck and the manager is named Al. Buck's first question is, "Well, Al, how do you think you'll do this year?" Al is not thrown by this. He says, "Well, I think we'll do pretty good. I think we'll do all right."
> Buck follows that up like a hawk. He says, a shade aggressively, "Well, are you predicting the pennant, Al?" Al replies that well, they won it last year, and the other teams are going to have to beat them. He knows one thing: They are not going to beat themselves
> . . . .

And so on. In the course of your research, watch for surprises and angles. Don't ask the Nobel Peace Prize winner how it felt to receive it;

ask her about the mime theater she endows back in Chagrin Falls, Ohio. Don't ask the Met tenor about his love for opera; ask him how he overcomes stage fright. Ask the mobbed rock star how he gets his hero sandwiches smuggled out of Lou's Pizza Heaven. Anything but the expected.

Barbara Walters, former ABC Evening News anchorwoman, once recommended certain "foolproof" questions for the over-interviewed, such as: "If you were recuperating in a hospital, who would you want in the bed next to you, excluding relatives?" Or: "When was the last time you cried?" I submit you can make a sap out of yourself if you go around passing out pointless interrogatories like these. Be fresh, not fatuous.

And about those tough questions you've saved for the end. Don't weasel when you ask them. Some interviewers want so badly to be liked, they will shore up their temerity with phrasing like this: "I'm sorry to have to ask you this, but my profession demands it." Or: "There are those who say that you've (been sticking beans in your ear, beating your great-aunt, smuggling hash, etc.). How do you respond to that?" Hold on to your dignity. Ask the question, don't slip it in like a prison shiv.

Thank the subject for his time and, if it was there, his candor. Then, once you've got the interview in the bag, sit down with your notes as soon as you can and go over them. If you find holes, call the subject back and fill them in. You may feel the need for a second conversation. If so, ask for it; the worst that can happen is a refusal, and you're too tough to be crushed by that.

On and off the record

You are obligated by the ethics of the profession not to print comments made "off the record."

So get as much on the record as you can. Then try to get the source to stand behind the rest. Be impatient with the subject who appends "that's off the record" to every negligibly controversial comment he makes. Such relentless auditory editing makes thin gruel out of the stew. People ought to be responsible for what they say, after all; side-of-the-mouth stuff is strictly for backchat tabloids and movie magazines.

Jack Newfield, senior editor of *The Village Voice*, offers a good rule of thumb:

There are certain people, like public officials, whom I won't take anything off the record from. If I'm interviewing a source I don't trust, like [Stanley] Steingut or [Patrick] Cunningham, I will tell them: Nothing is off the record. Most of my real sources are cooperating voluntarily, and when I'm dealing with a court stenographer or a nurse's aide, I give them my word I will not reveal their name because their job is at stake.

When there is a good reason to protect the source, do so.

But if there isn't, don't let the matter ride. Columnist Liz Smith of the *New York Daily News* always tries to talk reluctant sources into going on the record:

I tell them it's paranoid or irrational, and ask them what difference will it make. They're weakening the story, they're weakening their personality, and so forth. I hate to see a good quote get killed. If people say something outrageous, I rush over and keep them talking to get their minds off it.

There are times when it is legitimate to withhold names. For reasons of compassion, J.Y. Smith did not record the names of the ambulance patrons in his story at the end of chapter two. I left out the names of the injured in chapter three's emergency room story for the same reasons. And the name of the principal in chapter five's South Boston story was changed to protect him from possible reprisal. Editors are properly leery of the unattributed story, but they will go along with it if you make the motive behind it clear and attest to the complete truth of the contents.

Never give the subject approval of your copy before it goes to press. The ones that ask for it will tell you they want to see the story to make sure they weren't misquoted. But sure as you're sitting there they will end up demanding you delete every controversial thing they said. Tell them your deadline doesn't permit the time to get the story back to them. Tell them it's against newspaper policy. Both statements are true.

An old dodge is to send the story over as it goes to press, when it's too late to make any changes. But why play games? When they ask for the right to prior censorship, simply tell them: No.

Capturing the clam

When most people are told somebody doesn't want to talk to them, they'll go away and that will be the end of it.

Reporters aren't most people.

Don't take no for an answer, even the second time. The paradigm case is Bob Woodward's relentless pursuit of attorney Douglas Caddy at the arraignment of the five accused Watergate burglars. Woodward spotted him in the courtroom. What follows is recorded in his and Carl Bernstein's book *All the President's Men:*

Caddy didn't want to talk. "Please don't take it personally," he told Woodward. "It would be a mistake to do that. I just don't have anything to say."

Woodward asked Caddy about his clients.

"They are not my clients," he said.

But you are a lawyer? Woodward asked.

"I'm not going to talk to you."

Caddy walked back into the courtroom. Woodward followed.

"Please, I have nothing to say."

Would the five men be able to post bond? Woodward asked.

After politely refusing to answer several more times, Caddy replied quickly that the men were all employed and had families— factors that would be taken into consideration by the judge in setting bond. He walked back into the corridor.

Woodward followed: Just tell me about yourself, how you got into the case.

"I'm not in the case."

Why are you here?

"Look," Caddy said, "I met one of the defendants, Bernard Barker, at a social occasion."

Where?

"In D.C. It was cocktails at the Army-Navy Club. We had a sympathetic conversation . . . that's all I'm going to say."

How did you get into the case?

Caddy pivoted and walked back in. After half an hour, he went out again.

Woodward asked how he got into the case.

Here's a short one that appeared in the *Chicago Sun-Times* by columnist Bob Greene. The subject is not only reluctant, he's openly hostile. And that is the angle: Greene didn't lose the story, he gained a better one than he expected:

I wanted to talk to an expert about the national crime wave. Suddenly crime is the hottest topic in the country; *Time* magazine devotes a special cover story this week to Crime in America, and most public opinion polls show that citizens worry about crime more than anything else. Fear of crime is rampant in the nation.

Most of the people being quoted about crime, however, seemed to be Harvard professors or Princeton sociologists. The opinions of these scholars may be perfectly valid, but I thought it would be a disservice not to contact the most astute authority on violent crime that I know. I dialed a number in South Carolina.

"What is it?" Mickey Spillane said.

I identified myself, and said that I wanted to talk about crime. Spillane, 57, is the creator of the Mike Hammer private eye books, a series of blood-drenched, gore-soaked crime novels that have sold more than 130 million copies. Spillane himself is a crew-cut, politically conservative, fedora-wearing representation of what Mike Hammer might look like in real life. I asked Spillane if he, like so many other Americans, is afraid to walk the streets at night.

"Ha, ha," Spillane said. "Don't be stupid. If you screw me, kid, I'll jump on you like a ton of bricks. I'll tear your ears off." He sounded as if he had just consumed six or seven carloads of the beer he endorses on television.

I asked him again if he is afraid to walk the streets.

"That's ridiculous," Spillane said. "Ha. I never had any fears. I'm not afraid of anything. You're making a mistake, kid, if you think you got more power than I do. You have no power next to me. I'll slaughter you."

I began to realize that the interview might not go well. Nevertheless, I brought up the *Time* cover story, and asked Spillane if he had any solutions to the new flare-up in the crime problem.

"Who needs this garbage?" Spillane said. "I'm taping every word you say. They're always trying to get me, but they won't be able to this time."

I asked him who was trying to get him.

"The Canadians," Spillane said. "They do things."

I asked him what the Canadians had done to him.

"They can't do nothing to me," Spillane said, and the line went dead.

I called him back. I asked him for his specific thinking about street crime.

"I don't feel fear at any time," Spillane said. "New York is falling apart. You don't have one chance against me, kid."

I asked him how citizens could protect themselves against criminals.

"We don't need to protect ourselves against crime," he said. "Can you fight? When was your last fight? Did you win? How big are you? Don't try to hustle me."

I brought up the subject of the decay of America's cities.

"Tell me what you ever did to protect your city," Spillane said. "Did you ever kill anyone? Were you ever in a war? No war? Well, isn't that wild. No war. I'm an old fighter pilot. I'm recording everything you say. You even try to hurt me, I'll knock the hell out of you. If you think I can't, you're crazy. You'd better be pretty big, because I'm a big one."

I asked him if he had a way to solve the crime problem.

"Yeah, I've got a way," he said. "It's the only way. I'm going to send you some literature. In the mail. I'm a Jehovah's Witness. Read Revelations, read Timothy. That's the way to fight crime."

I asked Spillane if he was concerned about crime.

"Who cares?" he said. "I don't give a hoot. Crime? I'm not for it or against it. Who needs it?"

I asked him if he felt safer living in South Carolina than he did when he was living in New York.

"Why didn't you volunteer for the service?" Spillane said. "I volunteered for the Air Force. I'll tear you up. I'm going to end this conversation."

I asked him to answer one more question.

"What's that?" Spillane said.

I asked if Mike Hammer would have been scared by the current crime wave in America.

"Boy, what a stupid thing to say to me," Spillane said. "Was he ever afraid? No way. I'm ending this conversation. I'm 56 years old. I will tear you up. I love you. I got you on tape. I will kick your ass."

Note: Spillane makes a statement, Greene follows it up. Spillane hangs up, Greene calls back. Spillane threatens to end the conversation, Green asks one more question.

I was once assigned to do a series of stories for the *Kentucky Post* on a mining mogul with a curious background. I did some digging and found the background more curious than anyone had supposed. There was dealing in it, and desertion, but I started with the man's surface; the first part follows, showing how much can be gotten from witnesses who won't talk:

MOREHEAD — As the brand-new burgundy Cadillac churned toward him down the new-fenced gravel drive at the Canada Cattle Ranch in Morehead, the reporter let out a long slow breath.

It was the car he had been told the coal king drove.

The reporter had made a mad three-hour early-morning run at the edge of control all the way up from Pikeville along black-tar blind-curve coal country backroads on the promise of an interview with mystery millionaire Claude Shelton Canada. The mine owner had not been in his registered rooms at the Morehead Holiday Inn, so the reporter camped for two hours more at Canada's vast cattle farm miles out Hwy. 801.

Canada did not respond to the reporter's wave of greeting as he pulled his dust-smeared limousine to a halt beside the big white Travco van he often stayed in at the ranch.

"What do you want?" he growled, looking not at the reporter but dead ahead over the steering wheel and through the front wall of the trailer-home office.

"I want to talk to you," the reporter said.

The silver-haired, wet-combed Canada did not move. His eyes, lost to expression behind large black-framed lenses, stayed to the front like a soldier's at inspection.

"Why do you want to talk to me?" he demanded. "There's oodlin's of people like me."

Which was not precisely true. Not everyone's right ring finger flashed a diamond the size of the one the reporter could see through Canada's still-rolled Cadillac window. The stone was as big as a glass eye in a stuffed grizzly, a perfect 15-carat, six-point solitaire delivered to Canada at one of his mines under armed guard. He had paid a reported $148,000 for it.

"You're a colorful man," the reporter told him. And an elusive one, he thought.

Canada came out of his car with a gesture of impatience. Levi'd and leather-coated, at 56 the agrarian-mod coal owner was shorter than middle height and less prepossessing than his legend. The hair was moving back from his forehead and his stomach pooched out slightly over a beaten-gold belt buckle with a striding stallion on it. A gold watch and wristband kept close company with the smaller but still impressive lemon-drop diamond on his left hand, the one appraised at a five-carat $10,000.

"I don't have that much money," Canada protested, his broken-veined Jack Daniel's face set in a florid frown. "I'm not a millionaire — not nearly."

Which was also not precisely true. Besides the burgundy Cadillac, Canada also owned a car custom-built by the late George Young of England reputed to be worth a quarter of a million dollars. That was only one of a fleet of other expensive cars he acquired including a low-slung fire-red Porsche, a Mercedes-Benz 450 SL, and at least 16 — *sixteen* — Rolls Royces.

Exclusive of its Pikeville mining operation, the Canada Coal Co. purchased three-quarters of a million dollars in Rowan County land between May and October of last year. Canada personally paid out $186,000 at a stroke for one parcel at public auction.

Still, since he surfaced in Morehead Aug. 1 with a thick sheaf of Traveler's checks and the winning bid on the 114-acre Ezra Martt farm, Canada has kept to himself and his ranch, intended one day to become an area showplace. The locals have left him alone.

"We're grateful," noted one. "The prices he paid for his land raised the value of ours."

"He hasn't taken much part in community life," conceded Adron Doran, president of Morehead State University where Canada's mother once matriculated.

"I don't know a thing about him," said town mayor James Cornett.

The reporter explained to the coal owner he had been assured by Canada's wife Leona late the night before that Canada would see him that day for an interview.

"She told you that to get rid of you," Canada snapped, irritated. "I don't want any stories about me."

He began to rail at the press, claiming that the recent visit of the CBS "60 Minutes" crew to his ranch cost him $75,000 to $80,000 in lost man-hours and work.

"They brought everything in here," he complained, gesturing out across the artificial lake he created months earlier. "Everywhere I go, somebody's after me."

He meant the grifters and the poor, not the networks. Canada's reputation as a rags-to-riches eccentric made him prey to scores of demands for money and investment. He objects to the intrusion of begging strangers like the woman who wrote him to insist he place $6,000 in her account at a nearby bank.

"There were five or six people at the motel this morning bothering me," Canada said resentfully. "When I got off the plane in St. Louis there was a man who wanted me to set him up with a piece of coal. He said if I could do it, he could do it.

"So I'm supposed to lease him the land, fly him to it and consult with him if he has any problems. I'm supposed to do that? I can't spend my time that way."

He looked at the reporter's notebook.

"See? You're writing. You put my name in the paper and they'll be lookin' and findin'."

Canada shook his white head.

"Some dunce might come after me," he said, his mouth closing like a carp's on a doughball.

Paranoia hung heavy in the winter-crisp air.

Standing with his back to the trailer office in which was stored files and two large tanks of bull semen refrigerated by liquid nitrogen, Canada confessed his deep dread of "kooks and kidnapers."

"They're all over," he grumbled. "I wish I was back the way I was when I started in the mining business."

Canada had refused to talk to the reporter, but he had said a great deal. Now he stood with his arms stiffly at his sides in the center of his holdings, scores of white wooly Charolais cattle wandering the rolling grounds under a sky blue as a bird's egg.

A quarter of a mile distant a just-completed green barn stretched its incredibly long length over the field's edge. Canada has instructed Morehead contractor Ed Maybry to pass out no information about the structure. Even such innocuous data as the specifications of a barn had become intelligence for the enemy.

The story resides in Canada's reluctance. It reveals him to be an individual confined rather than liberated by his riches, a man somehow diminished rather than enlarged. If the interview is abortive or impossible to get, think: That in itself may be the story.

You're never out to do a hatchet job, but if you're interviewing somebody with really outrageous ideas, let him hang himself. Pursue his views, get them down without comment, and they will speak for themselves. *Cincinnati Post-Times Star* reporter Lew Moores once interviewed Matt Koehl, then head of the American Nazi Party. Koehl didn't rave during his elaboration on the evangelism of bigotry; he didn't even raise his voice. But talking quietly with him was like sitting alone in a room to the measured tick of something that sooner or later just might go off. In one exchange, a straight-faced Moores reveals something of Koehl's views by forcing him to be very precise about them:

Moores: Are there any requirements [for membership in your organization] in terms of race and religious preference?
Koehl: Well, obviously we have only white people, non-Jewish.
Moores: How white?
Koehl: I would say any perceptible amount of Negro blood would not qualify. . . .
Moores: Or Jewish blood?
Koehl: Down to perhaps say a minority of Jewish blood. Normally we haven't had this problem. We from time to time have individual cases where there are persons who have a fraction of say Indian blood or Jewish blood or something like this, but this is rather a rare case. It doesn't crop up too often.
Moores: How about Puerto Rican, Spanish . . . ?
Koehl: Well, I've known Puerto Ricans whom I've considered white and Aryan, but the typical Puerto Rican is not. He's non-Aryan.
Moores: But a Puerto Rican wouldn't be allowed in the membership if he believed in National Socialism?
Koehl: If he were a Spanish-European type Puerto Rican of white blood, but as I say, the typical Puerto Rican would not be admitted on racial grounds.
Moores: How about an Oriental?
Koehl: No.

Thus is Koehl's position made perfectly clear.

Remember, too, the very subterfuges of the subject may expose him to an alert reporter.

An Amarillo lawyer named A.D. Payne set off for work on foot one June morning in 1930. He was accustomed to driving — the office was three miles away — but he said he needed the exercise. He left the car for his wife, who got in it with her young son, drove six blocks, and was blown through the roof by a dynamite bomb set inside. The boy survived.

A.B. Macdonald of the *Kansas City Star* went to work on the case. He interviewed Payne and noted the man's "even-toned voice," which seemed to him "unnatural." Macdonald noted in a *Star* story later:

> No matter what question was asked him he always dwelt on how he loved his wife, how much she loved him, and how they just lived for each other. He overdid that.

Macdonald noticed something else.

> His eldest daughter, who will be 14 next February, was getting dinner. Every once in a while she would come to the door and gaze in at us where we sat talking, and I imagined that there was a frightened look in her eyes.

The reporter found out that Mrs. Payne had narrowly escaped death only the preceding March when she had opened a closet door and a shotgun went off inside, wounding her in the hand. Payne went to great lengths to explain the gun had fallen from a sewing machine, but Macdonald became convinced the "accident" had been a trap.

> I could see that the whole household was on high tension, and that the two girls had been coached by Payne to tell their stories a certain way. . . . I felt then, and I know now, that both knew their father had killed their mother and were in mortal fear lest they might say something that would disclose it.

Macdonald became convinced that the insurance alone was not motive enough for the killing and set about finding a love interest. He asked Payne if he had ever been involved with another woman.

"No," he said emphatically, "I was never untrue to my dear wife even in thought, let alone in deed."

Macdonald pressed him for a list of his stenographers, noting carefully what the lawyer said about them:

"I had several different stenographers in the last year. The first one was Vera Holcomb. She stayed with me only a short while. I don't know what became of her. The next was Verona Thompson. She came to work for me last August a year ago, and I let her out in December. She is 24 or 25 years old, just an ordinary-looking woman. No man would ever get sweet on her. The next was Mabel Bush, who lives on Pierce Street. She's young and very attractive, a redhead full of pep and wide-awake. She is only about 19 or 20. My stenographer now is Miss Ocie Humphries."

That was the tip. Payne was trying to divert the reporter's attention away from the Thompson woman. When Macdonald left, Payne was sure he would be writing a piece that would clear him of all suspicion— but Macdonald tracked down the stenographer instead.

She was no wallflower.

Thompson's admission that Payne had been her lover was the thing that broke him. He confessed. Macdonald had unearthed the proof that had eluded police and won a 1931 Pulitzer for reporting.

Good talk and bad

Your subject is the story, but don't let him control it. That is, don't fall into the trap of quoting him *in extenso* as if you were making an entry into the *Congressional Record;* create a rhythm of direct and indirect quotation, with asides on ambience and expository background.

Your notes will give you your point; aim the construction of the story toward supporting that point. As in everything else, you are selective in what you set down as direct quotation. Generally, conversation worthy of quotation either reveals something crucial about the subject or expresses a thought better than you can. Here's Terry Southern quoting an Ole Miss graduate student in *Esquire:*

"*We* nevuh had no Negra problem heah. . . . Theah just *weren't* no problem— wasn't till these *agi-ta-tors* come down heah started all this problem business."

Southern couldn't have said it as precisely any other way. Nicholas Tomalin, an investigative reporter for the *Sunday Times,* recognized the same precision in the words of an infantry brigadier general during the Vietnam war:

"The way I see it, I'm just like any other company boss, gingering up the boys all the time, except I don't make money. I just kill people, and save lives."

Leaning from a helicopter with his M-16 on semi-automatic, the general goes "Zapp, zapp, zapp." Yessireebob. .

The quotes should be absolutely accurate. Not close — exact. Some writers clean up the grammar and delete the expletives. Don't. If you don't like the quote as it was spoken, rewrite it as indirect discourse. Anything else is misrepresentation.

Long quotes should be used only when they work as well as short ones. They should be neither tedious nor disconnected — unless that is your point concerning the individual who offered them. They provide an excellent opportunity to convey the tone of voice of the subject. Listen to this magnificent rendition of a two-fisted New York detective second grade by James Mills, from a story he wrote for *Life:*

"A woman OD'd on Broadway and there's a guy there who is built like a cigaret machine and he has six cops at bay, just standing listening to him swear at them. There's a crowd and the cops are afraid to do anything, even question him, because he's yelling about brutality and swearing at them and the crowd is watching and he feels like a great man because everyone's seeing him abuse those six cops who are afraid to go near him. I didn't want to jump into the middle and act like a big hero or something. So I stepped into a doorway and told one of the cops to bring him in to me. Just for openers I was going to hit him in the stomach. . . ."

Taut, isn't it? The manner of the man's talk is as powerful as the subject matter. Equally successful is this fragment from a piece on an off-track pro by *Boston Globe* reporter Will McDonough:

"Ahhh, it's been like that all year," said the Bookie, slowly walking around the bar, talking out loud to the empty seats. "I'm glad the thing's over. No kiddin'. This was a gambler's year. The bookie got nothin'. The gamblers made it.

"I mean, like I'm gettin' sick of the whole routine. I got stiffed for about five grand. You don't go crazy enough every weekend without worryin' about guys walkin' around the streets with five grand of your money in their pockets."

It's all right to yield the floor now and then if you have a good reason, but don't let go of the gavel.

Remember your reportorial obligation to be fair. You have incredible power: You can make anybody look like a turkey forever to thousands of readers. If the individual has behaved fowlly, paint him that way. Just don't be sticking feathers about where they aren't warranted.

Be careful not to sensationalize the insignificant. Sometimes it is the decent thing to withhold your knowledge that the vicar subscribes to *Raunch.* Avoid where possible indecent exposure of the soul.

This is an ellipsis— . . .— and it is better not to see one in your copy. The ellipsis tells readers words have been left out, and readers, being the alert folk they are, get to wondering *what* words were deleted. Some may suspect deliberate distortion. Obviate the construction by bridging your quote with some brief exposition in place of the gap.

Tom Wolfe, whose pyrotechnic influence has long exerted itself on the "new" journalism, frequently employs a literary device called "third-person point of view," which is a means of telling the story not through the reporter's eyes but through the subject's or those of some other individual. He has argued it is legitimate to report another person's thoughts because individuals can be interviewed about their thoughts and emotions along with the rest of it. Wolfe is an otherwise exemplary craftsman, but this particular method is out of bounds for the purist. What were *you* thinking about over breakfast yesterday? Since it is quite impossible to get accurately inside another person's head, and since people tend to be imprecise about what their thoughts were at a given moment, don't cross the line into fiction by pretending to convey the immeasureable.

One final matter. On certain investigative stories dealing with damaging accusations — which, of course, you've checked out — it is wise to get notarized affadavits from your sources spelling out their testimony. These will protect you should the subject of your investigation decide to sue. It happens.

Gravely Speaking, Hitch Digs Fright
by Robert Kerwin

[Here's a swell story on Hollywood's own fell kewpie by freelancer Robert Kerwin. The legendary Master of Suspense is portrayed against the backdrop of a press conference — notice our friend the PR man hovering just off camera.

Alfred Hitchcock is cooperatively anecdotal, but the reporter's questions are the catalysts. They capture both the great director's evident sense of craft and his insistent self-deprecation. "After all, they're only movies."

Or superbly staged dreams.]

The fat man climbed briskly from a black limousine and marched pompously toward Universal's graveyard set. Alfred Hitchcock has killed so many people that the studio brass thought it appropriate to kick off his 53rd picture against a **News peg—** death background.

The organist, in mourning and elevated on a platform by the wrought-iron cemetery gate, stopped playing the funeral dirges when the noted director arrived, and segued fast into the Hitchcock signature tune from all those hundreds of TV episodes: "Gooooood ev-en-ing."

Hitchcock passed up the two bars and headed for the receiving line. At the head of the line stood bosses Lew Wassermann and Jules Stein, who run Universal-MCA. Next in line was a star of the 53rd film, Bruce Dern, dressed in mourning, followed by costar Karen Black, a thick black veil down from the hennaed hair onto her face.

Ambience— The lunch tables were draped in black and set amid the crosses, headstones, and plastic-flowery graves of the backlot cemetery, the one they show to people on the Universal tour, where they shoot all those sad burial scenes.

"How about a drink, Hitch?" somebody asked, as Hitchcock plumped down at the head table, his red face puffing. He wanted one, he needed one, but said, "No thanks. **Note wine references—** I'm going to be good today for a change. Wine only. I've got to get through this." He sat like a corpulent bishop, satisfied, letting his eyes and head rise curiously as he heard the false electronic bird sounds emanating from strategically placed hidden speakers.

Ambience— Lunch was served in the graveyard by quiet, stern waitresses in black veils.

The well-wishers kept aiming at hitchcock's past — *Torn Curtain, North by Northwest, Notorious, Psycho, The Birds,* ets. — but hitchcock was being paid today to hype No. 53, *Family Plot* [now showing on Chicago and outlying screens].

The corpulent man has a special niche in Hollywood. He's a living half-century of terrorizing film. As he used to say of himself, "Ours is not to reason why, ours is merely to scare hell out of people."

How does he always get that great suspense, as he did, say, in "The Birds"?

Note wine— Hitchcock sipped red wine and pontificated: "In the *movies,* they would do things differently. But I'm not in the *movies.* In the *movies* they would crosscut: the girl, the birds increasing, back and forth. Well— I didn't show any birds just then.

Good talk— "The women look out the schoolroom window, and one turns to the kids and says, 'Get out, go home, go home.' And I cut back immediately, as the kids trooped out, to the birds on this playpen thing, then I wait time enough for the kids to go down the steps and down the street. When you heard the patter of feet, that's when you cut to your long shot, and here are the birds coming over the schoolhouse. I stayed on those birds instead of showing the progress of the children, because I wanted the audience to say: 'Where are the children? Are they all out? Are they safe?' That's the way I make an audience worry: by *withholding* facts at the right times.

"I just keep doing that same thing over and over again, every picture. Very simple. I've set a style for myself. All I need is a good basic idea [most of which I get from reading thrillers]. Who was it who said that self-plagiarism is style? Naturally I have been plagiarizing myself for years."

Again wine— Do people tend to remember whole pictures of his or just moments?

"People remember moments," he said, gulping more red wine, "because moments stand out. You see, we're in a churchyard here. I've got a scene in a graveyard in this latest picture, *Family Plot.* This taxi driver is out doing a bit of investigating, trying to find a missing heir. What surprises him is that there are two headstones — one with a couple's names, one with an individual's name — but the stories are different. One headstone is old; the otheer is brand new. Yet the dates are the same. Now figure that one out."

"Never mind that, Hitch," someone said, and then asked Hitchcock if he's going Hollywood in his old age.

"Nope, I'll never go Hollywood," he replied, sipping still more wine. "I've been here since 1939 when i did *Rebecca.* It was very pleasant to see that it was the best picture of the year, and quite interesting to watch the producer walk up and take the award.

"Hollywood hasn't changed me — as a person, as a filmmaker. I'm not around Hollywood and Los Angeles. I live at home. No, I haven't gone Hollywood. In other words, I don't stroll up and down the Sunset Strip.

"Nothing changes much for me. I'm still making pictures the same way as always. What has changed in films is the idiom — of speech, of behavior, that sort of thing. The only changes you see are in manner, customs, clothes and behavior. We all know that language in pictures has changed. I can remember the days when you couldn't have two people — even though they were married— in bed together.

"They do many thing gratuitously now — language and violence and sex. I never did that. My feeling is that, to make an audience scared, it's only fair to give them an example. That's the reason for putting something in a film. I wouldn't do a ghastly scene just for the hell of it, you know. I made *Psycho* in black and white for one reason only: I did not want to show that blood going down the bathroom drain. It would have been to unpleasant."

Again— Hitchcock ordered another split of red, listened for a time to the bird sounds, cut himself a chunk of porterhouse, and talked about critics.

"I read them now and again. I won't say that I *don't* read them, because I do. Very often I'm surprised when they dissect my films and find all sorts of meanings in my shots, which, of course, don't exist at all. I don't bother with those who probe deeply.

"It's like I used to say to Ingrid Bergman. She used to pace and say to me, 'Oh, I don't know *what* to do with this scene.' She used to just walk up and down, up and down, you know, and get into some kind of agony. I'd say, 'Ingrid, it's only a *movie!*' What else can you say? Then, in the same vein, she'd say to me, 'I *cawn't* do this scene the way I want to, the way I feel it.' I said, 'Ingrid, fake it.'

"Once I had Charles Laughton, who was absolutely the most difficult person I have ever worked with. I pleaded with him all one day to get together this one scene where he had to tell a woman he loved her, while crying. We tried everything and so did he. It took eight hours to try to get him in the mood for the one small scene.

"Well, he finally got the inspiration from somewhere and did the scene perfectly in one take. I asked him how he managed to get himself up for it finally, and he answered, 'I just thought about the times when I was a little boy and used to wet my knickers.'"

Encouraging the anecdote—
The Cary Grant-Ingrid Bergman telephone kissing scene in *Notorious* had to be brought up eventually, and it was. Some woman said that she couldn't think of any greater screen romance, and that she'd never forget that torrid telephone scene.

"Well, do you know what they said to me when I set that up?" Hitchcock said. "That I was crazy, that it wouldn't work. Well, I just kept the one camera closeup. I'll tell you what exactly went through my mind. I said, 'People in an embrace don't want to break it off; they want to continue it— whatever they're doing. For all I know, they might even have to go to the toilet — and still not break the embrace.' But the important thing was: the camera shouldn't break the embrace, either. That's why I kept the camera on a tight two, as though the camera was in the embrace with them, wherever they went."

Would he say that *Psycho* had romance in it?

"No. No romance. *Psycho* was an amusement. Whether you have romance in it depends on the story, the telling. *North by Northwest* was no horror story. *The Lady Vanishes,* one of by most successful pictures, was practically a comedy. It depends."

Hitchcock then launched into a discussion of his favorite films. "One of my favorites is a film called *Shadow of a Doubt.* Because I wrote it with Thornton Wilder, which was a most enjoyable experience. He was such a humble man. And for once we were able to delve into character in a thriller which very often you aren't given the opportunity to do. You can't devote the footage to it.

"I think *Shadow of a Doubt* comes nearest my favorite. But I like the film *Rear Window* because out of that came one of one's favorite technical tricks, which Truffaut learned: the subjective treatment. That is, something becomes pure cinema when you put the camera in the eye of the beholder. You have your closeups, and you have what the beholder sees. In that way, whatever he sees, you create a mental process of reaction on his part."

Has it ever been a secret desire of his to make a straight comedy?

"I did it. Carole Lombard persuaded me to make a film. I'd never make another. In a comedy, there's nothing for me to do. Just photograph them going through their antics. Bedroom farce, what else can you do? That's the trouble with a lot of films, as I see them. They're photographs of people talking. That's all they are, certainly. I think it's terrible."

How about a good musical?

"Listen, if I did a musical, they'd want to know which girl in the line would fall dead. That would be a good shot, wouldn't it? Shooting right along the chorus line, and boom! One falls. No, comedies and musicals are not for me."

A ghost story? The supernatural?

"No, though there's a touch of it in the beginning of this new picture, *Family Plot.* There's a seance between a medium and a rich old lady, and she speaks through her mouthpiece from the other side, in a man's voice.

"As I say, we shouldn't take these movies too seriously. After all, they're only *movies.* That brings to mind a young actress I was working with not long ago. At one point in a scene, she said to me, 'What's my motivation?' 'Your what?' I asked her. 'My motivation,' she repeated. 'What motivates my action in the scene?' I told her: 'Your salary.'"

As Hitchcock threw down the last of his second split of red, he was approached by Universal publicity officers to make a speech. He wiped his mouth with a napkin, and told them: "I'm not going to say much, you know. Just introduce Lew and the others and then—"

"And you'll introduce the cast who are here, won't you?" a publicity man suggested.

"You want me to mention *them?* They're *actors*. That's undignified. Should I have the indignity of introducing *actors?* OK, I'll do it. Should I stand up for this? Do I have to sit or stand?"

Hitchcock approached the microphone.

"Goooooooood ev-en-ing. All those with their mouths full, stop chewing. Ladies and gentlemen, I'm terribly sorry, but I'm a man of very few words. But I'll refer to some of our principal guests, then our cast — who are interred in this cemetery."

He introduced the brass and cast members, then said, "I'm glad to see you come here. To quote Gray's 'Elegy,' 'To strew the hungry churchyard with your bones.'

"Being in a graveyard recalls to me a very famous story of an English comedian who was killed in an air raid in World War II. Naturally, at the cemetery, the grave was surrounded by mourners who consisted mostly of fellow comedians. And a young, rather brash one leaned to an older one beside him and said, 'How old are you, Charlie?' And the old boy said, 'I'm 89 years old.' The young one then said, 'Hardly seems worthwhile going home, does it?'

"And that's what I want to say to you all this afternoon. Thank you very much."

Angel Cordero: Tactical Genius With a "Dominant Will to Win"
by Steve Cady

[New York Times *reporter Steve Cady delivers the following incisive analysis of a jockey's skill literally on the man's own turf. He picks one race — the one showing his subject to the best advantage — and invests his packed story with all the detailed immediacy of a motion picture.* '

*Cordero, caught in action instead of afterward, is not nearly as lo-
quacious as Robert Kerwin's Hitchcock. Still each quote counts, and
Cady fleshes out his research with the corollary comments of others.]*

In a few minutes, a man will stick his head into the jockey
room at Aqueduct and drone, "Let's go, riders."

The riders, none of them weighing more than about 115
pounds, earn anywhere from $10,000 to $300,000 a year
maneuvering brakeless half-ton racehorses around dirt or grass
tracks at 40 miles an hour. Nobody does it with more flair,
Detail—dedication or consistent competence than Angel Cordero Jr.,
the volatile little man now buttoning another stable's racing
silks over a tee shirt lettered "Kiss Me, I'm Puerto Rican."

"He has a dominant will to win, one of those undefinable
qualities," observes Jack O'Hara, the warden of New York's
News   racing colony, trying to define the "difference."
peg—   So at the age of 33, Angel Thomas Cordero ranks as a year-
round virtuoso whose skills set him apart from all but a handful
of America's 2,500 other licensed jockeys and one of the elite
of professional sports.

Some of those skills involve obvious physical assets:
strength, especially in the fingers, wrists and legs; stamina,
agility, superb reflexes, perfect balance. If Cordero had been a
foot taller and 100 pounds heavier, he might have become a top
football or basketball player instead of a four-time New York
riding champion. Except for size (5 feet 3 inches, 112 pounds),
all the elements of conventional athletic success are there.

The less obvious clues to what sets Cordero apart would include:

• His horsemanship, a talent developed almost from the
cradle in Puerto Rico, where he was handling a pony alone at 3
years of age in Santurce, riding in races at 17.

• An iron-man resiliency that enables him to recover more
rapidly than others from injuries.

• Freedom to eat as much as he wants of whatever he wants
without risking the weight problems that haunt most jockeys.

• A gabby, salesman's charm in persuading trainers to put
him on horses he thinks can win.

• That sixth-sense timing that tells a player when to swing
the bat, pass the ball or leap for a rebound.

"He can do everything," says Tony Matos, the jockey agent who gets a fourth of Cordero's income for picking and choosing most of the mounts he rides. "He does things sitting on the back of a horse that other people couldn't do standing on the ground."

"You gotta be prepared," Cordero says, echoing the old Boy Scout motto. "You gotta know your horses, your trainers and your riders. They don't change habit."

Getting ready now for the next race, Cordero continues his preparation by pondering tactical questions. Which horses have the early speed to go to the front in this one-mile race, and which will be allowed to come out of the starting gate more leisurely? Where will the other jockeys try to position their mounts? When can they be expected to make their bids?

"A lot of times," he explains, "trainers give you really foolish instructions. Like there could be five horses with speed in the race, and he'll tell you, 'Put this horse on the lead.' You know your horse don't got that kind of speed, and if you use him early, you gonna come up empty. But if you don't try it, the trainer's gonna get mad at you. I blowed a lot of races trying to follow instructions from trainers. It comes to a situation, like, you gotta use your own judgment."

In Cordero's judgment, distilled from 16 years of race-riding, a jockey with only one battle plan is inviting disaster. "Things not always come out the way you plan it. It don't come out, you got a loser. So I prepare myself to ride three ways: if I'm on the lead, or just off it; if I'm in between, laying third or fourth; or if my horse happen not to show speed that day and I got to come from way back."

A classic example of this resourcefulness came in the 100th Kentucky Derby two years ago, when Cordero steered Cannonade out of a 16th-place jam into the winner's circle with a daring inside run along a rail deserted by 22 other jockeys. Paper-throwing fans had broken through a fence on the backstretch, so the rest of the jockeys were staying clear of the rail.

"Angel's so aggressive," says Woody Stephens, the trainer who saddled Cannonade that day. "Always so full of that idea of 'Get out there and do it.' Boys like that, they may have a bad

Cries
out for
quoting—

week, but they'll never have a bad month."

Measuring human greatness can be difficult in a sport where perhaps 90 percent of the winning equation comes from the horse. Eddie Arcaro once startled a complaining trainer by snapping, "If I could of carried your horse on my back the last eighth of a mile, we might've won it." Jockeys can become wealthy with a winning average of 12 percent (about one in eight), and even the highest can't go through a season with an average much higher than 20 percent. Yet the jockey's part of the equation can make the difference in a world where millions of dollars often hangs on photo-finish inches.

Cases could be made for other big-league riders. Laffit Pincay, the only jockey besides Cordero whose mounts have earned $4 million in a single season, probably has more muscle, more rhythm. Willie Shoemaker has a silkier touch on the reins, Braulio Baeza more style, Jorge Velasquez probably more finesse, Eddie Maple perhaps more patience. On balance, though, no jockey brings so many varied skills to his trade as Cordero.

Now, in the prerace bustle of the jockey room, a different side of Cordero emerges as Joe Imparato, a second-echelon rider, wanders over. Cordero greets him with a theatrical burst of vocalizing. Imparato laughs, and Baeza, at the next bench, allows himself a rare half-smile.

The tee shirt and the singing reflect a public image of exuberance, even clownishness. But the happy-go-lucky flamboyance masks a family man's stability (wife, two young children) and a perfectionist's attention to detail.

Point: intense concentration—

Even as he waits the next race, Cordero checks notations he has made on the appropriate past-performance page of the Daily Racing Form. Initials designating the rival jockeys (BB for Baeza, EM for Maple and so forth) have been scrawled beside each horse's name, listed in order of past position. Large S's, denoting early speed, have been inked in red alongside the names of several horses. Two more, considered particularly dangerous, have an X marked next to them. Another's weight, unusually light, has been circled.

Plant—

Cordero has already watched the taped rerun of the previous race, noting the step-by-step performance of every horse, including his own, and mentally filing the data for future reference. His mind is a memory book of information on horses, trainers and jockeys. This horse likes the inside. That trainer likes his horses to run on the outside. This horse is lazy, and must be ridden hard all the way. That one stops trying if he's hit with whip.

It's almost time to go out. Cordero tilts his head back and squeezes a drop or two of eyewash into each eye. Few jockeys watch the opposition as closely during a race as Cordero, and the eyedrops help keep his 20/20 vision clear. On muddy days, he wears as many as seven goggles in a race instead of the usual three, flipping the lenses down one by one as they gather mud.

"When I'm behind," he explains, "I watch the horses in front of me and next to me. I know who the riders are, who the trainers are. Other jockeys, they don't see as much. When I'm in front of a horse, I figure out, according with the rider and the trainer and the habit of the horse, I figure out when he'll be coming. You guess. It's like a hitter in baseball, he guess the pitch he's gonna get."

Now the jockey-room aide calls out, "Let's go, riders." Cordero takes a swig of honey ("good for the resistance") from a jar in his locker and strides towards the paddock.

Cordero's mount is not a "big horse" in the race-track definition of top quality. He is just another cheap claimer, going against others of his class. But to Cordero, who startled the racing world last year by bringing home 46 winners in one 14-day stretch at Aqueduct, every horse he rides is a big one.

In the parade to the post, Cordero limits his mount's warm-up to easy jogging because he has decided not to try for the lead: too much early speed in the race.

"You wanna go to the lead," he says, "you gotta warm up your horse one way. Gallop him good, get him on his toes. When you don't wanna go to the lead, you *prepare* not to go to the lead. You walk, jog, talk to your horse, keep him calm so he'll relax coming out of the gate. They don't answer, but they listen."

What this particular horse hears is a soothing "Easy." If he came from a barn where most of the help spoke Spanish, Cordero would calm him with a word like *suare,* meaning slow.

The jockey's occasional warnings to other riders during a race are also bilingual, depending upon the rival.

The doors of the starting gate bang open, and the 12 horses lunge forward: "The first jump, you just hold on to see what happen. After the first jump, you make your mind what you gonna do."

Observed in action—

This time, it's almost as routine as a milk run. Cordero gets his mount out of the gate alertly and settles him into fifth place, an ideal spot for keeping an eye on the opposition up front and listening for (but not looking back at) the contenders to the rear.

Not being on the lead, he will not have to contend with "bad riders running at me early." Cordero knows his horse: "Sometimes they lie to you. You got a good hold on a horse, you never ask him to run, and when you finally ask him to run, he got nothing left. He already run what he was gonna run."

This $7,500 claimer doesn't lie, though. Halfway down the backstretch, where Cordero likes to "go by horses without using your own horse," the jockey eases his mount past two faltering rivals. From there, the rest of the basic Cordero riding strategy takes shape: approaching the turn, "save ground" along the inside; at the quarter-pole, near the top of the home stretch, "get position to make a run"; and near the finish, try to keep the horse from dropping his head and changing his stride.

"What you usually keep in mind when you ready to turn for home," he explains, "is just to be in a spot that if you're running, you gonna be clear."

Once again, Cordero finds the right spot. The front-runners tire, and Cordero's mount has enough left to fight off a late challenge from a closer. Another winner.

But Cordero, the methodical perfectionist, never rests. Within minutes, he is back in the jockey-room lounge studying the video-tape rerun, looking for clues to future winners.

7. Color

Legwork

The night of January 6, 1906, magician and escape artist Harry Houdini was locked naked in Cell Number Two of Murderer's Row in the United States Jail, Washington, D.C. It was the same cell in which Charles Guiteau, the assassin of President James Garfield, had been kept for almost a year.

Photographs of Houdini taken around that time show a wiry sharp-featured man of less than middle height with intense, almost incandescent eyes and a full head of thick, wooly hair.

As warden J.H. Harris and Superintendent Richard Sylvester were to attest later, Houdini was out of the cell within 20 minutes.

He had also acquired his clothes, which had been locked in another cell.

And he had opened the doors of the eight other cells as well, switching all the occupants.

One way Houdini got himself out of these situations was by means of a hooked key. The hook was soldered to the rest like an iron lure, and just before he was frisked, Houdini would brush the back of his examiner, leaving the key hanging unheeded from the shoulder of the man's suitcoat. After the pat-down Houdini would retrieve the key and conceal it in his luxuriant hair by casually passing a hand through it.

Simple, but very, very clever.

Just as Houdini required a key to exotic obstacles, so too the writer— a literary conjurer — requires one for revealing events and occasions to his readers. It's as simple to get hold of as Houdini's metal pick, but requires just as much imagination in the use. The key is legwork, and its adhering hook is the informed source.

Go to the expert. If you are lost in any community, you can always get good directions from the local firehouse— firefighters have to know their way about. If you're sick, you're going to consult a doctor, not the stars. Similarly, at the center of any place or proceeding is somebody who can tell you all about it. The trick is to use a little logic in locating that individual.

Let's travel together on a sample journey. Your assignment is to get the story on Pikeville, Kentucky, a place you've never heard of but one your editor says has become newsworthy because coal miners are getting rich there hand over fist. He wants a lively piece on the town and its people. He wants to know what makes Pikeville tick. And he doesn't want you to waste a lot of time finding out. Time, he reminds you deathlessly, is money.

So you drive down there through tree-strewn shack-scattered hill country to Pikeville, a canyon-shaped pocket carved by the Big Sandy beneath Peach Orchard Mountain. It's a boomtown, all right. The first thing you notice is that the narrow streets are choked with traffic, and this Monday all the motel rooms in town are booked for the week, not by tourists but by legions of briefcase-bearing men who come to buy and sell.

You locate the reconstructed C&O railroad car office of the Pike County Chamber of Commerce at the south end of Main Street. That's the logical place to get a map and some background. Hugh Collett, 49, the Chamber's bespectacled executive director, tells you coal prices have gone up as oil has grown scarce, and Pikeville's sudden economic explosion has made it the mark for every loser and dreamer with an aim or an angle. Some local businessmen, he notes, have detected an influx of a new and unsavory element— sleek up-North sharpers out looking for live ones. They're there because the coal surge has produced more than 90 millionaires in the immediate area and three local banks with over a million dollars apiece in assets. In two years the licensed coal operators in Pike County have increased from 178 to 400 in what is the world's largest producer of underground coal. Scores of letters from all over the world barrage Collett daily setting down schemes and asking for help from a place and population conceived to be fabulously wealthy.

"Take a look at this," sighs Collett, and hands over the top mailing on his morning stack.

It's from a 30-year-old gospel singer in Lagos, Nigeria. All he wants is $120,000 for musical instruments to equip his dance band.

Collett puts you on to the town historian, 78-year-old Frank Forsyth, and you use your map to locate his white frame house at 128 Park St. Forsyth, a genial white-haired wire-rimmed gentleman with a symbolic coal scuttle on his front porch, tells you Pikeville was a trade center for Kentucky commerce long before the mud streets turned to asphalt and coal became its major export. He tells of the old days a century before when huge falls of white oak and hickory timber were sent down the Big Sandy on big lumber barges bound up by poplar pegs and steel "chain dogs."

Forsyth fondles one of them as he talks, its spike end and heavy links clanking like Morley's shackles in his hand.

"If these could talk," he says, "they could really tell you something. There was a day when a thousand rafts all tied up at Catlettsburg at the same time, closing the whole river to traffic."

But at length the trees were timbered off the top of the hills and the hard search for survival beneath the surface began. Coal men worked around the clock, right through the "hoot owl shift." Up at dark, down in the mines before dawn and out after dusk, such men developed bent backs and callused knees clawing out coal in 30-inch shafts with no sight of the sun. They were the pioneers, the pilgrims of the mountain country.

They were the unprosperous ancestors of the ones subscribing to today's *Pike County News* with its strange and wonderful advertisements in the back: offers for starting chinchilla farms, sales lists on lush out-of-state retirement tracts, and half-page send-offs for Mercedes-Benz.

You're ready now to hit the street and have a look for yourself. It takes you an hour just to get into town and park, so heavy is the influx of shoppers, salesmen and just plain passers-by into this sudden center of Pike County activity. Walking up and down Main, you count no fewer than five jewelry stores in that small town, and the curbs are lined with long expensive Eldorados and Mark IVs.

In a display case just beyond the door of Hefner's on Caroline Avenue, you find a $14,000 three-carat diamond looking not at all lonely or even remarkable among the even ranks of water-bright stones; and Gus Poulos, owner of the "Camera and Diamond Center," admits he has sold finger rings for upwards of $30,000— in cash. George Wells of

Wells Plymouth-Chrysler Imperial around the corner sells "a couple hundred" new cars a year. No recession here.

"When the mines are good, business is good," says Wells.

The mines are good. After hitting peaks of $75 and $85 last year, the Chamber of Commerce reports coal prices have leveled off to a respectable $23 a ton. This is an area that the brochures tell you has paid Kentucky attorneys $7,789,122 in black-lung fees during the past two years. And business is good. At the W.B. Call Co. ("Everything for the fancy bath") up the street, luxuries like cultured marble bathroom vanities, chandeliers and embossed toilet seats are prominently displayed, and guitars and banjos sell by the score at Gene and Mike's House of Music nearby. You stop in the Pikeville National Bank and Trust Co. and get a Comparative Statement of Condition: In one year the assets have made a whopping jump from $74 million to $160 million!

You locate the Chief of Police in a small green office on 11 Division St. in a building he shares with the fire department and the jail.

"Our biggest problem is traffic," claims gold-badged Jess Johnson, 63. He heads a force of 11 officers and two meter maids. Lacing his arms across his chest, he concedes crime is on the upswing: "The juvenile situation is gettin' a little bad. Mostly automobile pilferin', breakin' and enterin'— theft."

(You ask around find out the *Pike County News* reported a one-man crime wave recently when whispers of a mysterous masher sent Pikeville women home after dark to lock themselves away from another fancied Jack the Ripper.

The "masher" turned out to be a sad deaf-mute day laborer who only wanted a kiss.)

"Our biggest problem is narcotics," insists Sheriff Bill Deskins, 45, in his quarters on the second floor of the Pike County Courthouse.

In the foyer you spot a wanted poster for "Greasy" Lawrence, mail thief, and a pipe-smoking deputy with a can of Prince Albert protruding from his pocket.

"We're cracking down on it," Deskins says. "Twenty were indicted by the grand jury last month."

You ask what kind of "narcotics" has been nabbed.

"Mostly marijuana and a few assorted pills," admits the sheriff.

But you know what the biggest problem really is— running whiskey. At each election the Baptists and the bootleggers get together to vote

Pike County dry, while West Virginia is within easy hauling distance 40 miles away.

You find this out from a source who would surely know things: your rougher-'n-a-cob room clerk. He offers you "a number to call," and you can have anything you want delivered to your door— at double the licensed price.

"I'd stay away from the 'shine," advises your benefactor. "Stick with the bonded whiskeys. You want to know your bootlegger before you buy any moon to make sure he keeps a clean still. A lot of these guys filter their stuff through some car radiator, and it's the best way I know to get lead poisoning."

Pressed, the sheriff agrees it's of some concern.

"We [he and his six deputies] raid the boots every once in a while, maybe 75 times last year," Deskins says. "We caught one hauler setting right in front of the courthouse with a full load. We pulled 50 cases of beer out on the steps."

You determine that the Schlitz 16-ounce can is the most popular bootleg item. You've observed from your motel window grown men in suits and ties stealing back to their rooms with brown paper bags, just like so many high-school kids sneaking a six-pack after a dance.

You nose around some more, talk to a few citizens and repair to your room to pound out your perceptions. Now it's just a matter of organization. You sew up your piece this way:

The essential character of Pikeville goes beyond the overnight wealth that pushes some of its people into expressing their affluence with flashy acquisitions and fashionable jet flights to Jordan to be baptised. That character also outstrips the town's confined cultural interest in bluegrass music and Carrie Ten Boom's *Tramp for the Lord.*

It can be found in the steel-toed boots and mud-splattered jeeps of the miners who pulled coal from the earth, not for diamond rings or sleek sportscars but to feed their families, and who ruined their lungs and their backs working the shafts.

For while suited salesmen talk deals in the lofty Landmark Restaurant where the top sirloin goes for $8.50 and almonds turn up in the string beans, the best part of Pikeville congregates next door at Jerry's in denim and open-necked flannel shirts, joking over fried chicken and ice-box pie.

You've used your head, talking to people who know things, making sure you got not only the vested interests but the others. You've also used your eyes and ears to pull in enough detail to paint a proper picture. It's a wrap: You'll file it in the morning. Time elapsed, with travel: 24 hours.

Morgues and other museums

To properly prepare for a story or an event, locality or occasion, get as close as you can to your material. Immerse yourself up to the eyes in the subject matter.

Every building you've ever been in has a story behind it. If bricks could talk, writers would be out of business, so endlessly fascinating would be the yarns they could reveal about the romance that remains always just an inch beyond routine.

Well, bricks can't talk, but you can make them murmur. Open your senses; run your fingers over the surfaces. And *ask questions.* Acquire the habit of cataloging impressions as well as information. In this way it is possible to reconstruct Rome from a fallen pedestal.

Real Paper contributor Judy Jarvis took an insightful look inside the Boston morgue that provided a good deal more than a mere explanation of how the place functions. It was interesting enough to learn bodies may enter through a secret underground corridor that connects with Boston City Hospital and that they are kept in 101 boxes at 32 degrees; but it was Ms. Jarvis' awareness at the scene that convincingly conveyed a sense of Being There:

> The morgue has an odd smell from the caustic cleaner used to remove any flesh and fiber left on the litters or on the linoleum floor. The walls of the large main morgue are white tile bricks, shiny from just having been cleaned. Joseph Flannagan, tour guide and mortuary assistant supervisor, said that a commercial cleaning company had just steam-cleaned the morgue. He thought the cleaner smelled like bubble gum.

Fascinating. Suddenly you're right there with her: Welcome, dear reader, to Stiff City.

On-site observation can reveal the essence of an event through apparently casual elements. Everything counts; sudden relevance pops up in obscure places. Covering the Kentucky Derby for the *Boston*

Phoenix, David Rosenbaum caught the single-minded commercialism of the entire affair simply by showing the parking situation and some of the stuff for sale:

"Park right here," said an old coot waving at cars from his front porch. "Never mind the rose bushes." Never mind the lawns, the hedges, the tulips, the white picket fences. Park anywhere you like, buddy. It'll only cost you five, 10, 15 or 20 bucks 'cause, you see, there just ain't no parking at Churchill Downs. And if you save your money and take a bus to the track, you can always get rid of that heavy bread weighing down your wallet by buying, say, a plastic Derby tote bag, a Derby tee-shirt, a Derby pennant, a Bicentennial souvenir Derby mint julep glass (I got six), or a parimutuel ticket on any nag running in any of the 10 races on the card.

By consciously absorbing every impression and selecting those that seem salient, you can recreate your own emotions in the reader. Look on each locality as an exhibit with a series of revelations scattered inside. Then proceed to share them.

There are no dull subjects, only dull writers. To an artist's curious mind, *everything* is interesting, and his craft is to pass that enthusiasm on to an audience. Every place and time has a peculiar texture, the quality of which will be always intriguing. Suppose you're out of assignments one New Year's Eve after several seasons of Watergate politics and economic recession. So you drive down to the airport in a drizzle. The place is all but empty. No story? That *is* the story:

The slate-gray sky was a Confederate shroud over the Greater Cincinnati Airport, leaking cold rain the last day of the year. The few thick-coated travelers turned their collars against the chill while planes moved in and out of the overcast like shell-shaped ghosts. New Year's Eve at the airport was the uncomfortable end of an uncomfortable year.

"We sell a lot less insurance on days like this," Evelyn Wischer said.

Mrs. Wischer, 51, of 1392 Pleasant Valley Rd., Florence, sells air policies from a cubicle in C Terminal. The sheet-metal sky guaranteed few sales this day.

"On an overcast or snowy day they won't buy flight insurance," Mrs. Wischer noted. "On sunny days they want all they can get, plus more."

Travelers evidently feel the buying of insurance on a bad-weather day comes too close to acknowledging an already gloomy possibility.

But those customers Evelyn Wischer has tend to linger at her counter.

"They seem to want to talk," she said. "And about personal things— illnesses and deaths in the family. Tragic things."

The nature of her work and the understanding in Mrs. Wischer's face account for that this cheerless day. But New Year's Eve was turning out to be a quiet day, except for sad confidences.

"I deadheaded out and in three times," said shuttle-bus driver Fred Hamilton, 44, of 126 Fairfield St., Bellevue.

("Deadheading" means driving empty.)

"Sixty per cent or better of our passengers are business people coming in for the week. Between Christmas and New Year's, business drops."

That it had. Travelers on New Year's Eve tend to be loners or people with sudden trouble. Earl Pleiman, 65, was seeing his wife off to Fort Lauderdale where their daughter awaited an operation for a fused vertebra following an automobile accident.

Robert Elzy, 52, was on his way back from Birmingham where he had attended the post-Christmas funeral of a niece. The long, carpeted terminal halls were as uncrowded as a museum at closing.

Elizabeth Doak, 89, was returning to Seminole, Fla., after a seasonal visit with her son. Frail but eyesnap sharp, Mrs. Doak paused for a grim observation on the old year.

"It's been a terrible year for these United States," she said, birdlike and erect. "Our only hope for 1975 is if they get this inflation under control— and I don't know who is going to do it."

Asked what she would be doing late this night, Mrs. Doak supplied a wink that had none of the octogenarian in it.

"They're having a little party on at my condominium tonight," she smiled waspishly. "I think I'll go."

But bartender Bill Limerick, 60, of the American Airlines Sky Chef, regarded the New Year with a mixologist's most-wary eye. His midnight celebrating would be held strictly at home.

"I'm going out the next night," he confided, passing a cloth over the bright surface of the bar. "Then I won't be paying two prices and running the risk of getting run over by a bunch of drunks."

Despite the commercial slowdown in the airport shops, where penny candy now sells for three cents and some shelves stand empty after the year's-end inventory, it is business as usual across the rain-wet runways now bright with a steel-mirror shine.

"We're set up to operate under these conditions all the time," said George W. Hessler, 57, chief controller at the Federal Communications Control Tower.

He pointed out through the wraparound glass of the tower 124 feet up where visibility had closed to a fuzzy half mile. New Year's cloud cover or not, the big Boeing 727 is still slid through the smear one by one. The radar crew still worked, and would be working through the night.

The sparsely-filled aircraft continued their intermittent movement outward bound, soaring beyond the old year to wrest some away from trouble and take others relentlessly toward it.

Snippets of time like this are the stuff of daily history, poignant Matthew Brady photographs of particular moments pointing up the enduring drama of the everyday. Humdrum? Insignificant? Only to those for whom life itself is insignificant, and they don't read.

Putting people in it

An upended mahogany box about the size of a capacious coffin is not in itself remarkable,. even with a front panel of glass an inch thick revealing a steel cage inside.

Fill the box with water and it is still unremarkable. It is furniture, nothing more, and not very functional at that.

But— lower Harry Houdini inside it upside down, his feet fastened in heavy stocks. Lock the lid. Draw a curtain, and play "Asleep in the Deep" for two endurable minutes. . . .

Suddenly the box is remarkable indeed.

Houdini used what were ostensibly the bars of his cage as a ladder to haul himself upward where he could free his feet. He would then invert himself in the cell; there would be air to breathe at the top from the splashed-out water he displaced when he was lowered into the tank. In this position he worked the trick locks of the lid and escaped.

The point is that there is no drama whatever without a performer. Just as the stage set only moves us initially, serving as the backdrop rather than the substance of a play, so any story to stay lively must summon forth actors as soon as possible. A subject is sold by the people you put in it, and they can sell anything.

That is the essence of showmanship.

It is also the essence of good feature writing.

Landscapes are breathtaking, but people make us laugh and cry. I could go on and on about the purple mesas and cactus-strewn sands, but your ears won't begin to prick until I put in the lone rider who looks a little like Clint Eastwood and a little like you. Then, when I add a few assorted Indians with warpaint, and maybe a grizzled old busybody of a sidekick, I've got you. And if I start the bunch of them shooting at each other, I'll keep you.

Suppose one day you're sitting over by the teletype thinking pure thoughts as newspaper people do when you get a call from a woman who thinks there might be a story in a chair she's got. The idea interests you as a challenge: how to get an amusing piece out of a hunk of old furniture?

The answer is to use the chair as a wedge on the people who used it:

The cracking, wire-wound wooden chair is empty now, but for more than 40 years it was the sentry-seat for butcher Mike Finke.

Located strategically in the hall of his meat market at 824 Main St., Covington, the chair offered Finke a clear view of his shop and of the old fire station at Emma and Main across the street.

Finke was a fixture in that chair, his body canted back against the wall and fingers laced calmly across his chest. Two things brought the chair down with a bang, sending Finke abruptly to his feet: the entrance of a customer and the shrill ring of the fire bell at Engine Co. Four.

For when the firefighters roared out on a run, it was Finke who crossed the road in their wake to shut off the siren and close the firehouse door.

The chair banged out its intermittent tattoo from 1920 to the day of Finke's death on April 1, 1962. Now Finke's Quality Meats is gone from Main Street, and last week the firehouse closed down.

But the chair survives in the possession of Finke's oldest daughter, Mrs. Martha Finke Oehler.

"I'm almost getting too broad for it," she admitted. "I hang out a little on the sides."

Mrs. Oehler, 54, keeps her father's chair in the living room of her remodeled farmhouse home at 2439 Dixie Hwy., Fort Mitchell. On the front lawn outside rests more antique evidence of the pursuits of Mike Finke — the iron pot he cooked in.

"Nobody around here knew what goetta was until my great-grandmother brought it over from Germany," Mrs. Finke said. "My father used to cook it once a week in that pot, 100 pounds at a time."

Mike Finke's goetta, a slow-simmered combination of sausage meats and oatmeal, became the favorite breakfast fare for many Covingtonians. But frequent was the startled passer-by who, sighting pungent goettawurst smoke seeping up from Finke's store, ran scared straight across the street to sound the engine company alarm.

"The firemen were always our friends," recalled Mrs. Oehler, who still won't pass a firehouse without waving — although the firemen she knew as a child are now retired or dead. "They say never look back, but I always do. My memories are important to me."

Surrounded by her houseful of heirlooms, Mrs. Oehler reflected wistfully on the old days when Mike Finke ran his tireless circuit from the front hall to the firehouse and back. If her brightly-colored psychedelic tunic placed her family in the present, her furniture and affections time-traveled her momentarily into the past.

"I think people were happier then," she said, and looked at the empty chair.

Simple enough. What sells the story is not the chair but the robust German butcher who launched himself in and out of it for four decades. He lives, and so does his daughter, your source, whose backward looks imbue the piece with a kind of wistful longing for a less complicated, unrecoverable past.

At any event you'll find people present. Nail 'em. Note 'em and quote 'em. They'll save your story, adding life to what might otherwise be as unreadable as the minutes of a faculty meeting. Here's how Sean Toolan of the *Chicago Tribune* starts a remarkably informative story about showing dogs:

The woman from Detroit was complaining that her "darling dog" would have won "best in group" if only she had been able to get a thin coat of black powder to dust his coat!

The bone of contention was that another lady in the next row of benches at the International Dog Show in the International Amphitheater was allowed to dust her dog's white coat with ordinary, run-of-the-mill chalk.

"But where are you going to find a stick of black chalk?" the disgruntled owner asked.

Good question, and one that reflects the frustration and anxiety of people who show dogs.

Toolan describes the show, the dogs, the judging criteria, the American Kennel Club, and the history of the contest — but he is careful to include a variety of colorful characters to keep our attention from straying. He eavesdrops to excellent effect.

Witness a few random remarks at the International Show last weekend:

A shrieking woman to a passing child, obviously longing to pet her precious poodle: "Keep away from him, he doesn't like people just before he goes into the ring."

A growling man to a photographer lining up to snap a picture of a drooling Newfoundland dog, wearing a baby's white bib: "What are you doing, trying to make a fool of my dog?"

The owner of a doberman pinscher worrying about her dog's weight: "When he doesn't eat I have to force-feed him and literally stuff the food down his throat with my fingers."

He even makes a whole category of show-connected escorts as immediately recognizable as a single individual:

You can spot the professional handlers by the cut of their coats. One shoulder is usually drooping because one arm is usually held higher than the other, trying to keep the dog's head high and dignified. Handlers also smell of liver, because they carry pocketsful of stuff to "bait" the dog. That means getting the dog to stretch head and body into a near-perfect stance as the judge walks around the ring.

Very nicely done. The piece is populated, so it moves.

In covering a breaking feature, keep your eye on the people in the situation, especially as they present themselves in scenes. On charged occasions we all act out our own instant movies; the effective writer will offer up the scenes intact as the best way of revealing events— in action. The closing down of a firehouse would seem on the surface of it a minimal opportunity for a story. It could be done in three graphs at the desk. But you're a feature writer, and you go down there to see the place for yourself. And all you have to do is watch and listen:

"It's the end of an era," said Engineer Mike Newcomb of Engine Company No. 4 at Emma and Main Streets, Covington.

Lack of manpower made Friday the final shift for the firehouse, which would be shut down and boarded up in the morning.

"This was one of the last of the old-time firehouses where you knew the names of everybody in the neighborhood," Newcomb continued. "We treated skinned knees here, cut the glass from kids' feet, drove home lost old men."

And answered an average of 450 fire alarms a year since the building of the station in 1888.

Now the wall lockers were empty and the beds upstairs stripped as firemen sat in the day room talking wistfully of old times. Cigarette smoke hung in the air like the ghost of old emergencies. In an adjoining kitchen a sweet-sharp bowl of chili bubbled for the final meal. A thousand conversations had been held around the same worn table in coffee-drinking camaraderie as firemen talked off the tension after rugged runs; this would be the last and loneliest.

"I've been here for 11 years," firefighter Jack Balderson said. "I'm sad about it, yes. I hate to see any rescue facility closed."

Master Mechanic Bill Glindmeyer agreed.

"Especially since this is the one closest to my house," he said wryly.

The small square room in which they sat was once the hay loft for the horses that pulled the old firewagons. At the sound of the bell their traces fell from the ceiling on the backs of the horses, so well trained they never disgraced themselves on what was then a wooden floor.

"The firemen held buckets behind them," Balderson explained, "and the horses filled them on schedule."

Symbolic of those animals are the poured-concrete engine heads that grace the front of the firehouse. During Kentucky Derby season, firemen used to hang the names of projected winners from the necks of the statues, frozen forever and straining above the door.

"It's like losing a landmark," sighed Chief Phil Gardner. "You've got to have a bad feeling about it. This is a place where men eat, sleep, breathe together."

"Firemen have to be close," supplied Balderson. "Each man's life depends on the others."

"You can't hold grudges here," Gardner nodded. "I can't afford to carry on a mad against the man who may be pulling me out of the smoke tomorrow."

Firemen at Engine Company No. 4 often became the father confessors of their area, consulted on everything from domestic spats to minor repairs.

"I wore out a crescent wrench fixing bikes for kids," Balderson recalled.

Talking softly now at the end of their tenure, the firemen spoke of the scared boy who showed up late one night lost and caught in a dog collar. They spoke of the fireplug at the corner they opened up for swim-suited children to play around and of the stunned householder standing before the smoking wreck of his home with three burnt dollar bills squeezed tight in his hand. And they spoke of the fires: the Ohio Scroll and Lumber Co. on Russell Street that burned to the ground, the blaze at Welch Fan on 2nd and Scott.

"Well," said a gruff voice suddenly, "is this the last one?"

The heads of the firemen snapped up.

Hellos and handshakes raised themselves instantly in greeting, for the voice belonged to retired fire marshal William Bailey, 73, a 20-year veteran and no stranger to the pumper company on Emma and Main.

"Just stoppin' by," he said off-handedly.

But the immaculately erect ex-captain of firefighters had not merely happened on the house. In spite of a dental appointment that had left his mouth feeling like a well-batted hardball, he was making sure he showed in time to say goodbye to a building that had been an important part of his life.

He recalled the time a fireman's pet monkey had gotten loose in the station and they had to cut a hole in the ceiling with an axe to catch him. When the laughter subsided, he recalled something else

that still lights up his face like the solar ball on a smile button.
"We were on a rescue run to 3rd and Main," he remembered.
"Woman there was having a baby. I delivered it, and darned if on
the way to the hospital I didn't deliver another one. Twins!"
At their first communion, Bailey was named godfather.
Bailey's expression became more sober as he discussed the com-
missioners' meeting he had attended the night before.
"I told Mayor Grimm that the fire department is just like a ball
team. When you're in bad trouble you need a certain amount of
backup on the bench."
Capt. William Bailey's eyes traveled the walls of the room.
"Well, this pumper company was our bench. And we've lost it."
Jack Balderson stopped sweeping the tiled day room floor and
hurled the broom against the wall.
"I'm not mad," he said, and stalked off.
The whine of a power saw rose like a seabird's scream as
Engineer Jim Watters cut long lengths of plywood to nail over the
windows. Pumper truck four rose clean and crimson behind him,
waiting to be driven out for the last time. Its final call had occurred
at 12:53 the night before— a false alarm.
Capt. John Meyer, a 28-year veteran who answered fire calls on
a bicycle as a boy, passed by carrying boards. Outside the large
electric door another boy, tow-headed and tin-badged, stood on the
sidewalk like Meyer's younger self, looking up at the firehouse
with eyes as big as snowballs. But there would be no more sounding
sirens at Emma and Main, no more roar of trucks on a run.
The ticker-tape machine by the door wrote *finis* for the firehouse
that once held the newest and fastest pumper in the city. The
epitaph was short and without ceremony:
"P4 off the track at 8:00 a.m. The new run schedule is now in
effect."

Anybody else might have said nothing happened, but you as a feature
writer found significance in Jack Balderson's thrown broom and a rich
old edifice came to life because you recorded what was said inside it.
You're getting stubborn, you are.

Seasonal stuff

Holidays and festive occasions make sure-fire feature stories if you can find the proper angle. Every Saint Patrick's Day you can be sure somebody is going to write a parade story; you want yours to distinguish itself from all the others.

Take Christmas. Santa stories, right? You get word of a college basketball player hiring out in the beard and the red flannel and you go out to talk to him — on site, of course — with that in mind as your angle: a boy Santa. But when you locate him, the angle turns out to be something much better:

> The kid on Santa's lap was screaming. Santa's eyes rolled Heavenward. He rang his reindeer bells, he cooed, he brandished toys.
> The kid screamed on.
> "Smile," the child's mother said.
> In a stockroom later, beyond the gaze of his subjects, Santa took off his scalp. The beard followed, and he mopped his brow.
> "It isn't the kids that make this job painful," Greg Anderson said. "It's the mommies."
> Anderson, 21, seems at first blush an unlikely candidate for the role of Santa Claus. At six-foot five, the rangy ex-athlete still answers to his basketball nickname of "Bones." But as a psychology and communications major at Trevecca College in Nashville, he brings the understanding arts to bear on children. A little clown-white makeup, some rouge and a strategically located feather pillow complete the transformation.
> Greg is working his school vacation at J.C. Penney's Monmouth store in Newport. There he does daily battle with that most dangerous of strange beasts— the oversolicitous matriarch.
> "They want that picture," Anderson explained.
> He referred to the shots taken of Santa and the children by a camera stationed in front of his green throne, two dollars for a five-by-seven or a wallet-sized sheet.
> "Even if the kid is scared to death, they're going to get that picture," Greg Anderson groaned. "So you've got this terrified kid beating on Santa with his parents looking approvingly on. It really destroys the spirit of Christmas."
> Still, Greg enjoys the job. Once a forward averaging ten points and 12 rebounds a game, he now looks toward a career in broadcasting. He sees the Santa work as a valuable supplement to his

psychology studies.

A lot of weirdos wander into Toyland. One 16-year old girl insisted on sitting on Santa's lap.

"Ho, ho, ho!" said Santa, and prepared to ask her what she was doing later.

"She was married and had a kid," Anderson added.

Gregg finds the boys most often ask for fire trucks. The girls seem intent on either Rub-a-Dub Dolly or Baby Alive. Rub-a-Dub Dolly is washable ("Two in a bathtub is more fun than one," deadpans the ad), and Baby Alive consumes a formula which she promptly defecates, placing the child in the closest possible touch with reality.

The job is not without its ancillary tribulations.

"I got up for a break once and my pants fell down," Gregg said.

He stumbled on the situation by accident. Victor Temporaries told him they had "a position" at Penney's. An eight-hour job. Sit the whole time. $2.50 an hour. The constant company of two good-looking female photographers. And a tailor-made suit.

"When they pulled out the Santa costume I about fell over," Gregg admitted.

Penney's assistant manager Pat Wildman had only a few admonitions.

"He wanted me to make sure my hair didn't fall out from under my wig. And he told me to be friendly. Last year's Santa was a little mean and grumpy."

He was also a little sauced, which was bad for Santa's image.

Anderson dandles the children on his knee while the pictures are taken, then gives them a small toy — monster teeth, a squirting cigar, or a tiny plastic game. Some of the games are mystifying.

Asked by one kid for instructions, Gregg examined the game doubtfully.

"I just make 'em, I don't play 'em," he said.

Beside Santa's chair is a record player ($244) playing Christmas carols and a fan ($19.88) to keep Santa from suffocating in his suit. Next to that is a display of Little Golden Books (35 cents), one of the most enduring of which is "Bedtime Stories," in which Foxy Loxy solves Chicken Little's sky-falling problem by eating him.

Meanwhile Mommy is back with her screaming charge.

"Smile real big for Santa," says the photographer, fruitlessly trying to distract the erupting infant with a stuffed dog waved in the air.

"Take it crying or not," says Mommy.

Santa sighs.

Again, don't preconceive the story; let the point emerge from what happens, not what you expect. But in any case, insist on that which is fresh. All the old subjects are legitimate — winter weather, Salvation Army bands, groundhogs, chopped cherry trees, July Fourth fireworks, you name it— but look at them from a *new perspective*.

That's not as hard to find as you might think. One December, 21 days before Christmas, my editor came up with a crippler of an assignment: All he wanted out of me was a full-length Christmas story every day until the 25th. In the process I was to come up with a blockbuster for Christmas Day that would embody the spirit of the season.

It was rough, but I used my head and people following the series phoned in tips. Every day when I left the office I worked my way further down the street in front of it, interviewing tree salesmen, shop keepers and social workers; that would at length provide a color piece on what was going on up and down the city's main drag. I went to orphanages and toy shops, soup kitchens and company parties. I found an authentic Scrooge and an authentic Santa. I drove around and talked to people, and there was always something ready in time for deadline, because while occasions express themselves in cliches, people don't; no two of them do the same thing quite the same way twice.

But I wasn't saving anything up. That Christmas Day story could well have been any of the ones I was turning in, but I never had a backlog and I was beginning to dread coming up empty. Which I almost did. An hour before copy had to go out Christmas Eve I sat in front of the typewriter with nothing in my head, not even visions of sugarplums. In fact I was sick of the whole thing, and if anybody's elf had poked his benign face over my out box I would have cheerfully stabbed the little monkey.

Then somebody dropped an envelope on my desk. It contained a scrawled note and a check — and I knew I had my story. It had been there all the time, but I hadn't seen it because the Maginot Line of my imagination had faced me fixedly off in the opposite direction.

I had preconceived the story. I had expected it to be somewhere outside, and there it was, right inside the city room. Because that hadn't been the first envelope I'd been sent.

I bent over the typewriter and began banging away:

"Find me Christmas," the editor said, and sent the reporter out into the snow.

He looked in churches and social service centers, in department stores and nursing homes, bus stations, back alleys and barrooms, in search of the seasonal spirit. The idea was to come up with *the* Christmas story that best expressed the giving heart this December, a story that would demonstrate clearly that there was something beyond the shop windows and roadsign Santas with products peeking out of their packs.

The reporter wrote some stories. There was one about a woman who made dolls, another about a family in trouble 21 miles from Bethlehem, Kentucky. There was one about a small boy in an isolation ward, one about a dying woman and her husband about to be evicted, one about a family of eight without furniture and food. There were others.

And what emerged was that *the* Christmas story did not reside in these articles, but in the readers' response to them.

Anna Frost, 86, lives in the Old Ladies' Home, 7th and Garrard Streets, and makes dolls for disadvantaged children. Little Diana Smith, 12, of 437 Greenup, read the story and visited Mrs. Frost, bringing fruit and friendship. Other children followed.

Ray Smith of Gratz lost his right hand to a cornpicker shortly after his wife had undergone a series of brain operations. His once-secure family suddenly found themselves strapped, with two young children to feed. Readers from all over northern Kentucky sent checks for the Smiths to the First Farmer's Bank and Trust Company in Owenton which, at this writing, amount to more than $2,000.

Young Bobby Baker, 7, lay alone in the isolation ward at Children's Hospital, Cincinnati, afflicted with viral penumonia. The gunmetal gray walls of the room sealed him in like a steel coffin, cheerless and bare. Bobby made a modest Christmas request: He wanted somebody to send him cards. Readers responded with scores of them and toys, too; strung across the room and over the wall facing his bed, they set up a varicolored holiday mosaic around a manger scene and menageries of stuffed critters. Bobby, one arm taped to an intravenous tube, has become adept at opening mail with his teeth, a plastic car and pocket radio stored safely away beside him. His smile is another sun.

Thelma Holmes, terminally ill and tended by her recently-fired husband Blaine, awaited eviction by his employers at Blue Grass Manor. Medical bills mounted and desperation with them as the end of the month drew nearer. The Rev. Gene Barbour and the members of Erlanger Methodist Church on Commonwealth Street read the story and have arranged to pay for medicine and rent for the Holmeses; they are also seeking employment for Blaine.

Doris Gray, 40, in need of furniture, food and clothing for her family of seven children, found all three through the quick intervention of Catholic Social Services, the Downtown Neighborhood Center, the Be-Con Christmas Store and Goodwill Industries. Jim Schworer of Goodwill contacted Burt Rosenberg of Marx Furniture and Tony Maza of Value City, both of whom donated generously.

The reporter had gone in search of Christmas and it had found him instead.

And he wanted to thank these people, but there weren't any words left to do it. The photograph of Bobby Baker might go a way toward it, and the communicated gratitude of all those the readers reached; but it had moved beyond the power of print.

"Merry Christmas," the reporter said, and came in out of the cold.

Sometimes the power of the press can be a beautiful thing. It had almost wrecked my season, then saved it instead.

The reporter as goat

Rolling Stone contributor Hunter Thompson applied the term "Gonzo journalism" to that species of writing in which the reporter actively injects himself into a situation for the predetermined purpose of writing about it. That was not an idea new or peculiar to Thompson; George Orwell did it in *Down and Out in London and Paris*. Ernest Hemingway did it in *The Green Hills of Africa*, Jack London did it in *The People of the Abyss*, and James Boswell did it in *The Life of Samuel Johnson*. Jack Kerouac made an entire literary career of it. There were others, but perhaps the clearest expression of the attitude such an experiment demands was articulated by Jack London in the preface to his willing descent into an East End hell:

> I went down into the under-world of London with an attitude of mind which I may best liken to that of the explorer. I was open to be convinced by the evidence of my eyes, rather than by the teachings of those who had not seen, or by the words of those who had seen and gone before.

He entered into the project forthrightly and with courage; his aim was nothing less than to live as a poor man among the poor. London's single reservation was to sew a gold sovereign into his shirt in case of emergency. Later he would give it away.

The virtue of this sort of enterprise is that a writer, that most equipped of observers, can glean the essence of a situation in a relatively short time. His sensations and impressions act as a diving bell for the landlocked, allowing the rest of us to see under various surfaces vividly and immediately.

What, for example, is it like to be present inside a Ku Klux Klan meeting? *New York World* reporter Lindsay Denison wangled his way into a "Klavern" on a New Jersey farm in the predawn hours of May 3, 1923. There was a burning cross 62 feet high, an excess of ceremony, and some rather revealing conversation among the hooded minions of the "Invisible Empire":

> One thing was clear then and remained clear throughout the night. The members of the Klan take themselves very seriously, even in their friendly chat. It is no frolicsome lark for them. They are quite sure that they "are getting this country on the right road at last." They keep saying it.
>
> "Where's Jim?" asked a man in a sheepskin coat. "Thought he was coming."
>
> "Why, say, I thought you knew," was the answer. "His wife wouldn't let him."
>
> "Why, what's the matter with her?" asked the inquirer. "Always thought she was a kinder sensible woman."
>
> The other man whispered something.
>
> "Is that so? Well, now, do you know I never knew she followed the Pope? What do you know about that!"

Denison takes us with him among the knights errant of ignorance for an intimate look. Or what does one experience inside the steel womb of an airship bound out to disaster? William L. Lawrence of the *New York Times* flew aboard the B-29 flagship *Great Artiste* bearing the atomic bomb to be dropped on Nagasaki. He wrote of the haunting phenomenon of St. Elmo's fire about the bomber en route:

> I noted a strange eerie light coming through the window high above the navigator's cabin, and as I peered through the dark all around us I saw a startling phenomenon. The whirling giant propellers had somehow become great luminous disks of blue flame. The same luminous blue flame appeared on the plexiglas windows in the nose of the ship, and on the tips of the giant wings. It looked as though we were riding the whirlwind through space on a chariot of blue fire.

Later he would see the bomb dropped through arc welder's lenses. His final look recalls the simultaneous attraction-repulsion of a poetically rendered bacillus:

> As the first mushroom floated off into the blue it changed its shape into a flowerlike form, its giant petals curving downward, creamy white outside, rose-colored inside. It still retained the shape when we last gazed at it from a distance of about two hundred miles. The boiling pillar of many colors could be seen at that distance, a giant mountain of jumbled rainbows in travail. Much living substance had gone into those rainbows. The quivering top of the pillar was protruding to a great height through the white clouds, giving the appearance of a monstrous prehistoric creature with a ruff around its neck, a fleecy ruff extending in all directions, as far as the eye could see.

Lawrence puts us right at the elbow of history. Or how about discovering what it's like to fight a fire? I took a turn for the *Kentucky Post* with Asst. Chief Donald Brown of the Covington Fire Department at a training area outside the city:

> As a white eel of water hissed out of the turret nozzle of the pumper truck at 350 gallons a minute (it's capable of 1,000), Chief Brown took the reporter through the fireless smokehouse. The walls were black with the char of many training schedules.
> "Here at least you don't have to worry about the flashover from

superheated wallpaper and paint," Chief Brown observed.

The inside of the two-floor structure resembled any gutted fire site. A worn maroon overstuffed chair sat incongruously in one corner.

Chief Brown well knew his way through, but not alone as an instructor. A fireman finds himself automatically noting the exits in any room; he may have to get out of it one day.

"You want to feel your way along the walls," Chief Brown advised. "Otherwise you could get hopelessly lost in the smoke."

And you'll move at a crouch — or a crawl. The ceiling temperature in a high-burning fire can approach 2,000 degrees Fahrenheit. At eight feet the temperature will be 1,600 degrees; at four, 400. So unless a fireman wants his ears crisped down to pork rinds, he will stay low.

The firehat helps. That long bill in back keeps the water from running down a fireman's neck from a ceiling which may be boiling hot. And the hat can be reversed, employing the bill as a heat shield.

Chief Brown lit a pile of boards and scrap in a back room. Black tendrils grew from it like the legs of a groping scorpion.

"Care to learn what fighting a fire feels like?" he asked the reporter, and like a fool the reporter said yes.

With the assistance of the white-haired chief, the reporter donned a rubber turnout coat and boots, a firehat and the twin tanks of a Survive-Air 30-minute smoke mask.

"But it never lasts 30 minutes," observed the chief comfortlessly.

A buzzer goes off when you're out of air. The reporter's sincere wish was that he would not have occasion to hear the buzzer.

He and Chief Brown stood on the roof of the smokehouse, which was already crooking black fingers around the edges. The reporter pulled on the mask, cinching the rubber straps tight.

"Let's go," said the chief, and in they went.

Forget all the TV shows you've ever seen about firefighting, because the reality of the inside of a house on fire is invisibility — smoke and heat and nothing but. You can see absolutely nothing — not the walls, not the hand in front of your face. It is like being wound within a thermal gray shroud.

Somewhere ahead of him the chief was moving down the stairs. The reporter could hear nothing but the loud laboring of his own lungs. The equipment was heavy on his back and the heat was fierce. The thick boots were rubber shackles on his feet. He felt his way along the walls; the doorframes were stove-hot to the touch.

"Back," said the chief.

A wall of fire sprayed across the bottom of the stairwell like a lambent orange sheet. Retreating, they entered again from the back. This time someone handed the reporter an inch-and-a-half hose. As he pulled the handle at the end of it he was not quite knocked down. He trained the stream of water toward a dim orange luminescence located only by the heat. He saw nothing, nothing at all, although there were firemen all around him.

His hat was falling off, and he knew if he dropped it he would never find it again. He crouched in the scorch, which pressed against the edges of his face like a flatiron, looking less like Steve McQueen in *Towering Inferno* than a tourist in Hell.

The hose was heavy, the oxygen tanks were heavy, the hat on his head was heavy, and his face mask was starting to steam up. The fire was beyond visibility now, only faintly detectable by a constant crackling sound somewhere behind the smear. It was beginning to irritate the reporter. The fire wasn't paying attention to him. He sprayed it, splashed it and smothered it, but the smoke bloomed on like a contained mushroom cloud.

At length it was out, and the reporter emerged from the smokehouse like a black-garbed, face-masked Martian. He had just an inkling of what a very small fire was like, and Chief Brown, who had personally saved the lives of four children only a week before, smiled at him.

And the reporter, looking back at the steaming mess he had left, had pause to grasp what "smokeeater" meant.

In each case, the reporter's willingness to actually participate in the event he is writing about makes for an exciting story with the aura of absolute authenticity about it.

The drawback to this kind of effort is of course occasional physical danger. Theatrical reporters like to point to the flathead saps they carry in the same pocket with their pipe and halfpad notebooks, hinting around at midnight standoffs; but the kind of reporter who engages in "Gonzo" is aware that legitimate, for-keeps trouble can accrue to these assignments. R.T. Sale, who is white, went deep into ghetto Chicago with a gang leader to write *The Blackstone Rangers,* a book about black militants in the early '70s. More than once he was greeted without enthusiasm:

> We came into a small dark meeting room. It was hard to see after the brightness outside. Flags hung limp from staffs at the front. Plain folding chairs were neatly arranged in rows of four. At the back, on the right, a few black men stood near two large cluttered wood desks. They saw us and stopped still. Joel went in first, moving up a narrow aisle between the empty chairs on the right and an old low sofa on the left. Two boys sprawled on the sofa, looking up, pulled in their legs to let him pass.
>
> Joel left me and went up to the group of young men to talk. More blacks appeared. I turned away, walking over to where old photos were fastened to the plaster wall with pins. I made myself stand and look at the pictures. All were old and faded and a few were framed. In each of them a short, pudgy black man with a pleasant face stood exhibiting his teeth, shaking hands with one famous figure after another. A voice at my elbow said:
>
> "Man, we ain't no animals in no zoo for you to be comin' here lookin' at."

Uh hunh. That is the point at which the investigative spirit may flag. Hunter Thompson finished out his examination of the Hell's Angels motorcycle club when he got himself stomped by the membership.

But there are opportunities short of pure mayhem for a reporter to use himself as goat for a story. Curtis Wilkie of the *Boston Globe* went upstate once to check on police protection of the President in the wake of two abortive assassination attempts:

> NASHUA, N.H. — The editors asked me to run up to New Hampshire and find out how tight was security for President Ford's visit yesterday.
>
> Pretty tight.
>
> Within 15 minutes of my arrival in Nashua I was in handcuffs and under arrest.

Wilkie was busted for nothing more than asking to see the police chief. In the process he got the story, a much better one than the security arrangements piece he had planned. Alan Richman, also writing for the *Boston Globe,* heard rumors that Celtics basketball star Dave Cowens, who made $300,000 a year, was driving a cab to relax. He set out in search of him.

From 8:30 until 9:30, I searched Chinatown and the Combat Zone. I was walking up Tremont Street towards the waterfront when cab No. 352 turned onto the street and went by a rather abnormal rate of speed. By the time I could hail him he was two blocks away. I gave chase and caught him at a red light.

He did not know me. Despite his longshoreman's cap, I knew him.

"Hi, how you doin'," Cowens asked his customer. "What you been doin' this evening?"

Richman's successful hunt for the eccentric basketball player made a good story in itself, with the bonus of an interview at the end. And *Louisville Courier-Journal* columnist Billy Reed shared insights into problems of the handicapped by participating in "Wheelchair Awareness Week" at the University of Kentucky.

I soon discovered that the perspective from a wheelchair is different, even frightening. Other people always seem to be looking down at you, in more ways than one. And as chattering bunches of people whirl past, you get the feeling that you're out of sync, moving at 33 rpm in a 78 rpm world.

People in wheelchairs notice all sorts of little things that escape everyone else. A crack in a sidewalk looks like a yawning chasm. Street corners, narrow doors and sloping sidewalks are formidable obstacles. After a short while, my hands were dirty and sore, my shoulders aching.

We stopped at the corner of Limestone and Euclid so I could try to use a phone booth from a wheelchair. It was impossible to get in the booth or reach the phone.

The intense eyewitness quality of these articles make for fine reading. While earlier the reporter was encouraged to stay out of the story unless he affected it in some crucial way, here he is invited to take a deliberate turn center stage— all it takes is imagination and a little moxie.

Harry Houdini of course made a very good living of using himself exclusively as goat, not infrequently placing his person in real peril. Houdini advertised all over the world that he could escape from anything, accept any challenge, elude any lock. His ingenuity always

saved him. Then, in 1902, with characteristic humorlessness, Kaiser
·Wilhelm's Imperial Police claimed Houdini's publicized stunts were
"swindles." The magician sued for slander.

Houdini spent weeks before the litigation in preparation for it,
studying extensively under German locksmiths. Then, as he expected,
lawyers for the police submitted a test. If Houdini could escape from a
set of handcuffs supplied by their clients, they would concede the case.
The magician accepted. Manacles were snapped shut on his wrists and
he stepped into the judges' chambers to get free.

There was a catch. Only the lawyers knew police had designed the
bracelets with a difference: Once they were locked, *no key could open
them.* They were one-time-only cuffs that would require hard work with
a hacksaw to part.

An unfair test, perhaps, but an existential one.

Houdini emerged from the judges' chambers in three minutes, the
handcuffs held triumphantly over his head. They were still shut.

The Imperial Police were compelled to publicly advertise "an
honorary apology" and pay court costs.

How did he do it?

By employing the same ingredient a feature writer uses in getting
across the color story. And you know very well what that is.

Magic. . . .

Drive-Ins: Evenings of True Grit
by Richard Dyer

['Fess up: you've been to the drive-in more than once.

*What an opportunity for a color story! The sights, the sounds, the
scents . . . the crazies. I once interviewed a projectionist at one of these
alfresco auditoria whose signal responsibility was to edit out all the skin
scenes; they backed up traffic on the interstate for miles. He noted with
pride he had cut down* Japanese Doll House *from an hour and a half to
45 minutes. . . .*

Richard Dyer of the Boston Globe *paints a vivid picture of this
quintessentially American experience.]*

The night of June 6, 1936, just over 40 years ago, was an
historic one for the Boston area. That evening, in Weymouth,
was the gala opening of New England's first drive-in theater.

Research— Ushers on bicycles led motorists to their places on the seven levels that faced "the largest movie screen in the world." The crowd paid 35 cents apiece to see a newsreel, a Disney cartoon, a Three Stooges short, and the English dancing star Jessie Matthews in the main feature *First a Girl*. The press commented that "every sound of the talkies was audible in the furthermost corner . . . the sounding of horns of almost every description took the place of the usual hand-clapping and cheering as the audience showed approval."

On-site observation— Things have changed. Three nights last week I went to drive-ins. There were no ushers, but at the first drive-in I visited there was a cheery lad to take $5 for my carload and tell me, "*The Creature from Black Lake* is really great!" There was no cartoon, newsreel or short — though there were a lot of ads — and there

Note second reference to Jessie— was the promise of a "co-hit" on the marquee. "What's the co-hit?" we asked. "It's no hit," came the reply, "but you'll like it anyway. *The Night Evelyn Came Out of the Grave.*" Jessie Matthews probably wouldn't have cared for it.

Drive-ins hit the peak of their popularity in the years immediately after World War II. Land was cheap; people wanted to be entertained; returning servicemen were responsible for a lot of kids who weren't of an age to be taken into movie houses. Nowadays, though, drive-ins have fallen on hard times. The theaters in the shopping malls and the dollar cinemas in the suburbs compete for the moviegoing audience; land and taxes are costly. Drive-ins look around for daytime uses as churches, parking lots and flea markets. But drive-ins will always have their audience because the experience they have to offer is at

Detail— once uniquely sociable and uniquely private. People bring their lawn furniture and sit facing the screen and the stars; children wrap themselves up in blankets and go to sleep on the roofs of station wagons. There is repartee with the serene and, if you want, with the next car over. If you don't want, there is privacy. Nobody cares what you look like after a hard day's work, and your car is your own property.

The audience at the suburban drive-in is in its way as exclusive as the crowd in Cambridge at the Brattle or the Orson Welles, though the former represents a wider age-span. You're more likely to see a tee shirt proclaiming South Boston "The Irish Riviera" than a pipe and beard; you don't see many foreign cars.

A sign in a drive-in ticket window tells you what to expect. Vans and trucks are directed to the last row ("Because people can't see through you"). Families should go to the center rear ("Close to bathrooms and the snack bar"). Lovers should go to the left front; single guys are directed there as well ("If the movie is lousy you can make lots of noise to bum out the lovers"). Single girls go first to the right rear ("Later to the left front— see above").

Adults like drive-ins because you can smoke, eat, drink and take the kids. Babies can scream their little heads off without disturbing anybody else. Older children clamber over rickety Playlands, oblivious to the R-rated shadows flickering on the screen above them. ("Free Rides," a poster proclaims. That meant there was a slide, a rusted jungle gym, some unstable-looking swing sets and a warped merry-go-round.)

Putting in people—

A report from my emissary to the ladies' room suggests that early teens never change: Three 14-year-old girls were sneaking cigarettes. In the men's room, some young boys were talking about escalating the attack on the girls waiting back in the cars.

Teenagers have their own reasons for liking drive-ins, you see; in my day we called them "passion pits." Out of the oppressive house you went and into the car and into the free and permissive world of the drive-in. The only problem was getting your girlfriend to be permissive, too.

Specificity—

The movie, obviously, is only part of the fun. To begin with, you have to wait for it to come on. You sit through ads for the Jimmy Fund, ads encouraging you to be a woman on the Aerospace Team, ads telling you how to be beautiful and where to hire your wedding clothes, where to eat and buy a motorcycle. Most of all, there are blandishments to visit the refreshment stand. "It's only a few short steps," the voice confides, "why not add to your enjoyment?"

"Only two minutes to showtime," the warning comes. "Purchase a delicious confection and drink at our attractive refreshment stand." The rock music shuts off and the off-to-the-snack-bar march strikes up. "Tempt your taste with a wide variety of delicious foods at popular prices at our refreshment stand." ("Popular prices" can mean coffee at 35 cents, french fries at 75 cents and popcorn for $1.50 a bucket). "Your favorite beverage awaits you," comes the next line.

Irony— Finally the speaker drops the fancy language about "beverages" and "confections." Ghastly color photographs of hamburgers and slices of pizza revolve around the screen and the voice grows friendly, confidential, reassuring. "Only one minute to showtime, folks, but the refreshment stand will remain open for your pleasure."

Again observation— The refreshment stand in a modern drive-in is in fact a triumph of engineering. Soft drinks are shot out of a gun that looks like a prop borrowed from a space movie; the line leading to the cash register takes you by not only what you knew you wanted to eat but what you decided you wanted when you saw it.

The movies, in their own way, keep up the enticement to eat. To begin with, they are generally awful, and you flee to the refreshment stand to escape them. There seems to be a general principle that the better the movie is, the *worse* it is as a "drive-in picture." The place itself offers too many distractions that get in the way of concentration.

The films thrive on dialog you don't need to listen to because you've heard it all before. "Try to forget," says someone to decadent Lord Cunningham in *The Night Evelyn Came Out of the Grave*. His lips say something in Italian — it's a dubbed movie — and the voice comes out of the speaker in reply, "That's just the trouble . . . I can't forget."

Third reference to Jessie. Point: change, and lost innocence— Still more drive-in movies thrive on action, violence, horror and sex; these scenes earn the same symphony of horns that sweet Jessie Matthews once did.

Most of all, though, drive-in movies thrive on eating. There's a character in *The Creature from Black Lake* who only talks about how much he wants a hamburger, coke and fries; so, after a while, do you. *Pom Pom Girls* might just as well be called *Cheeseburger*. The ultimate drive-in movie was released just a few weeks ago: It's already grossed more than a million dollars at the box office. It's called *Drive-In*.

There's something wonderful about that fact, and it made me realize what I had missed in the elaborate preperformance show at the Neponset Drive-In. It began with "Our National Anthem." The words unfurled themselves across the bottom of the screen, and we saw the Statue of Liberty, the Lincoln Memorial, the Rockies, the Capitol at sunset, the fruited plain, the Golden Gate Bridge. It would have been just as essentially American, I thought, to show a drive-in. . . .

Show-within-a-show snapper—

Just a Quiet Dinner for Two in Paris:
31 Dishes, Nine Wines, a $4,000 Check
by Craig Claiborne

[Hunter Thompson to the contrary, using yourself as the impetus for a story need be neither hazardous nor unpleasant; witness this example by New York Times *Food Editor Craig Claiborne. If you've been wondering what it would be like to eat a $4,000 meal, here's the answer. Bon appetit.]*

If one were offered dinner for two at any price, to be eaten in any restaurant anywhere in the world, what would the choice be? And in these days of ever-higher prices, what would the cost be?

By submitting the highest bid on Channel 13's fund-raising auction last June, we found ourselves in a position earlier this week to answer these questions. The place: Chez Denis in Paris. The cost: $4,000.

Single sentence graph for emphasis—

Our winning bid was $300.

Our factor in the selection of the restaurant should be noted quickly: The donor of the dinner that Channel 13 auctioned was American Express, which set forth as its only condition the requirement that the establishment be one that accepts its credit card.

In turn, when American Express ultimately learned what we had done, its reaction went from mild astonishment to being cheerful about the outcome. "Four thousand— was that francs or dollars?" asked Iris Burkat, a company official, at one point.

Royal "we" suited to subject—

At any rate, the selection of the restaurant dominated our fantasies for weeks as in our minds we dined on a hundred meals or more. At times we were in Paris, then in Alsace. We considered Rome, Tokyo and Hong Kong, Copenhagen and Stockholm, Brussels and London.

The consideration of restaurants competed with thoughts of the greatest of champagne and still wines, visions of caviar and foie gras, dreams of elaborate desserts. Perhaps we would choose nothing but vodka or champagne with caviar followed by foie gras with Chateau d'Yquem — but no, any old millionaire could do that.

In addition to excluding those that did not recognize the credit card of the donor, we dismissed from our potential list of restaurants several celebrated places, simply, perhaps, because of their celebrity.

In time we considered Chez Denis, which is a great favorite among several food writers (Henri Gault, Christian Millau and Waverly Root among them), but it is nonetheless not well known. It is a tiny place on the Rue Gustave Flaubert, not far from the Arc de Triomphe.

We visited Chez Denis in a party of three to reconnoiter. It was not hard to go incognito, for we suspect that the proprietor, Denis Lahana, does not credit any Americans with even the most elementary knowledge of French wine and food.

The investigatory dinner was sumptuous. There was a chiffonade of lobster (a salad of cold lobster, cubed foie gras, a touch of cognac and, we suspect, cayenne, and a tarragon mayonnaise flavored with tomato, tossed with lettuce).

In addition, there was fresh foie gras with aspic, braised sweetbreads with a light truffle sauce, roast quail and those delectable tiny birds from the Landes region of France, ortolans. There was also a great personal favorite, andouillettes served with an outstanding sorrel sauce. The wine was a fine Pommard.

Detail— The meal having passed the test, we were able to ignore the few plastic boughs and plastic flowers tucked in beams here and there.

We wondered how it was that the place did not merit one, two or three stars in the Guide Michelin. It is not even listed. Mr. Denis would not comment on a story we had heard about inspectors from Michelin having somehow offended the proprietor and having been asked to leave.

After dinner, we asked Mr. Denis, offhandedly, how much he would charge for the most lavish dinner for two that he and his chef could prepare. He spoke in terms of $2,000 to $3,000.

We told him that we were about to celebrate a birthday and that money was no obstacle in ordering the finest dinner in Europe. Mr. Denis, with little hesitation, pulled up a chair and sat down. He took us seriously.

We asked him to consider the matter at this convenience and write to us with his proposal. When he did, his letter stated:

"In accordance with your demand, I propose to organize for you a prestigious dinner. In the land of my birth, the region of Bordeaux, one speaks of a *repas de vins,* a meal during the course of which a number of wines of great prestige are served, generally nine wines.

"I am suggesting nine such wines, to be served in the course of a dinner *à la Française* in the classic tradition. To dine properly in this style, many dishes are offered and served to the guests, chosen with the sole thought that each dish be on the same high level as the wines and those most likely to give pleasure as the wines are tasted."

Organization of meal as organization for story—

He suggested a dinner of 31 dishes that would start with an hors d'oeuvre and go on to three "services," the first consisting of soups, savory, an assortment of substantial main dishes, and ices or sherbets to clear the palate.

This would be followed by the second service: hot roasts or baked dishes, vegetables, cold, light, meaty dishes in aspic and desserts.

And then the third service: decorated confections, petits fours and fruits.

The youngest wine would be a six-year-old white burgundy, the oldest a 140-year-old madeira.

Mr. Denis set a price of $4,000. This, we must hasten to add, included service and taxes. We accepted.

The proprietor suggested that the meal be served to four persons — all for the same price — because the food must be prepared in a certain quantity and would be enough to serve as many as 10 persons, while the wines were enough for four.

Revealing punctilio—

We declined, because the rules set by American Express called for dinner for two. The dinner party would be made up of me and my colleague, Pierre Franey. Anything left over, we knew, would not go to waste.

Mr. Denis noted that it was not required that all foods be sampled and that the quantity of the food served would depend on the guests' appetite.

And so, we sat down to our $4,000 dinner.

The hors d'oeuvre was presented: fresh Beluga caviar in crystal, enclosed in shaved ice, with toast. The wine was a superb 1966 Champagne Comtesse Marie de France.

First
service—
Then came the first service, which started with three soups. There was consommé Denis, an inordinately good, rich, full-bodied, clear consomme of wild duck with shreds of fine crepes and herbs. It was clarified with raw duck and duck bones and then lightly thickened, as many classic soups are, with fine tapioca.

The second soup (still of the first service) was a crème Andalouse, an outstanding cream of tomato soup with shreds of sweet pimento and fines herbes, including fresh chives and chervil.

The first two soups were superb but the third, cold *germiny* (a cream of sorrel), seemed bland and anticlimactic. One spoonful of that sufficed.

The only wine served at this point was a touch of champagne. The soups having been disposed of, we moved on to a spectacularly delicate parfait of sweetbreads, an equally compelling mousse of quail in a small tarte, and a somewhat salty, almost abrasive but highly complementary tarte of Italian ham, mushrooms and a border of truffles.

The wine was a 1918 Chateau Latour, and it was perhaps the best bordeaux we had ever known. It was very much alive, with the least trace of tannin.

The next segment of the first service included a fascinating dish that the proprietor said he had created, Belon oysters broiled quickly in the shell and served with a pure *beurre blanc*, the creamy, lightly thickened butter sauce.

Also in this segment were a lobster in a creamy, cardinal-red sauce that was heavily laden with chopped truffles and, after that, another startling but excellent dish, a sort of Provencale pie made with red mullet and baked with tomato, black olives and herbs, including fennel or anise seed, rosemary, sage and thyme.

The accompanying wine was a 1969 Montrachet Baron Thenard, which was extraordinary (to our taste, all first-rate Montrachet whites are extraordinary).

The final part of the first service consisted of what was termed *filets et sots l'y laissent de poulard de Bresse, sauce suprême aux cêpes* (the so-called "fillet" strips of chicken plus the "oysters" found in the after-backbone of chicken blended in a cream sauce containing sliced wilk mushrooms).

There followed another curious but oddly appealing dish, a classic chartreuse of partridge, the pieces of roasted game nested in a bed of cooked cabbage and baked in a mosaic pattern, intricately styled, of carrot and turnip cut into fancy shapes.

And a tender rare-roasted fillet of Limousin beef with a rich truffle sauce.

The wine with the meat and game was a 1928 Chateau Mouton Rothschild. It was ageless and beautiful.

The first service finally ended with sherbets in three flavors — raspberry, orange and lemon. The purpose of this was to revive the palate for the second service, and it did. We were two hours into the meal and going at the food, it seemed, at a devilish pace.

Second service— The second service included the ortolans en brochette, an element of the dinner to be anticipated with a relish almost equal to that of the caviar or the foie gras.

The small birds, which dine on berries through their brief lives, are cooked whole, with the head on, and without cleaning except for removing the feathers. They are as fat as butter and an absolute joy to bite into because of the succulence of the flesh. Even the bones, except for the tiny leg bones, are chewed and swallowed. There is one bird to one bite.

The second service also included fillets of wild duck *en salmis* in a rich brown game sauce. The final dish in this segment was a *rogonâde de veau,* or roasted boned loin of veal wrapped in puff pastry with fresh black truffles about the size of golf balls.

The vegetables served were *pommes Anna* — the potatoes

cut into small rounds and baked in butter — and a *purée rachel,* a puree of artichokes.

Then came the cold meat delicacies. There was butter-rich fresh foie gras in clear aspic, breast meat of woodcocks that was cooked until rare and served with a natural *chaud-froid,* another aspic and cold pheasant with fresh hazelnuts.

The wines for this segment consisted of a 1947 Chateau Lafite-Rothschild, a 1961 Chateau Petrus, and the most magnificent wine of the evening, a 1929 Romanée Conti.

The dinner drew near an end with three sweets— a cold glazed charlotte with strawberries, an *île flottante* and *poires alma.* The wine for the sweets was a beautiful unctuous 1928 Chateau d'Yquem, which was quite sweet yet "dry."

Third service— The last service consisted of the pastry confections and fruits, served with an 1835 madeira. With coffee came a choice of a 100-year-old calvados or an *hors d' âge* cognac.

And for the $4,000, logic asks if it was a perfect meal in all respects?

The answer is no.

The crystal was Baccarat and the silver was family sterling, but the presentation of the dishes, particularly the cold dishes such as the sweetbread parfait and quail mousse tarte, was mundane.

The foods were elegant to look at, but the over-all display was undistinguished, if not to say shabby.

The chartreuse of pheasant, which can be displayed stunningly, was presented on a most ordinary dish.

The food itself was generally exemplary, although there were regrettable lapses there, too. The lobster in the gratin was chewy and even the sauce could not compensate for that. The oysters, of necessity, had to be cooked as briefly as possible to prevent toughening, but the *beurre blanc* should have been very hot. The dish was almost lukewarm when it reached the table, and so was the chartreuse of pheasant.

We've spent many hours reckoning the cost of the meal and find that we cannot break it down. We have decided this: we feel we could not have made a better choice, given the circumstance of time and place.

Mr. Denis declined to apply a cost to each of the wines, explaining that they contributed greatly to the total cost of the meal because it was necessary to open three bottles of the 1918 Latour in order to find one in proper condition.

Over all, it was an unforgettable evening and we have high praise for Claude Mornay, the 37-year-old genius behind the meal.

Insight— We reminded ourselves of one thing during the course of that evening: if you were Henry VIII, Lucullus, Gargantua and Bacchus all rolled into one, you cannot possibly sustain, start to finish, a state of ecstasy while dining on a series of 31 dishes.

Wines, illusion or not, became increasingly interesting, although we were laudably sober at the end of the meal.

8. Explanation

Of black eyes and B-girls

It is four o'clock on Christmas morning. The gifts are wrapped, the tree is up, but you can't go to bed because you still have to assemble Erecto, the Mechanical Pony. Erecto comes in a crate the size of a streetcar with printed instructions for putting together 312 moving parts. That, the manufacturer assures you, is "so easy a child of five could do it."

By six a.m., lost in the center of a steel scrapyard that resembles nothing remotely equine, you know why a child of five would have the edge: he can't read.

Explanations are hard to write.

To do the thing well, the first rule is to keep it simple. Simplicity is accomplished through crisp, uncluttered diction and a step-by-step approach. That's not as easy to accomplish as one might think — the myriad versions of hopelessly baffling Erecto manuals are evidence — but with effort it can be applied to the most sophisticated application of solar energy. And the result need not be dull.

For example, a reader wrote the *Boston Globe's* "Ask the Globe" column to find out if beefsteak really works as a remedy for a black eye. Here is the paper's lucid response:

> Medically, a black eye is the bleeding that occurs under the eyelids and the surrounding skin when a blow strikes the area around the eye. When the blow is sustained, blood escapes from small blood vessels and seeps into loose spaces under the skin. The displaced blood gives the skin its bluish color.
>
> The British Medical Association reports that the "time-honored

beefsteak remedy is both expensive and useless." Most doctors believe that beefsteak achieves whatever success it does by acting as a wet compress. A wet towel would work as well, and it's a lot cheaper.

A rather complex matter is thus rendered with disarming ease. Stay away from all technical terms, mechanical, legal or methodological. Try breaking the problem down and arranging it in the order of approach. The step-by-step method can be effective, as this *Kentucky Post* sidebar suggests:

Pete Cahill, greens superintendent of Summit Hills Country Club, knows a great deal about grass. Here is his advice on how to grow and maintain your lawn:

1. Choose a high quality seed with a high germination percentage. This will be printed on the bag label. Cheap seed has an 80 per cent germination; the best seed goes up to 98 per cent.

2. The best time to plant is in the early fall, although the spring season is also favorable.

3. Loosen the ground to prepare the seed bed by either raking or roto-tilling.

4. Fertilize the ground with balanced fertilizer at ten pounds per thousand square feet. All commercial fertilizer is balanced. Rake in or roto-till.

5. Seed at half the recommended rate, raking in lightly. Immediately seed the surface with the remaining half.

6. Cover the seeded ground with clean straw or mulch.

7. Irrigate the ground if possible and keep it damp.

8. Fertilize again with balanced fertilizer at ten pounds per 1,000 square feet.

The idea is to achieve a kind of forceful economy that informs without belaboring the subject.

Explanatory information is best passed on in scene, offering a dramatic context for material that might otherwise be dry. Note the casually inserted info in this snippet from a story on a race horse:

The ruddy-jawed trainer, flannel-garbed like a lumberjack against the evening chill, watched as groom Louis Glass pried packed earth from the horse's hooves and rubbed his nostrils with a mentholated balm to ease his breathing.

Or the information can be woven in more formally among quotes, using an individual as a sort of instructor:

> Fog was blurring the landing lights below. There the field was a mazework of radiant globes, yellow for the airstrips and blue for the taxiways. An indicator before him tells traffic controller Tom Braunom exactly how far a pilot can see when landing. The distance is measured by photoelectric lights that take automatic readings on runways 18 and 36.
>
> "Before take-off I give the pilot weather information, the route to fly, and issue clearance," Braunom explained.
>
> This includes the altitude and heading. The pilot has already filed a flight plan, ratified by computer. A ground controller taxies him to the point where he goes through his run-up, checking the equipment on the aircraft. Then the tower clears for take-off.
>
> "Pilots are also required to file an alternate flight plan," Braunom pointed out.
>
> That's done to cover nights like these. When the weather is bad an airport might shut down, and the ship must have another field in mind to land on.

Or you might provide a paradigm as a vehicle for factual matter, as in this explanation of the behavior of professional hostesses in Newport night clubs:

> There will be a dancer, this time a tall coltish black woman bound out on James Brown's "I'm Ready." As she turns under the hot lights on stage, the other girls, sleek in heels and halters, make their slow circuit of the tables.
>
> "Would you like some company?" they ask.
>
> Well, who wouldn't? But the "company" costs: The price of it is a drink for the lady, which runs $4.25 in a no-admission location, $2.50 elsewhere.
>
> "It's no rip-off," one long-legged nymph insisted. "We're providing companionship, and you're providing something to go with it."
>
> If you don't buy the drink, say goodbye to the girl, who may or may not call you a cheapskate.
>
> But if you buy it, she will stay and talk with you about whatever

you find especially moving at the moment, which will probably center on her — unless you prefer astrophysics or the early works of Chaucer.

The effect is to create the illusion of a relationship without its substance. Because there will be a hostess who will show up in five minutes or so to ask you if you want to buy the lady another drink. If you don't, farewell, my lovely; that friendly warmth against your leg might have been a dream.

Remember, Angel's under pressure. At Bourbon Street she has to make 60 points on drinks in the course of an evening. Which works out to 20 drinks a night, the average expectation for many clubs. That's a lot of company.

If most of us would find it a tad rough being sociable after 20 drinks — some have been known to nibble at the legs of chairs after a mere ten — there is pause for the mathematician to reflect that the lady's drink he is buying may be no stiffer than the mixer.

Eschew the pedantic and simplify, simplify.

The use of figures in explanations can be tedious unless they are related to realities the reader can identify with. In a revelatory *New Times* article on special dispensations to House and Senate members called "The Imperial Congress," Robert Shrum put his evidence in context, making the piece interesting as well as informative. "A filet of sole stuffed with crabmeat goes for $10.95 in New York or San Francisco," he notes. "In the Senators' dining room, it costs $2.75." This discount is typical of the meal markdown for both Congressional bodies; "with all the standard expenses added in, the House restaurants are losing thousands of dollars a year, and the Senate $800,000, which works out to a culinary subsidy of $8,000 per senator per year." Later Shrum makes the figures a forceful rebuke by personalizing them in a way no more statistical tally could:

One colleague recalls riding with Utah's Wallace Bennett on the Senate subway shortly before Bennett was to retire. A senior citizens' delegation had just been to see Bennett, and the senator was riled. "These people," he grumbled, "keep asking for more and more Social Security. They've got to stop." But Bennett, already a millionaire after an earlier career in private business, did not wince at the idea of accepting his forthcoming senatorial pension of nearly $18,000 a year, a sum seven times the average Social

Security benefit. Typical congressional pensions can reach $11,000 annually after six years of service, $20,000 after 15 years, and can soar as high as $38,000.

When Shrum reveals Senate authorization for a $50,000 design study of a proposed third congressional underground garage, he adds: "If built, each parking space in the new garage will cost some $22,000, or about half the price of the average American home." These and other emoluments for the American public servant add up to a formidable bill, rendered once again in careful, devastating context by Shrum:

> This year, it will cost U.S. taxpayers at least a million and a half dollars to finance each Capitol Hill legislator. Congress clearly believes that God helps those who help themselves; for in 1977, it has appropriated almost a billion dollars to maintain itself, shoeshines and all, a total that exceeds the entire municipal budget of Philadelphia.

Shrum makes numbers work for him by providing a frame of reference for each figure. A billion dollars boggles the mind, but only briefly; dividing that up into a per-legislator cost and comparing it to a city budget brings the boggle back and hits us up the side of the head with it.

One way of making explanations immediate is to render them in the second person. Used judiciously, the pronoun "you" can place the reader right inside the story; overused, it becomes a gimmicky mannerism. Sportswriter Roger Kahn wrote a fine column for *Esquire* describing his tribulations on the way to the second Ali-Frazier Heavyweight championship fight; somebody stole his wife's wallet. It was an excuse for Kahn to examine the craft of picking pockets. He told of the School of the Ten Bells in Bogota, Columbia, where initiates to the cutpurse profession must pick the pockets of a hanging dummy without ringing the small bells sewn inside. Kahn then explained how the members of the old school operate, adroitly employing a second-person stunt of his own:

> All right. You've dropped your wallet into your back pocket and you're going to the track. The number six horse in the first race has the same name as the uncle who paid half your freshman tuition. The three horse in the second race has been running well, according to the bartender last night. So you have information. Good information. You're in a hurry to make the daily double. Your wallet

sits innocently in the right hip pocket of your new trim-tailored slacks.

You are now a mark. Gathered for a reunion, three graduates from Ten Bells spot you. One walks in front of you for several strides. Then he stoops to tie his shoelace. You bump into him, groin first. While you bump Pickpocket I frontally, Pickpocket II lifts the wallet from your backside. You feel nothing. Pickpocket II hands your wallet to Pickpocket III, who walks away. Should you realize that you've been hit, should you happen to find a cop, and should the particular cop want to help, where is the evidence? Colombia exports stronger stuff than coffee beans.

Kahn gets it across without tedium or even any evident effort. This is the art of the raconteur applied to the knowledge of the scholar — the writer as skilled information merchant.

Always the example

The best way to reveal a problem, phenomenon or social circumstance is to illustrate it with a single, specific instance. Just as one exemplary detail serves to focus a description, so does one representative situation afford the most effective insight into a larger course of events.

Generalities bore. It's the apple, not the orchard, that catches our eye — Odysseus, not the Ithacans.

Air Travel Journal had a point to make about passenger restraint in flight. Here's how it was done:

The male passenger who thinks his airline ticket gives him the right to make passes at the stewardess is inviting more trouble than if he smoked in the fueling area.

Patting a stewardess on the fanny while a plane is airborne is a Federal offense, punishable by up to 10 years in prison under the U.S. air piracy statute.

Aubry Brumbard, a Texas oil worker, found that out last week when he was taken before U.S. Magistrate Peter Palermo in Miami for whacking three National Airlines stewardesses on the derriere.

The flight attendants reported the incidents to the captain, who radioed ahead to have the FBI arrest the man soon as the plane landed.

The *Journal* went on to reveal Brumbard pled guilty to a lesser charge of assault and was fined $500. That's $166.66 a fanny, a fair object lesson.

Try to ignore the beginning of this *Boston Globe* article by John M. Allen, assistant managing editor of *Reader's Digest:*

> PAWLING, N.Y. — I killed your cat early this morning. You know, the small black-and-white one, sleek-furred and friendly — about three months old, I'd say. I laid it down on the front section of yesterday's newspaper and folded a part of the paper over its head — the white side up — and then I took an old walking stick and I bashed the paper over the head as hard as I could. Four times, just to make sure. It broke the old walking stick.

Allen goes on to explain that the killing was not a matter of choice; the kitten had run afoul of two dogs, who had hopelessly mauled it, and he had been forced to stop the animal's suffering. But Allen's point was that this kitten was one of thousands of house pets simply set free by un-caring owners every year, owners responsible for animal misery they never see and consequently pretend does not exist. Many a vacationing family acquires a dog or cat for their summer home only to leave the pet behind the following fall, assuming, quite wrongly, it will survive wild — or find a home with someone else. Allen addresses his article to these in-dividuals directly as a gimmick to get the story read, and we, guilty or not, are made aware of the substantial problem beyond the single defunct feline.

Boston Globe columnist Mike Barnicle traveled to Los Angeles and examined human isolation there by interviewing a tuna fisherman and a professional hostess at a place called Morrie's ballroom. Andy Turco rolls in weekly from San Pedro for a little companionship.

> "I come here to dance every Friday night," he said. "I don't drink. So I come here for my enjoyment. It's terrific. You meet some real nice girls in here. They're all nice to you, you know?"

At nine cents a minute, the hostess doesn't share his sentimental perspective.

> "They all look the same to me," Connie Webster said. "A job's a job."

Barnicle finds in an illustrative vignette the full fruition of his theme, which is that L.A. is a city of strangers:

> Loneliness is to Los Angeles what gambling is to Las Vegas. It's a principal product of this sprawling, smoggy urban accident. It's as much a part of the town as the tinsel of Hollywood; LA is a place by the ocean, home to thousands of people who've literally come to the end of the earth looking for something or someone, only to end up with less than they hoped for.

It's a town where nobody knows your name, caught in capsule for a few sad moments at a dance hall by a savvy writer. Nothing else is necessary.

The disarmed private eye

Hank Messick of the *Miami Herald* poses as a Newport racketeer and sits in on a vice deal with a bagman and some local hoods and pols to get a story on how to buy a brothel in south Florida.

Carl Bernstein and Bob Woodward of the *Washington Post* go to work on a bungled burglary story and, after early-morning meetings in underground garages and a web of nocturnal suburban interviews, prove the existence of a campaign sabotage team in the White House.

Seymour Hersh of the *New York Times* moves among the Washington intelligence community, gets wind of dossiers kept on Americans by the CIA and unearths a massive illegal domestic surveillance operation against the antiwar movement.

Sexy stories all by tough investigative reporters with certain shared qualities that made them stand out long before they achieved national recognition. First, they were all insistent self-starters who completed the assignments handed to them by editors and then went out to dig up better stories on their own initiative and their own time. Wrote Leonard Downie, Jr., metropolitan editor of the *Washington Post*, "Bob Woodward had accumulated more front-page bylines than any of the other 60 reporters on the newspaper's metropolitan staff" — in his first nine months on the job *before* Watergate. Woodward and the others were never nine-to-fivers and they were never satisfied with routine assignments. "It's a cliche," Bernstein told Downie, "but every day as you walk around, you see fascinating things that havent been written about."

Next, none of them knew what it meant to give up. They were able to get people to open up to them. That's why you're reading about them. Third, they all crawled out from behind the desk and into the field. Messick talked to mobsters on their own turf. Woodward and Bernstein went into the homes of workers for the Committee to Re-Elect the President. And Hersh flew all over the country to talk personally with witnesses to the massacre at Mylai 4.

This kind of reporting can sometimes get a writer into real trouble. Investigative reporting is aimed at revealing facts somebody wants kept quiet. The reporter who specializes in it can expect threats, lost friends and the surprising boredom or even resentment of a public that doesn't want to face unpleasant facts.

Jack Anderson associate Les Whitten was once arrested by the FBI for receiving and possessing stolen property. Whitten had been covering the return of documents taken from the Bureau of Indian Affairs by a coalition of protest groups, documents which revealed national neglect and instiutional bad faith toward the American Indian. Relentlessly the writer, Whitten was taking notes on the bust even as federal agents clamped the cuffs on. Anderson accused Presidential Chief of Staff H.R. Haldeman of orchestrating the arrest as part of a vendetta against the Anderson team, and in the two weeks that ensued until the grand jury refused to indict him, Whitten knew the discomfort of waiting out a trumped-up felony rap.

Jean-Pierre Charbonneau, of Montreal's *Le Devoir* and later *La Presse,* reported there was nothing random about the crime in his city, documenting an organized underworld there that worked exactly like a large corporation. In *The Canadian Connection,* a bestselling book on drug traffic, Charbonneau named 800 names. Then somebody walked into the city room one night and shot him. Fortunately, Charbonneau survived.

Arizona Republic reporter Don Bolles spent 14 years lifting various high-level lids on organized crime and land fraud in and around Phoenix. On June 2, 1976, in response to a tip, Bolles drove to the Clarendon Hotel where nobody was waiting for him but a phone call kept him busy for a few minutes. When he got back into his brand-new white four-speed Datsun 710 and turned the key, three sticks of dynamite went off underneath him. Eleven days later, Bolles was dead.

That doesn't mean the investigative reporter emulates his enemies in self-defense. *Newsday* editor Bob Greene, Pulitzer Prize-winning head of the Investigative Reporters and Editors team that went into Arizona to expose massive high-level corruption there, has insisted:

> We don't carry guns and we don't intend to; I think you approach
> this thing with a certain fatalistic sense, you know. You are doing
> the thing that you like. If, and I think the odds are very much
> against it, but if you die or get hurt doing the thing that you like,
> then that is the way to die far better than lying around in bed in a
> nursing home eating gruel and having 15 tubes going in and out of
> you.

Most investigative reporting, however, is a lot less dramatic than these
pages would indicate. The essence of good investigative work lies less in
midnight encounters and face-offs with hoods than in patient, painstak-
ing scrutiny of public records.

Two of the best men in the business are the Philadelphia *Inquirer's*
Donald L. Barlett and James B. Steele, reporters who specialize in cold,
careful analysis of files and statistics, the interpretation of which often
requires expert, computerized assistance. Writing for *The Quill,*
Bartlett and Steele conveyed the humdrum reality of their invaluable
work:

> In the spring of 1972, the two of us trudged up a narrow, wooden
> stairway at the rear of Philadelphia's labyrinthine City Hall to an
> isolated alcove nestled under one of the building's great domes.
>
> There, in row after row of brown, aging, legal-size file folders,
> stacked seven to eight feet high on dusty metal shelves above a con-
> crete floor, was the record of violent crime in Philadelphia for the
> last quarter century.
>
> Occupying an aged, wooden desk and two disabled chairs, we
> began to read, take notes and systematically extract information
> from the files on murders, rapes, robberies and assaults which took
> place in Philadelphia during one year and how the city's criminal
> justice system dealt with those cases.
>
> For nearly six months, we repeated this ritual: arriving about 9
> a.m. each day to begin work, taking a brief luncheon break at 1
> p.m., then returning to our secluded garret for a few more hours of
> research. Late in the afternoon, we would walk the four blocks
> north to the Philadelphia Inquirer building to study the day's
> cases, type notes on the more interesting ones and jot down those
> that might require a follow-up.

Such is the glamorous life of an investigative reporter.

Barlett and Steele's cloistered efforts produced extraordinary evidence of widespread discrimination in the criminal courts. Based on more than 1,000 cases, their seven-part series exposed inept judges and prosecutors, disproportionately long sentences for blacks, liberation of habitual criminals, and, in general, overwhelming documentation of maladministered justice in Philadelphia. The stories won the Heywood Broun Award for exploring injustice through unusually enterprising reporting and the Sidney Hillman Foundation Award for authoritatively presenting an important social problem. Similar techniques produced a later series on inequities in Internal Revenue Service enforcement methods which won them a Pulitzer Prize.

Investigative reporters are individuals of nerve, drive and intelligence with a passionate interest in detail. By the definition of this book, all good reporters are investigative reporters.

The investigative story

And all good stories are investigative ones.

That is, they get beneath the surface. They don't settle for the superficial.

But the in-depth examinations we're talking about now are more ambitious than personality pieces or color stories. Their goal is the exposure of abuse, and a lot more gets in the way of the reporter than the mere limits of his imagination.

The reporter's attitude toward obstacles should follow the example of David Chandler in his *Rolling Stone* story on what may be a 100-ton cache of gold bullion buried on Victorio Peak inside the White Sands Missile Range. Certain evidence suggested soldiers there might have found something, but the Army wasn't letting anybody in. Chandler went there.

I found Lt. Col. Donald Keller in the hallway of the headquarters building. Col. Keller was a short, trim man wearing summer khakis. His face was red, his back bowed, his fists shoved out.

"You're the sonofabitch," he screamed, "who called the Congress! Don't deny it! You got the general stirred up," he screamed, "with your goddam political interference. The Army doesn't like political pressure and I don't like you one fucking bit." I suggested we get to work and led the way into his office.

Never give an inch— unless appearing to might gain you some ground. Some ethical considerations. Don't steal documents, but if they come to you, use them. Be particularly wary of any personal conflict of interest; writers of investigative stories should be free of all affiliations that might suggest bias in their work. Jealously protect all sources, even against the corporate lawyers for your own newspaper; expose one and you'll lose them all. Should you be called upon to name sources in court under oath, refuse; let them throw you in the slam for contempt — that's a hell of a story. And don't try to push legislation beyond the publication of your piece. You're a writer, not a pol.

Investigative reporters are tempted to pull strings — "work behind the scenes" as Jack Anderson calls it — because the impetus behind their efforts is often a reformer's missionary zeal. Sometimes the publication of exposes results in indictments — even Presidential resignations — but more often little comes of them. Don Bolles considered getting out of investigative work shortly before his death because 14 years of public apathy and political ineptitude seemed to him to make the personal risks pointless; "Nothing ever happens," he said. But while the reporter cannot count on his stories getting results, he should not turn himself into an activist to insure them — it will interfere with his credibility.

Jack Newfield of the *Village Voice* disagrees. "Writing an article is less than half the job," he has said. "The follow-up, creating a constituency for an idea by lobbying and writing repeated stories, is essential." Anderson personally went after L. Patrick Gray during the Senate confirmation hearings on his appointment as FBI director. And Drew Pearson, Anderson's predecessor and creator of the "Washington Merry-Go-Round" column, made a career of personal vendettas against figures as widely disparate as Joseph McCarthy and Jacqueline Kennedy Onassis; ultimately he came to see himself as a molder of history and even warned General Douglas MacArthur off a libel suit with love letters the soldier had written a Eurasian girl. These alternating delusions of grandeur and forays into cheap vindictiveness brought Pearson's reliability into serious question. At best it turns the reporter into a literary nag with his endless thin followups trying to keep the pressure on.

A reporter's motive for getting a story should be to tell the truth, not to get things done. If the truth catches the public imagination, something *will* be done; if it does not, tough cheese. You can't put a gun to the head of the public, even for its own good.

The investigative story usually begins with a tip from one of three sources. The first is a beat acquaintance — any one of the scores of clerks, lawyers, prosecutors, local and federal investigators, politicans and assorted staffers you come in contact with in the course of your rounds. The second is a disgruntled employee; somebody is always willing to blow the whistle on the boss. The third, more rare, is what *Newsday* editor Bob Greene calls a *"kamikaze,"* a public-spirited citizen so outraged at some malfeasance he's encountered that he feels it is his duty to come forward with the goods. Each tip should be evaluated on its merits, not the motives behind it; even scoundrels can pass legitimate information.

A little preliminary checking is necessary to see if the tip merits a full-scale effort. The morgue clip file will tell you what's been done — you don't want to repeat an old story. Then begin with the phone book and start seeking out other sources. Try the criss-cross directory, which lists people in the alphabetical and numerical order of their street address — this can give you the numbers of a subject's neighbors. The city directory lists city residents alphabetically, by street address and by telephone number; the listings include the first name of the subject's spouse and the employer's name and business address — or at least a description of the subject's work. The telephone company publishes directories of phone numbers in numerical order listing the individual or firm each one belongs to and the address. City libraries carry back issues of most of these materials in the reference sections, so you can check back even on figures long dead.

Once you've spoken to enough people to satisfy yourself there is a story — people by the way you're sure won't be tipping off the object of your investigations — you've got to sell it to your editor, unless you're a freelance. If it's the former, good luck. Many editors are reluctant to free up writers for investigative stories because they tend to take a lot of time and a lot of money to document — the Xerox fees alone can be heavy, never mind the travel — and the results may be uncomfortable for the paper to print, particularly if it offends advertisers. Why should they send you off on a maybe when the city desk has a sure thing every day? The editor knows too investigative stories draw libel suits like blue serge draws lint, and they're expensive to fight even if you ultimately win. So don't expect big smiles from the higher ups; you're going to have to convince them any way you can. If you're a freelance you may press for an advance from an interested publication, but count on nothing. One possible outlet for you is to seek a grant from the Fund for Investigative Journalism in Washington, D.C. But let's suppose you've sold an editor; if it's good you'll work on it anyway on your own time — there's no stopping you. Then you'll get going on your research. There are masses of hot material on the public record, as Barlett and Steele have shown. There are birth and death certificates, deeds, federal contracts, licenses, business records, military records, marriage records, payroll records. Get friendly with the clerks at city hall and the state house — they'll tell you where to find them. And you'll be surprised how helpful a reference librarian can be in coming up with places to look for needed information.

This is the most important part of your investigation. Freelance investigative reporter Jack Tobin says, "If you can't prove it in the public records, you can't print it." That means too you should press your sources for documentation. They can get it, but they need to be encouraged; point out their civic duty, their moral responsibility to the future, etc.

Documentation can mean the difference between journalistic sainthood and literary *hara-kiri*. In 1971 Jack Anderson reported that contrary to public Presidential statements of neutrality, the Nixon administration was really supporting Pakistan in its battle with India over Bangladesh. In fact, Anderson wrote, the President had supplied the Pakistanis and dispatched a naval task force led by the nuclear carrier *Enterprise* to the Bay of Bengal, where the Soviet Union was establishing its own presence. In *The Anderson Papers,* Anderson wrote:

> [John F.] Kennedy's handling of the Cuban confrontation made a deep impression on Richard Nixon. He spoke admiringly of the cold courage Kennedy had demonstrated when he faced an imminent nuclear holocaust. In December 1971 President Nixon had an opportunity to stage his own nuclear showdown in the Bay of Bengal.

Anderson had transcripts of secret White House meetings to prove everything he said. He won the Pulitzer for national reporting. But in 1972 he broadcast nationally that Missouri Senator Thomas Eagleton,

Democratic Vice Presidential nominee and admitted shock therapy patient, had an alcohol problem substantiated by "photostats of half a dozen arrests for drunken and reckless driving." Anderson had based his assertion on what sources had told him; he didn't have the photostats. When he was asked to produce them he backed into a half-hearted retraction that made matters even worse. It was a mistake, a blackening of a man's reputation without evidence, and Anderson wound up looking less like a muckraker than one of his own targets.

Make sure the documention is *in your possession.* You'd be surprised how easy it is to walk off with records from some county courthouses— so xerox them while they still exist. Don't count on them being there the next time you want them. If your subject gets wind of what you're up to, he may be just as smart as you are at hunting down the paperwork— and getting rid of it.

Don't forget a very good reason for burning down some private firms is because the books are inside.

If you're paranoid, and it's a sensible thing to be on some stories, don't leave your documentation at your home or even in the city room. Put it in a safe deposit box. In a big bank.

When you've got everything you need to hang him, approach the principal or principals of your investigation. For two reasons: One, it makes a better story; two, it's only fair to get the other side. It may even clear up minor errors of fact. Whatever is said should go in the story, and a denial should not be buried deep inside but related soon after the lead. If the principal has no comment, or won't make himself accessible to you, mention that to show you've sought balance as fairly as you can. Then, having been the perfect soul of restraint, crucify the bastard with the evidence.

Now that you've got your story it's time to hassle some more with your editor, who's been pestering you for it for days. He'll be the devil's advocate, pointing out the holes and weaknesses. You'd better have it all, because a story, no matter how sexy, is worthless without ironclad evidence.

Warren Hinckle, one-time editor of *Ramparts,* wrote an autobiographical account of the storm-tossed '60s titled *If You Have a Lemon, Make Lemonade* in which he referred to a newspaper editor named Penn Jones, Jr., of Midlothian, Texas, a town about 25 miles from Dallas. Jones had come across a number of mysterious deaths related to the assassination of President Kennedy. One of them concerned a woman named Rose Chermi. Wrote Hinckle:

> According to police reports Penn had dug up, Ms. Chermi, a lady of less than tender years and experience, had been thrown from a moving automobile near Eunice, Louisiana, on November 20, 1963. A passing good Samaritan picked her up and drove her to a hospital, where she angrily volunteered information to the effect that she was in the employ of Dallas nightclub owner Jack Ruby and had been driving to Florida with two of Ruby's men to pick up a load of narcotics for their boss; during an argument, one of the men shoved her out the door of the speeding car. She also volunteered the information that President Kennedy and other officials were going to be killed on their impending visit to Dallas but two days hence. No one took her seriously. After the assassination, the Eunice authorities thought a little differently and Rose Chermi was questioned further. Shown a news story the day after Ruby shot [assassin Lee Harvey] Oswald, which quoted Ruby as denying having previously known Oswald, she laughed out loud. "They were bed mates," she said. What further information, if any, Rose Chermi provided was not later found in the official records of Eunice, Louisiana. And l'affair Chermi somehow escaped the attention of the Warren Commission.
>
> When Penn went looking for Rose, he found that she had been killed by an unidentified hit and run driver on September 4, 1965, while walking along the side of a highway near Big Sandy, Texas.

There were others. But the story is thin. The best source is dead, the rest is hearsay, and the only documentation is a couple of police reports. It's a place to start for a story, but it's not a story.

New Times printed a piece by Michael Drosnin called "A Military Mystery Story: Desktop." In it, Drosnin suggested that DESKTOP was the code name for a covert American military program the objective of which might have been to set up an illegal underwater nuclear weapons system on the floor of the Pacific Ocean. Drosnin's only evidence was some conversation with a 32-year-old yeoman first class. The story is well-written speculation; it's thin.

Contrast these with the locked-in Spotlight Team series for the *Boston Globe* on abuses of "VA-approved" private vocational schools that appeared in March 1974. *Globe* reporters applied for and took courses to find out how students were tested. The team showed applicants did not get the education they paid for with government assistance and, further, that sloppy government practice made the fleecing easy. ITT Tech was successfully sued by the Massachusetts Attorney General for substantial refunds to former students. The ITT school in Boston closed, along with others examined in the series. Legislation was engendered to curb vocational school abuse. All because the career school story had the facts and proof to back them. The premise is not as exotic as the ones for the preceding two stories, but the evidence is *bona fide*.

Suppose now you've got it all, but still the editor isn't nibbling. The story is documented. It's well-written — the prose is immediate, the evidence is presented simply, the whole con is set forth step by step, the figures are related to realities the reader can understand. What's wrong?

Maybe nothing. In 1967 Nicholas Gage, Hank Messick and James Savage formed an investigative reporting team on the *Boston Herald-Traveler*. They were all crack print men and today enjoy national reputations. They uncovered underworld ties to a prominent citizen; it was a story the paper refused to go with. The team split up to pursue separate destinies, but the reason for the *Herald* kill became clear later: The citizen was a stockholder in the paper.

In 1969 Jonathan Kwitny of the *Perth Amboy Evening News* did a series on some fast-shuffle land deals. The newspaper sat on it. Kwitny felt the general manager had stopped the stories to avoid angering the business community. Kwitny sold them to the *New York Post* and his editor fired him.

Now he works for the *Wall Street Journal*.

The reactions of these reporters were the right ones. If an editor stops what you consider to be a legitimate story, you have three options: One, live with it; two, rewrite it and sell it elsewhere; and three, quit. Option one rankles. Option two can get you fired, though it should not. Option three means no lunch for a long time.

But then maybe your editor is Ben Bradlee and you make a pile on the paperback and movie rights and appear on all the networks plugging your book. It's been done.

Son of Woodstein strikes back

Put on your trenchcoat and your best nobody's-fool newshawk face and we'll run through a fast front-pager. Our reportorial practice will be the best, but any resemblance of the characters, events and institutions that follow to reality is coincidental. Remember the advice of Barlett and Steele: "Never assume."

You're at your desk of a rainy Monday morning and you get a tip:

"I think you should look into that bombing on Dulaney Drive last month. Talk to Walsh. He knows things."

"Who is this?"

"Talk to Walsh. There's a cover-up."

The voice is female and all you've got is a name, but sound, crank or crazy you have to follow it up.

If there was a bombing chances are something would have appeared in your paper about it, so you walk down to the reference library and go through last month's issues. Sure enough, you find something buried on a back page:

Bomb Blasts Back Yard
of Ex-Mobster's House

A dynamite bomb went off this morning behind the fashionable Hempstead home of famed gangland figure Lou "The Hammer" Ianetti at 7 Seacliff Lane. Police in a passing patrol car arrested one of two men observed fleeing the scene.

Charged with wanton endangerment, willful destruction of property and illegal possession of an explosive device was Thomas Henry Walsh, 40, of 16 Harrison Ave.

The blast, which resulted in no injuries, was the second in the city this month.

Police sources speculate the bombings are connected to a power struggle between factions of the local Mafia.

Bombed March 3 were the Westwood Street offices of The Dudery, a boutique administered by Anthony "Threads" Bello, 50, convicted extortionist and reputed head of organized crime in the city.

Ianetti, 70, held that position until a rumored takeover occurred a year ago while the aging chieftain served out an 18-month sentence for income tax evasion in Evansville Prison.

Walsh was identified as an unemployed assembly line worker

with a narcotics record.

There are interesting things here. You still don't know whether you've got a story, but this fellow Walsh exists and it's clear he's worth talking to. Chances are he's out on bail; at any rate, the address is a place to start.

You go to 16 Harrison and find the place, a run-down tin-tier apartment complex with a forbidding fat woman sweeping the walk outside. She turns out to be Florence Levy, 62, the live-in rental agent. You talk to her:

> "It's the sixth floor, but he's not in, you know. Busted."
> "Is that right?"
> "Busted. Blew up some hood's house. God knows why. His wife's a suffering woman, I can tell you. A suffering woman."
> "Anne, wasn't it?"
> "Maureen. A suffering woman. He was out at all hours. Never knew where his money was coming from."
> "I'd like to talk to her."
> "Sixth floor. Suffering."

You've got the wife's name now in case Walsh isn't home. The mailboxes in the entry give you the room number, but upstairs nobody answers your knock.

You don't leave. Instead you try the other doors on the same floor. At this hour most of the tenants are at work, but at last you locate a neighbor, Lois Conroy, 26. She doesn't know your subject, but she's a noticer:

> "Mrs. Walsh left two days ago. Packed up lock, stock and barrel."

Which is peculiar. Your interest is piqued. Wives don't often walk off when their husbands are in trouble. Afterwards, yes. Her absence is curious, and she certainly can't have left with Walsh because he's under indictment.

It's time to try the city jail — maybe your man never made bail. On your way there you stop in the Westwood Street Dudery offices on the off chance mobster Tony Bello has observations on the new bombing — if it is a power play, he hired Walsh. You know he's not going to open up for you, but you're smelling a story now and you're starting to collect quotes. His eminence is in. He's even angry enough to talk.

"I don't know any Walsh. I don't know nothin'. But I'll tell you what I think: The Hammer bombed his own place to frame me. He doesn't want to get hung with blowin' my place two weeks ago. . . .

"No, I don't know why he'd do that. . . .

"Mafia? What's a Mafia?"

More grist for your mill. You've got an accusation, even if it sounds thin, and it's an excuse to get Ianetti talking later.

But you want very badly now to talk to Walsh. Chances are he's been told by a lawyer or public defender to say nothing to anybody, especially the press, but you don't write off possibilities without trying them. The jail is on the top floor of the city-county building and you're acquainted with the jailer, gregarious old Bill Pace, 46. He has some intriguing news:

"Walsh has been transferred. I can't talk about it. You'll have to talk with the Chief of Detectives. Sorry. I just can't talk about it."

"Transferred." Where? Why? By whom?

Police headquarters is on the second floor, but you know what to expect from the Chief: zero. He's paranoid about newsfolk and he hates you for the series you ran on a recent bungled search and seizure. You pump one of your pals outside the squad room. Det. Lt. Al Trask, 41:

"You're going to have to talk to Fender about that one."

This is unusual. Trask usually opens up like a poked *pinata*. So you go through the door with some resignation and talk to Chief of Detectives Pat Fender, who says, predictably:

"No comment."

But Sgt. Sid Pasco, 30, who owes you things, is around the corner from the booking desk, and you get this:

"This is off the record. Walsh is out. Never mind why."

"Something's askew, Sid. Come across."

"It's clean enough. All right— off the record, huh?"

"Off the record."

"He's an FBI informant. They're covering for him. The Feds have the lid on."

There's the reason for the pressure. And now you know you've got something, yes you have, and you can feel the fangs sharpen at the ends of your smile.

You head straight for the local office of the Federal Bureau of Investigation. You're no stranger there; other stories have taken you in and out of those scrubbed fatigue-green offices before. Ellen Tunney, 28, the regional director's secretary, gives you a familiar nod and sends you in. But the surprise is that there is a new regional director, Sam Eastlake, 39. The man you're used to talking to is missing. You go through the introductions. Then:

"Where's Jennings?"

"He retired."

"Why?"

"I guess he figured it was time for it."

"We have information indicating the arrested man in the Ianetti bombing case was an FBI informant. Is that true?"

"If he were, I could hardly confirm it. But let me tell you this: if he had information about a pending gang war, he'd be pretty useful to us, wouldn't he?"

"Has he offered any information?"

"I can't tell you that he has or hasn't."

"For the record: Has the FBI arranged for Walsh and his wife to be taken somewhere for their protection in connection with your investigation?"

"For the record: No."

He's danced you around pretty good, and he may or may not be telling you the truth. But this is curious: Ray Jennings is gone. And normally he would have tipped every paper in town on the retirement — yet he hasn't.

You pass Ellen Tunney a note on the way out inviting her for lunch at the Sirloin House. It would be a mistake to talk to her in the office. You've known her for years, and she's been a source before. Now that you think about it, the voice on the phone this morning had been vaguely familiar. . . .

"Yes, I called you. Jennings was fired. Or prevailed upon to resign. He arranged the bombings."

"Why?"

"He wanted to stimulate a war between the two leading mob factions so he could pick up the pieces. Each side was supposed to think the other was behind the blasts."

"And Walsh?"

"He was a narc informant. Jennings put him up to it. Jennings was a believer in getting the bad boys any way he could. When the Bureau found out, they unloaded him and spirited Walsh away with his wife to keep their skirts clean.

"Nobody was fooled except the public. Don't get my name mixed up in this. I just thought you ought to know.

"Besides, I despise Jennings. He was no fun to work for, I can tell you."

The old disgruntled employee gambit.

Now here's what you've got: some weird circumstances, some sources you can't quote, and a tremendous rush. But no story— not yet. You need proof.

You move around. Confirmation comes first from Irwin Davis, 31, a pinball concessionaire and associate of Walsh. But he's not what you could claim to be a reliable source. More digging gets you an on-the-record nod from Special Agent Arnold Reid, 45, a local Bureau man angry at the cover-up because he feels it demeans the organization — like the NYPD's Frank Serpico, an authentic *kamikaze.* You pull another affirmative from Special Agent Ted Lenz, 40, a competitor with Eastlake for the regional directorship.

That's two reliables, and Ellen Tunney, after persistent pushing by you, produces copies of correspondence between Jennings and Walsh that outline the whole thing.

Now you have it locked up, but you've got to call on Jennings, 38, of 1413 Dean Dr. It's a suburban split-level with one of those black cement coachmen out front. Jennings s on the third ring.

"You're crazy. Print that and I'll slap a suit on you that will fold your paper."

You're not terrified. When your editor kills the story because Jennings turns out to be publisher's brother-in-law, you sell it to a syndicate and wait for your call from the Pulitzer people.

Nice going, Ace.

Divorce Court— Where Nobody Really Wins
by William Ruehlmann

[This story uses a three-part structure to explain a new divorce code. I spent a long night with the law books trying to come up with accurate layman's language for the gist of it and got the help of a sympathetic judge who had been divorced himself. I sat through a case that served as an emblem for all the cases in those unhappy chambers and got inside the judge's reasoning to show how the law worked.
Elapsed time from idea to copy desk: two days.]

1. The Law

Scenario: A marriage is breaking up. The husband hires a private eye to follow the wife. The private eye takes pictures of her in bed with somebody else.

Meanwhile the wife gathers witnesses to the time she came to work with a black eye. She has a doctor certify various bruises on her body as having come from the blunt end of something very like that baseball bat the husband waves around when he's mad.

They go to divorce court.

"She's unfaithful!" screams the husband.

"He's a brute!" screams the wife.

And their teenage son looks on grimly.

It is an ugly sequence of events, and it has been played out before. But under the revised Kentucky law providing now for the "no-fault" divorce, it can't happen again.

The situation—

That law, which became effective here June 6, 1972, is based upon the Uniform Marriage and Divorce Act drafted by the National Conference of Commissions on Uniform State Laws. The conference felt that the traditional conception of divorce, based on blaming one of the two people involved, was misguided.

The necessity to blame someone for a broken marriage resulted in a lot of lying in court, some of it willful, some of it simple overstatement in the heat of anger. Further, mutual accusations added only to the anguish and not to the effectiveness of the proceedings.

Consulting the expert—

"The court seeks to sustain a relationship, not destroy it," Kenton County Circuit Court Judge Robert O. Lukowky affirms. "Courtroom recrimination can build a wall of its own between people. After you've publicly called somebody an SOB on the stand, chances are you won't communicate very well with him later."

The Uniform Marriage and Divorce Act seeks to settle matters in court amicably instead of making them worse. Under it, all that is demanded for the legal termination of a marriage today is testimony from the couple that their relationship is "irretrievably broken"; no grounds or causes for divorce are required.

"Now you can tell the truth," Judge Lukowsky notes. "You're able to say that your spouse is a great person, but you just can't make it with him."

Layman's language—

A finding of irretrievable breakdown means that the separated spouses have no reasonable prospect of getting back together. The marriage property is fairly divided the same way it might be between two members of any dissolved partnership. Alimony is not employed as a penalty or punishment.

"The attempt is to cut down on the adversary relationship of the principals," Judge Lukowsky points out. "After all, they may have to get along later. Financial situations continue, and, if there is a child, visitation will have to be worked out."

To reduce the hostile atmosphere of divorce court, the legal terminology has changed. The matter at hand is no longer an "action" — it is a "proceeding." The document bringing suit is not a "complaint" — it is a "petition." The court order does not employ the traditional combative case title of "John Smith versus Jane Smith," but applies instead the neutral head "In Re: the Marriage of John and Jane Smith."

And the prevailing situation is no longer a "divorce" — it is a "dissolution of marriage."

Conciliation is encouraged by the court, but if there is no possibility for it, custody is awarded according to the best interests of the child, not the wishes of the parents. The court will not consider conduct of a proposed custodian that does not affect his relationship to the child, so unless the child is in the room, that private eye can take his lens away from the transom; it isn't going to do any good.

Judge Lukowsky admits the parting of two people is no less

sad under the new law, but it is not nearly as uncivilized.

"At least the child no longer has to witness a public war between his parents."

The paradigm case—

2. *The Trial*

Lois Reed, 22, was in the ladies' room being sick while her husband Gerald, 31, waited in Kenton Circuit Court, Division 3. It was ten a.m., the hour appointed for the end of their marriage.

An empty jury box commanded one side of the cream-colored room, the bailiff's table the other. Between and above was the judge's bench. Robert O. Lukowsky sat behind it, black-robed and bespectacled.

Before him was the case file.

Mrs. Reed's petition asserted the dissolution of her marriage to Gerald and sought custody of their daughter Jena, who had been taken from her by the father. According to the petition, he retained the child "somewhere in the State of Ohio."

Gerald Reed's response concurred that the marriage was dissolved, but added that he was "the fit and proper person to have the care, custody and control of the minor child born of the marriage." He further requested the court to order the Department of Child Welfare to conduct an investigation concerning the custody of the child.

Drama revealed in scene—

Lois Reed, pinched and pale from her sudden illness, appeared with her mother, whose left arm hung down in a cast and sling. A lawyer led them to the table before the bench.

"What says the wife?" intoned the judge.

"We're ready," the lawyer responded.

"What says the husband?"

"We're ready."

The judge swore in his witnesses and Mrs. Reed took the stand.

She testified to her name, age and residence. She said she now worked for Blue Ribbon Towing in Chicago. She said she had married Gerald Reed October 3, 1972, and that they had separated June 13th of this year.

It was, she said, her second marriage.

She had one child, Jena Cassandra, aged 16 months. Her son

by a previous marriage died last Christmas.

What was Jena's present place of residence?

"I have no idea," Lois Reed testified. She indicated her husband. "He slipped her away."

Was their relationship irretrievably broken?

"Definitely."

The judge asked questions about the assets and debts of the couple, necessary information for an equitable property settlement.

Detail— Tense in a striped sweater and green pants, Mrs. Reed kept her hands tightly clasped in her lap. There was no ring on the left one.

She testified she and her husband had often been separated during their marriage.

"He'd come and go, staying maybe two, three nights," she said. "Then he'd leave for three or four more days."

She spoke of financial hardship in his absence.

"It got so I didn't have any money to feed my kids," she said.

At one point she had gone on welfare.

On October 19th, the day of his mother's birthday, Gerald Reed came for his daughter.

"He said he was just going to take her outside, and the next thing I knew he was gone."

On cross examination, Reed's lawyer asked her about trips to Chicago with a Junior Evans.

"He's a friend. That's it," Lois Reed said.

When the lawyer pursued that, Judge Lukowsky came down on him like a sliding Alp on a yeti.

"What in the name of God, Mr. Elfers, does this have to do

Point
of
illustration— with this case in a no-fault divorce proceeding?"

The lawyer claimed he intended to prove Mrs. Reed had been living with Junior Evans. The judge intended to curtail questioning along that line, unless it could be connected with the child.

Mrs. Reed was asked if, on occasion, she had said she did not want custody.

"When he first took her I tried to act like he couldn't hurt me," she said.

She burst into tears.

"And it does hurt," she said.

Did she ever have occasion to ask her husband where the child was?

She had— moments before, outside the courtroom.

"He said, 'You'll never find out!' "

Detail— Lois Reed left the stand with her blonde head high, but the crumpled tissue in her right hand suggested strain.

When Gerald Reed was called, he moved quickly to the witness seat. His face was flushed, his style modish in a suede jacket and leather boots. His wife watched him, one hand over her mouth.

Reed testified to the same preliminary matters his wife had, adding that he was employed at Nutone in Cincinnati as an assembler in the frame department.

Why had he taken the child Jena?

"I don't want her livin' with another man, and that Jena loved him more than she loved me as a father."

He testified he had done much of the child raising while his wife had been at the hospital with her ailing son, now dead.

"I feel I can bring the baby up," Reed said. "I can take care of it better than she did."

He went on to say that he had seen his wife once since their separation with her parents and the child at the Spinning Wheel Restaurant. Junior Evans had been with them.

Judge Lukowsky asked: "You've never seen your wife do anything improper with Junior Evans, have you?"

"No," Reed said.

The judge announced that his determination would be forthcoming and court was adjourned.

3. *The Determination*

In chambers, Judge Robert Lukowsky discussed his decision in the Reed custody matter.

"Everybody wants justice," he said, "but we administer only law."

Detail— Out of his robe and in shirtsleeves, the judge lit up a Camel. The nails were bitten down on his fingers.

"Here's what we know," the judge said. "We know the child is 16 months old. The father's lawyer has thrown up a smokescreen in which he attempts to show some misconduct on the part of the mother. But there is no convincing evidence — only the hearsay of the father, who admits he hasn't seen anything."

The judge waved a hand.

"Even if the evidence was compelling, there is no suggestion that the child has been affected at all."

He pointed to Section 402 of the Uniform Marriage and Divorce Act: "The court shall not consider conduct of a proposed custodian that does not affect his relationship to a child."

"The rule of thumb is that a small child ordinarily does best with the mother," the judge went on. "Has the husband shown the home in which he's keeping the child is substantially better than the one the wife could provide? I don't think he has."

He exhaled Camel smoke.

"You noticed the dichotomy in the testimony," he said. "He claimed she did not spend as much time with the child because she was with the other one in the hospital. But that's a pretty good indication of maternal interest right there."

He stubbed out the cigarette.

"He never denied stealing the child, either."

Judge Lukowsky's problem is to work for some judgment making a reasonably normal life for the offspring of a dissolved marriage.

"It's not easy to play God in these cases."

In this one his decision was firm:

"I'm going to let the child go to the mother and have him pay some reasonable support," he said.

Often divorcing parents use their children, consciously or not, to hurt each other. In this case the husband had snatched the little girl, but first the wife had told him Jena liked someone else better. Pain had been palpable in the courtroom, that sad chamber of averted eyes and lost relationships.

It had never been sadder than the moment before the bailiff's call to order, when Gerald Reed had leaned over to his lawyer and said:

Snapper— "I've got it in for her, but you know— I kind of like her."

Home Invasions: Why Elderly Live in Terror
by Anne Keegan

[Chicago Tribune *reporter Anne Keegan focuses on one unutterably horrifying situation to expose an increasing urban predicament of old people. It is extremely strong stuff, brutal but absolutely brilliant. Notice how she works in the facts and figures.]*

Action
opening—   Something woke Miss Ohge.

A creaking on the stairs? A rattling far below at a basement window? The faintest tap of a shoe hitting the hallway floor? Or was it the groan of a bannister under the weight of a silent hand?

Something — imperceptible — disturbed her aloneness, violated the solitude of the old brick mansion where she lay dozing on the second floor, her back up against the bed board, a book toppled into her lap.

She was asleep, but she felt it — as subtle as a warm breath on her cheek. Somebody was in her room!

The
paradigm—   Her eyes blinked open wide. And then she saw them, looking down at her where she lay confused on the bed beneath the reading light. Two men, one tall and heavy, with rolls of fat about his waist. The other— just short.

They were on her before she could move. One had something in his hand. He raised it and with a solid thwack he hit her on the head. And Miss Louise Ohge, 72, who lived alone, passed out.

The next morning, Sunday morning, Dec. 21, Mrs. Leola Alexander, who lives across the street, called Miss Ohge. There was no answer. But that was not unusual. Often Miss Ohge did not bother to answer her phone. So Mrs. Alexander went to church and thought nothing of it.

When she returned in the evening, she called again. She'd expected to hear from Miss Ohge, who usually called on Sundays to ask if a church dinner could be brought over. Again, no one answered the phone.

Monday morning she called again, but the phone just rang

and rang. "I'll check on her later," thought Mrs. Alexander, who had errands to do. But Monday evening, when the fourth call did not go through, Mrs. Alexander went across the street to talk to Mrs. Ann Mincey, who lived next door. The basement window in Miss Ohge's house had been kicked in, she said. Her husband had just noticed it. Perhaps there was something wrong.

Mrs. Alexander went outside and passed through the iron fence that wraps around Miss Ohge's yard. She had a key and quietly opened the door. There were no lights on inside.

She climbed the stairs to the second floor and called again. From somewhere came an answer.

Mrs. Alexander aimed her flashlight into Miss Ohge's room. The bedcovers were strewn about the floor, but nobody was there. She called out again and an answer came faintly from down the hall.

She went from bedroom to bedroom, "me calling and her answering." But still no Miss Ohge.

Finally, she passed into the bathroom. The door was closed but she pushed it open and shined the light around. There was Miss Ohge, lying on her back in the tub, blood crusted on her head.

"I put my arms around her and tried to help her out," said Mrs. Alexander. "She kept saying, 'Did you find the fire?' I said, 'Honey, there's no fire. But what has happened to you?'

"Then I saw. There was a stocking twisted around her neck. And her hands were tied under her. A coat had been put on her backwards and buttoned up the back — like a straight jacket. She'd been lying in that tub, on top of her hands, unable to move, for two days. And all that time I was calling her, and getting no answer, the water was dripping down on her head like a Chinese torture. I thought, 'Lord, what have they done to Miss Ohge?'"

The larger situation—

What was done to Miss Ohge was a home invasion — there are approximately nine a day in Chicago. The invaders beat her over the head that night — with an antique walking stick that belonged to her father. They kicked her around. They assaulted her. They tied her up, threw her in the bathtub, and left her to die.

Elderly and living alone, Miss Ohge was defenseless. Most old people are. But life for the elderly is no longer gentle. Crime has created a pervasive terror in their lives. It has become their major concern. A recent study in Chicago by the Mayor's Office for Senior Citizens and a nation-wide Harris Poll showed the elderly feel that more than food and shelter, money or health, crime is their No. 1 problem.

Why? Because they are vulnerable. Because they can't fight back. Because they're easy.

Consulting the expert— "The robber is the predator," says Chicago robbery Cdr. Ronald Rae. "He stalks the sickest, weakest, youngest or oldest. They are his prey. What has mankind always done with predators? Shoot them or put them in a cage. But with the courts the way they are, it doesn't happen any more.

"In changing neighborhoods especially, you've got old people living alone who are isolated. They won't move or can't move and their kids have gone off to the suburbs. They are alone and considered helpless by these predators.

"We're seeing a wave of home invasions now on old people because street robberies can be a hassle. But if they can get the old ones inside, the robber can take his time, take their purse or wallet, ransack the house for money and, sometimes, beat or torture the people demanding to know where the money is. It's really brutal."

There are no statistics in Chicago giving the number of elderly persons who are victims of crime. A study in Kansas City showed the number of senior citizens who were victims was not disproportionate to their population.

What was disproportionate, says Robert Ahrens, director of the Mayor's Office for Senior Citizens, is that the elderly suffer more as a result. Living on limited budgets, a robbery can leave them without money to eat or pay the rent. And any physical abuse, being thrown down or beaten, he says can lead to complications which, in some instances, bring death. The psychological damage they suffer, he says, is severe — they become paralyzed with fear.

A second expert— In New York, the increasing number of crimes against old people led robbery Sgt. James Bolte in the Bronx to head a special unit dealing only with home invasions against people 60 or over. It is the only such unit in the country.

"In 1975, we had 17 homicides of old people who were killed by home invaders," says Bolte.

"We've got 300,000 senior citizens in the Bronx out of two million, and they are prisoners here. We find some of them in their apartments with no food in the refrigerators, the garbage piled up because they are afraid to take it out. They are sleeping on newspapers because they won't go out to do the laundry. That's how great the fear is."

Bolte says part of his unit's job is to talk to senior citizens' groups about how to take precautions — always to lock their doors, to get extra locks for doors and windows, to always travel outside in groups of two or three. Not to let just anyone in who knocks on the door.

His detectives also follow up if a suspect is arrested.

"We give them a ride to court and we have it set up so when a senior citizen comes into court, his case comes right up rather than make him sit six or seven hours. We take him home and we let him know we're with him.

"That was part of the battle. They were afraid to testify or follow up. They didn't think the police would follow through. How much we are really stopping crime against the old — I don't know. What you really have to do is change people's values. And right now, there's no respect for the elderly left."

A third expert— Wentworth robbery investigator Larry Stomp agrees. Miss Ohge, he says, is a perfect example. When he arrived at her house the evening of Dec. 22, she was lying on a stretcher. She was incoherent. From her elbows down, her arms had turned black from lack of circulation. Her hands, he said, had swollen to twice their normal size and looked like black leather gloves that had split open.

Completing the frame story— Doctors amputated Miss Ohge's left arm just below the elbow the day after she was brought into the hospital. Since then they have been fighting to save the other one. She lies now on her back in a ward in Michael Reese Hospital trying to recover from that night.

"They knew she was living alone and figured she had a mattress full of money," says Stomp. "But she didn't. I don't think she kept more than two dollars around the house. She was just an independent old lady who liked to live alone with her cats. The shame of it is, she'll never be on her own again."

Miss Ohge says she lived in the house at 4306 S. Oakenwald Ave. for more than 40 years. When the neighborhood changed, she stayed on, because she "was accustomed to the place." It's where she'd lived with her books and her memories.

The books — 5,000 volumes — she recently gave to the University of Chicago. The memories she kept. But that's about all she has any more. Her cats are gone. She cannot hold a book to read. And her house has had visitors since she was attacked.

So Miss Ohge has no place to go. A hard fate for an independent old woman who liked living alone and keeping her own ways.

"Plans?" says Miss Ohge. "I'm making none. Sometimes I wish to God they'd cut off my other arm too — it would spare me the pain. Look at it, it is just a club now.

"I'll just stay in bed and watch the world go by. Now isn't that a lovely way to look at life? I can't help it any more. I've got no house left. T'ain't fair. That two men could break in when I'm old and everything would fall apart."

Nobody knows what time the robbers broke into Miss Ohge's house. Nobody knows who did it or what they were looking for. Whoever it was, they didn't find it. But they did find an easy prey, an elderly person, living alone, who couldn't fight back.

Driving it home— Nobody knows what will happen to Miss Ohge. But life for her will never be the same. Chances are, what's left will be lived from a hospital bed.

9. Judgment

The real role of the critic

There is this snob, see.

He thinks he knows things. He went to Harvard once and never recovered. He drinks herb tea with the pinkie pointed up. His mouth is so tightly pursed in disapproval you could mistake it for the bottom end of a bell pepper.

Because nothing, nothing is good enough for him.

That's the popular image of a critic. You've seen him in old movies played by George Sanders or Clifton Webb, wrinkling up his abnormally sensitive nose at theater openings and saying things like: "Miss Wonderly has all the musical charm of the retreating tide in a commode." By the end of the film he's been strangled or shot, and for good reason.

This insipid creature bears little resemblance to the authentic article. A critic is not a nay-saying snit, nor is he a rooter; he is an entertainer/teacher. His mission is to express an informed opinion with a measure of wit. He writes about a version of human creativity not because he is arrogant but because he loves the form. Since he loves the form, he wants to applaud excellence and deplore bad craft.

Critics operate under no delusion that they will influence audiences. They won't. A uniformly bad press for *Walking Tall,* a film about a tanktown lawman who beat up bad guys with a baseball bat, did not keep the crowds away; a uniformly good press for *Give 'Em Hell, Harry,* James Whitmore's Academy-Award-nominated one-man show on Truman, did not get people to go.

Audiences, bless 'em, will do what they want to do.

But a critic, alone with his typewriter, tries to bring to bear what he knows about aesthetics to express a thoughtful view about what he sees. He is not read because people agree with him, but because he writes well.

If he doesn't write well, nobody reads him, and there's an end on it. But if he does write well, readers like to match their views with his. They don't always agree; so what? It's the grip of the game, not the outcome, that counts.

The thing audiences and critics share is a love for art. If one loves art, one will always find something valuable in the worst of it and something that does not quite measure up to expectations in the best of it. That is the critical perspective. The critic's function is to collaborate with the artist in the pursuit of excellence.

We'll restrict our attention here to reviews of books, plays and films, since those have the broadest following— but the same principles apply to every type of critical writing. There was a time when some distinction was drawn between reviewing and "serious" criticism. The reviewer's job, preceptors said, was to give readers some idea of the subject matter and offer a perfunctory measure of the success of the execution. The critic's job, more profound and performed at greater length, was to express the artist's intention and comment on matters of form and style.

Today the distinction has generally disappeared and the reviewer serves both purposes. He must do something more than run over the obvious once lightly if he is to hold the attention of today's sophisticated audience. A review should be so informative that it will be of interest *even to those who have already attended or read the work discussed.* The reviewer is a vendor of insights; he should, by virtue of his specialized knowledge and fondness for the medium, be able to cast fresh light, to excite the reader to say: "Why, yes! I missed that, but it's there!"

The critic, then, teaches. He offers interpretations. But with sufficient humility to recognize he is not Handing Down the Tablets but sending out colorful cues to enhanced enjoyment.

Arguments against interpretation usually take a shape something like this: A flower is beautiful, but when you pick it apart you destroy it.

Nonsense. The more we know about the flower, the more we wonder at it: The higher the power of the microscope we place upon it, the more incredibly-wrought is the design revealed within. Works of artistic genius, like flowers, are inexhaustible. Look at the fun the centuries have had with Shakespeare.

Some general considerations:

1) If you aspire to be a critic, you must set about making yourself an expert. Laymen certainly have a right to their opinions, but those opinions are too often merely expressions of prejudice, not perception. *Know what you're talking about.* A book critic should know what *verso* and *recto* mean and what Henry James thought about the novel; a play critic should know what a flat is and why Harold Pinter makes a distinction between a dash and an ellipsis; a movie critic should know the difference between a pan and a dolly shot and what happened to Erich Von Stroheim's *Greed.* You are not entitled to teach off the top of your head.

2) Once you have it, don't flaunt your expertise. The occasional sesquipedalian word is permissible for style, but the context should make it clear. You know the terminology, well and good — share it in accessible language. Nobody is going to get excited about Arthur Miller's twist on the tragic hero in *Death of a Salesman* unless the classical concept of a tragic hero is made clear.

3) Don't talk down. Always assume your reader is as smart as you are. You may know things about James Joyce's *Dubliners,* but you don't hold exclusive rights to that knowledge. Bear that in mind, or — be certain of it — one day you will get a letter from some quartz miner in Colorado that will blow a stadium-sized hole smack through your old ego.

4) Avoid an overdependence on plot summary. There is a marked difference between acquainting a reader with the thrust of a story and recounting the whole thing in its entirety. Anybody can retell a tale; your interest is not so much in *what* happened, but *how* and *why.* And for decency's sake, don't ever tell the ending.

5) Two considerations are preeminent: a) Is the thing good entertainment? and b) Does it help us to understand ourselves or the world around us better? If it achieves both, it has a fair claim to being art.

6) Begin with a specific, arresting lead paragraph. End with a snap. This is a dumb lead:

I just loved *Mandibles.*

— Puce Vortices

This is a good lead:

Peter Brook's *King Lear* is gray and cold, and the actors have dead eyes.

— Pauline Kael

Time was when Those Who Knew Best insisted a review should lead with such matters as the title of the work, the author or director, the location of performance, and so forth; but the modern audience doesn't read formulas, and although these items should` be touched on somewhere in your text, anything goes. Here's an entire review by famed Sunpapers columnist H.L. Mencken:

Apologies for Love — by F.A. Myers. "'Do you remain long in Paris, Miss Wadsworth?' Earl Nero Pensive [!!!] inquired, as he seated himself beside her. His eyes, like beaming lights out of shadowless abysm, were transfixed upon her as by magic force. . . .'" Thus the story begins. God knows how it ends!

7) *Cite specific examples to support your views.* Your assessments are a lot less interesting than the reasoning behind them. You've got to show the reader why he should buy what you say. If you're audacious enough to have a point, you should also be rigorous enough to prove it.

8) Write well and cleverly. Just as your subject is expected to have style and structure, so must your review. A review should amuse as well as inform.

9) Take your stand with conviction. You can't throw a punch in two directions. A timid critic is of as much use as a necktie in a nudist camp.

10) Have a little charity. Remember a lot of effort on somebody's part probably went into what you're writing about. It's easy to be mordantly funny at another's expense. Remember too that the same high standards brought to bear on the finished work of professionals should not be applied to amateur efforts.

The following review of the film *Barry Lyndon* is carefully constructed to make its point. The lead graph has an angle and establishes the critic's attitude. The second graph touches on the plot. The third graph expresses the strength of the film, which is subordinated to its weakness in the fourth. The final graph offers the sum-up and finishes with an epigram:

The term "genius" has always been overused in reference to filmmakers, practitioners of a craft in which every innovator earns his own set of superlatives. Stanley Kubrick, recipient of insistent accolades for years, has directed some remarkable films, notably *Lolita* (1962), *Dr. Strangelove* (1964), *2001* (1968) and *Clockwork Orange* (1972). But Kubrick, ever the skilled technician, received rather more praise than he deserved. Dazzled by his lively sense of spectacle, reviewers and others made excuses for Kubrick's persistent failure to plot. Nowhere does this weakness appear more evident than in *Barry Lyndon,* Kubrick's most recent bid for cinematic immortality.

The film, based on William Makepiece Thackeray's first novel, concerns the abrupt rise of an unprincipled 18th century Irish opportunist to wealth and position and his subsequent fall to crippled poverty. Played with the resolute fresh-faced blandness of a varsity fullback by Ryan O'Neal, Barry Lyndon deserts armies and acquires mistresses with a certain air of stupified boyish abstraction that carries no hint of self-knowledge in it. Presided over by an intrusive narrator who acts as an auditory signpost for the action, Lyndon moves through his life dreamily, more pawn than person.

It is the drawback of the film that the characters are less real than the landscape they move in. Kubrick has a masterful eye for colonnades and moving carriages, Irish hills and English woods. There is a magnificent scene of marching redcoats, a brilliant duel sequence near the finish, and a marvelous moment with a tracking camera and a blackclad highwayman; Kubrick shows off several times with settings shot entirely by candlelight. These feats are embedded in a film of real technical virtuosity and attention to detail. Lyndon's rise, for example, is accompanied by an authentic Irish folk score; his fall plays to chamber music. But one can grow weary even of beauty. *Barry Lyndon* is more travelogue than epic; the subject is subordinate to the scenery, as Kubrick demonstrates in his favorite recurring shot: a closeup of Lyndon, then a zoom back to reveal the lushness of his surroundings.

Lyndon achieves status by marrying a wealthy countess (Marisa Berenson). His ambition, nowhere notable early in the film, emerges unaccountably, as does his willful maltreatment of her; Lyndon is simply unmotivated. As is she; Berenson is an alabaster beauty, but her suffering nobility reveals itself only in mute expressionless melancholy. Her sudden violent suicide attempt is consequently incredible. Berenson, like O'Neal, remains a mannequin; the two of them become Barbie and Ken in ruffles. Because we

258 Stalking the Feature Story

don't believe them, we can't care about them, and three hours is a long time to spend with such bloodless folk.

Lyndon comes a cropper when his stepson at long last goes after him, but the son is such a twit he is impossible to applaud, and Lyndon is so hapless a victim he is hard to pity. *Barry Lyndon* is an incredibly beautiful film to behold, but a hard one to sit through.

That's how it's done.

Patterns

We have argued in earlier chapters that the feature writer should concern himself first with form, the execution of which will express an effect. The critic determines what is going on in a work by working backward from the structure to the artist's implicit intention.

Watch for elements that recur. A green light that winks once at the end of a dock is a green light, but one that winks a couple of times in the course of things may be a symbol, like the one in *The Great Gatsby*. Every high school English student is familiar with the term "hidden meaning," which, some teachers imply, lurks mysteriously somewhere beneath the surface of the story as if the author were conspiring to keep us all in the dark about his motives. That's just absurd. Rather writers, dramatists and directors attempt to make their meaning *as clear as possible*, so they use every device at hand to do it — symbolism, statements of theme, character development, the works. And they restate their intention often just in case you missed it. The woven elaboration in a tapestry does not obscure the picture, it emphasizes it. So does the literary elaboration woven around a plot. Watch then for the emphases and preoccupations that repeat themselves in a work and return again to form a pattern.

The ending of course will be important and should provide valuable clues. Remember Poe.

Your assessment of matters of technique should be based on serious formal criteria you have set down and worked out in advance. In your mind's eye should be some Platonic vision of perfection that will be the measuring rod. The old smug expression "I don't know anything about art, but I know what I like" won't cut it in this business. That's for people who enjoy congratulating themselves on their ignorance.

The ways of structuring a review are as various as those for arranging any feature. Most important here of course is that avoidance of preconception we have warned against in general. If you go to *Hell's Angels Meet the Mummy* expecting disaster, you may be blind to some surprise values in it. For example, *Mr. Wong in Chinatown* (1939) was a low-budget imitation of the Charlie Chan films, which were B movies to begin with. The sets were cardboard, the scenes were all studio process-shot stuff, and the plot was as predictable as the progress of a marble down a metal groove. But the star was Boris Karloff, and the interesting thing was to watch what he did with his hands when the other actors had the lines. He was stealing scenes, and doing it brilliantly. Also he was playing a diminutive Oriental detective in spite of the fact that Karloff was tall and thin. He had to *act short.* He did it, too — a jewel among the ashes. And just as you should beware anticipating the worst, you should also control your specialized enthusiasms; if superstar Sal Monella can do no wrong for you, you're going to praise *Turkey Boy's Revenge* for reasons beyond anybody's apprehension.

The rule is to make it readable. There are all sorts of springboards for critical writing. In this *Chicago Daily News* book review of *The Final Days* by critic John Camper, the approach is corrective; Camper dismisses popular misconceptions and insists on an emphasis of his own:

> If your appetite for gossip and sensational disclosures about the Nixon administration has been whetted by widely disseminated excerpts from *The Final Days,* I have bad news for you. You won't find much more grist for cocktail party chitchat if you buy the book.
>
> Almost all of the "good parts" already have been published in *Newsweek* and the daily newspapers: Richard Nixon throwing himself on the floor and crying after kneeling down in prayer with Henry Kissinger; Nixon drinking too much and talking to the portraits of former Presidents; Kissinger calling Nixon a "meatball"; White House Chief of Staff Alexander Haig declaring Nixon "guilty as hell"; Pat Nixon sneaking tumblers of bourbon up to her room; Haig hiding all the pills in the White House to prevent a presidential suicide.
>
> Though the titillating excerpts undoubtedly will hype the book's sales, they also have given it an undeserved reputation as a tastelessly written *National Tattler* betwixt hard covers. Those who take the time to read the full 476-page book will find it to be the most clearly written and understandable Watergate book to

come along so far.

Watergate writers seem inevitably to get bogged down in complexities. Or they have trouble moving between the political and legal battles. Or they reprint too many of the tape transcripts or too much of the testimony we already have read.

Woodward and Bernstein, the *Washington Post* reporters who won a Pulitzer Prize for their investigation of the Watergate affair and wrote the best-selling *All the President's Men,* understood that a writer can make a complicated story much more interesting and understandable by focusing on the people involved.

The book is written, in the style of the "new journalism," like a novel. Woodward and Bernstein are omniscient observers who tell us not only what some figure said at a private meeting, but what he did, how he looked and even what he thought. The authors do not pass judgment, however, only the characters do that. Nothing is attributed to a source, though the identity of some sources is fairly clear (Special White House Counsel J. Fred Buzhardt obviously did a lot of talking).

This technique makes the book more readable, though it leaves the authors open to charges of inaccuracy, now being heard almost daily. We might put some stock in the charges if the pair had not proved through hundreds of newspaper stories to be energetic practitioners of the old journalism, constantly checking and rechecking their facts.

They say they based this book on interviews with 394 persons, and I know of no one who disputes that. They are saying, "Trust us," and I think we can. So, I am told, do many members of the Washington press corps.

Now let's make one thing perfectly clear: The book is not nearly so anti-Nixon as the published excerpts (and the stories about the published excerpts) would lead you to believe. It is, so far as I can recall, the only writing about Richard Nixon that has ever made me actually feel sorry for the man. He comes across almost as the classic tragic figure who has risen to a high position but is unable or unwilling to recognize the fatal character flaws that inevitably lead to his destruction.

Of course he was a despicable liar, and there is no need to feel pity for someone like that. But we get the feeling from the book that he believed his own lies and could not understand why others did not, and that is pathetic. Even the Kissinger-Nixon prayer scene, almost laughable in the excerpts, is strangely moving in the context of the entire book.

It is hard to understand why some of Nixon's family and former aides now are coming forth to deny that the former President ever was on the verge of suicide or mental illness or that he drank excessively near the end. Any normal person would be ready to "go bananas" (a term attributed to, but denied by, David Eisenhower) in a similar situation. But Nixon's friends seem intent on perpetuating the myth of his total implacability in the face of overwhelming adversity, thus depicting him as even more of an inhuman monster than he really was.

In the context of the book (but not the excerpts), when Kissinger calls Nixon "our meatball President" it reflects as poorly on Kissinger as on Nixon. In the book, Kissinger seems as bad as Nixon— arrogant, two-faced, "obsessed with his own prestige and image" and full of false machismo.

He calls others "craven," "cowardly" and "not manly enough" when they oppose his militaristic policies and expresses "enthusiasm at the size of the bomb craters that American B-52s left in North Vietnam." But when one aide makes a menacing gesture toward him (after being called cowardly), Kissinger quickly retreats behind a desk and says he was only kidding.

When Kissinger tells Nixon's personal secretary, Rose Mary Woods, that he will quit if Haig is named chief of staff, Miss Woods replies: "For once, Henry, behave like a man."

Another who comes off looking quite bad is James D. St. Clair, the high-powered and high-priced Boston lawyer brought in to defend Nixon. According to the book, St. Clair saw his appointment as an opportunity for greatness, a chance to shine as Joseph Welsh had shone in the Army-McCarthy hearings.

"St. Clair would save Richard Nixon and the presidency, and he would follow the President into the history books." But, according to *The Final Days,* he actually botched the case, lost the respect of Special Prosecutor Leon Jaworski and others, and finally directed his energies toward getting out of Washington with his professional reputation intact.

There is little mention of Nixon's former top aides H.R. Haldeman and John Ehrlichman (the book begins in late 1973

262 Stalking the Feature Story

after they resigned under fire), but both show up in cameo roles at
the end — seeking presidential pardons before Nixon resigns and
threatening to embarrass him if they don't get them.
Ehrlichman, the book tells us, had the gall to make the
blackmail threat to Nixon's loyal and heartbroken daughter Julie
the night before the President resigned. His behavior seems typical
of the kind of character that infected the Nixon administration.
With this book and others that have preceded it, the unraveling
of the Nixon administration is pretty well chronicled. Perhaps we
should now consider whether that administration was an aberra-
tion or whether there is something about the presidency, with all its
power, prestige and pressure, that tends to attract unbalanced people like Nixon and his cronies.
I have a feeling that the latter is true, and I think we should be
doing something about it.

Camper illustrates how specific examples support opinion and enliven
critical writing. He addresses himself to form and technique, and his
assertions that Nixon is made sympathetic by Woodward and Bernstein
and that his associates often come off even less creditably than the ex-
President are documented with evidence from the text.

In writing the following play review of *The Royal Family* for the
Boston Herald American, drama critic Elliot Norton offers extra information the average playgoer might not be expected to know. The
smooth presentation of well-researched background material is another
way to make a review interesting and informative.

The Drews and the Barrymores are all gone now, most of them
dead, a few still living quietly away from the stage, where their
fathers and their mothers and their uncles and their cousins— and
they had them by the dozens— made the family famous.
Diana, daughter of John, was the last of the Barrymores to
make a pitch for fame: sad, beautiful, decent Diana, who learned
eventually how to act but never how to live reasonably. She died
regrettably young.
Diana was in the fifth generation of this royal family of the
stage, whose four fathers and mothers were Drews, some of whom
married Barrymores, who had begun back in England as Blythes;
Barrymore was a stage name.
In our time, the Barrymores were the most spectacular: John,

the greatest American actor since Booth; Ethel, his regal sister; and their brother Lionel, who spent most of his later years in the movies. None of them wanted to be actors: John would have preferred to make a living as a newspaper cartoonist, and tried it for awhile; as a girl, Ethel aspired to be a concert pianist; Lionel spent a year in Europe studying art before he gave it up for acting.

George S. Kaufman and Edna Ferber were thinking about the Drews and Barrymores of course when they wrote *The Royal Family*. Although their story is fictional and fanciful, and their characters never existed, they created a wonderful ambience of truth to life.

There never was anyone exactly like "Fanny Cavendish," the grande dame of their play, but in her devotion to the theater and to her own family she suggests old Mrs. John Drew, who held the Drews and the Barrymores together while running her own theater in Philadelphia; a star herself, the wife of a star, the mother and grandmother of stars, to Ethel, John and Lionel she was "Grandma."

The daughter of Fanny in the play is "Julie," who resembles Ethel as Ethel must have been when she was young: pretty, talented, temperamental and loyal to the family. Julie Cavendish falls in love with a rich man of business but turns away from him in the end because he has no sympathy for her crazy family or crazier profession. Ethel Barrymore, who was wooed by such men of affairs as Winston Churchill, married a man of business, R.G. Colt of the Colt firearms firm.

The character Kaufman and Ferber call "Tony Cavendish" and whom they identify as the son of Fanny and brother of Julie is close enough in his lifestyle to John Barrymore, who was flamboyant and reckless offstage and sometimes on. No American actor of his generation matched John in greatness and there has been none since — except for Brando, who sold out to Hollywood for a million dollars a movie. None, not even Brando, behave as irresponsibly as he did.

Like his daughter Diana, John ruined himself eventually. In his final play, *My Dear Children,* he was a caricature, a self-mocking buffoon, his greatness drowned long since at the bottom of a bottle. In his heyday, he was erratic, unpredictable and irresponsible — but brilliant.

The Tony Cavendish of *The Royal Family* is on the run now from Hollywood, where he has slugged the director of a movie. He has come across the continent by train and plane — the time is 1927 — to hide in the family home in New York from process-servers and others bearing writs. He has to get a passport right away to be able to run away to Europe to escape pursuit by the agents of the law and a horde of reporters.

Except for his mother, Fanny, the grand old lady of this fictional royal family, all the Cavendishes are thrown into some kind of confusion by the sudden coming and going of Tony. He creates an uproar which, on the stage, is gloriously entertaining. Old Fanny is occasionally puzzled because Tony's problems are somewhat complex and his explanations not altogether coherent. But Fanny is a sweet, serene and good-humored and, as played in the new production at the Wilbur by Eva Le Gallienne, a great and loving creation. In the scatterbrained frenzy of *The Royal Family* she is all grace, goodness and dexterity.

A great star herself in the old tradition of the Drews and the Barrymores, she brings to the play more than 50 years of distinguished performance, and holds it in happy focus with loving care and affection for the men and women of the theater whom *The Royal Family* celebrates.

Slender, seeming at once frail and invincibly strong, she dominates the stage in a silken performance that meshes heart and art and, when the lines allow, speaks up for the grandeur and the glory of life in the theater with the fervor of the true believer.

Sam Levene, who has been on the stage for a few years too, gives another glorious performance as a manager to whom all the Cavendishes turn for comfort, solace, passports, money or common sense.

Carole Shelley is wonderful as Julie Cavendish, daughter of Fanny, mother of teen-aged Gwen and eventually grandma, too: a mercurial actress who would like to break away from the stage and its confusions but never will be able to make it.

As Tony Cavendish, who roars in and out of the action like a genially demented troubador, Leonard Frey does all the right things in the right way without ever creating the illusion of greatness which the role requires in this good and entertaining production of a good and entertaining old American comedy, which remains to be seen at the Wilbur by everyone who is or ever has been stagestruck, which is to say all the good and imaginative people of New England.

Norton imparts his knowledge gracefully and without pedantry, affording a richness of illustration that supports a sense of his own enthusiasm for this production and the theater in general. Just as specific detail is the essence of interesting description, so specific snippets of context, character and scene make for the most colorful criticism.

A third way to construct a review is to use it as the occasion for a tangent meditation on the subject matter of the work under discussion. In the following *Suffolk Journal* film review Robert Eckfeldt argues that the material of *Idi Amin Dada* transcends its somewhat sloppy execution. As the beginning and ending show, Eckfeldt is as concerned with the loss of a pristine, precolonial continent as he is with the efforts of the filmmaker.

East Africa — that beautiful, innocent land where Livingstone played out his poignant drama of missions, trade routes and the passion to end slavery forever — is a much-handled relic of colonialism. In Uganda, 90-odd years of British rule left a garage-sale heap of classes, sects, factions and interest groups at the door of independence in 1962.

Uganda's president, General Idi Amin, bursting like a cunning bull elephant out of this ferment in 1971, has, with the aid of his willing armed forces, kept his formidable tusks at his nation's throat ever since. His regime is a too-well publicized bedlam of ghastly cruelty and scary horsing around. A Clarabelle the Clown with a sten gun, he is terrifying and hilarious at once, and he won't be dismissed after the children's hour.

Making a film about Amin was a curiously original stroke. It was perhaps also inevitable in the type of overexposed media world we live in. As plain moviemaking goes, *Idi Amin Dada: A Self-Portrait* isn't really worth the price of a beer at the Orson Welles bar. It is shot with cheap process stock, frightfully edited, and rife with bad continuity; the camera is handled like a suitcase. It drags on much like a hot day in Kampala and never really decides just what it is up to. Considering the subject, however, that may be an artistic virtue.

Which is a pity, because director Barbet Schroeder is a man with impressive credentials in the French cinema. Yet Schroeder has succeeded brilliantly on another plane, quite without effort. He has permitted General Amin in an hour and a half to come very close to revealing himself as a man. Or so it seems. Amin the dictator is one type of puffed-up horror; Amin the man is precisely that — a flesh and blood human being. That he is a cunning, treacherous, cold-blooded murderer is not the point. Who can truly fathom human motives, let alone political ones? Dog must not eat dog.

He is a man. And a likeable man, an attractive man — a banal man. There is where *Idi Amin Dada* attains the honor of a master-piece — and a certain level of perfidy. It is a strange, compelling film. It is positively schizoid. It is billed as a documentary (a red herring of a term in the best of cases), but it is really an odd apologia by Amin himself and an unuttered statement about Africa and her ragtag European heritage.

Director Schroeder wished to execute a "portrait of power." In an interview with the San Francisco *Times and Sunday Chronicle* after the film's release in the U.S., he said he was "interested in the idea of all power concentrated in one man. In every case it leads to something completely crazy when there is no restraint."

To this end he prudently approached General Amin with the proposal that Amin himself direct the greater part of the film. Naturally Amin flung himself into the task with frightening gusto. "I was putting fiction in a documentary, and it was not my fiction," reflected Schroeder. "It was Amin's."

And what fiction! It makes *Monty Python's Flying Circus* look like a Lutheran church service. At times the film creepily resembles movie satires such as *Dr. Strangelove* or, more pointedly, *The Mouse That Roared.* The General arranged "sequences" for Schroeder to film. A mock attack on the Golan Heights, based on Amin's "master plan" for retaking Israel, features Amin and four Centurion tanks. It resembles a gang of boys charging a neighborhood sandbox with toy guns and couldn't be funnier if Amin had announced the objective to be Brooklyn Heights. Amin seems to think it pretty funny, too.

"I never knew when he was joking," said Schroeder. Apparently Amin wasn't too sure of that himself. He cavorted for the camera like a manic starlet. His sheer physical presence is awesome, drawfing his environment, and he is a genuine, natural-born performer. This is undoubtedly a measure of his power.

Perform he does. He presides over an outlandish Cabinet meeting like some Viking king laying down the law. Ministers are advised to show up on time or they're out of office— and to watch for spies. They are also ordered to ensure that the people love their leaders: "Everybody must be loved!" The Cabinet is seen to be studiously taking notes all the while.

At a conference with Kampala's physicians, Amin tells them to stay sober — so they can apply all that "primary and secondary school." He attends seemingly endless displays of military pomp and fury, parades and drills, with the meticulous attention Winston Churchill is said to have lavished on his toy soldiers as a child. That isn't as absurd as it seems. It is in scenes such as these, I think, that the film declares itself, although subtly.

General Amin, like certain Latin American dictators we dismiss as savages, personifies a swollen travesty of our own Western institutions. He is literally a deadly political satire. The Amins, the Stroessners, the Francos flourish because ours is an unhinged world where on one hand men are going to the moon and on the other they are still hunting game with bone spears.

But there is human warmth to this curious film as well, moments genuinely touching. Amin talks about his childhood of dingy poverty. He shows off some of his 19 children, adorable tykes. He is seen playing the accordion at a party and joking richly with members of the national football club. ("You must KO your opponents!") He takes us on a boat ride, happily pointing out the animals on shore, like Adam in Eden.

He rumbles with laughter when asked about his now notorious telegrams to world leaders — particularly that sent to UN Secretary-General Kurt Waldheim concerning the Jews and Hitler. He seems to fob them off as practical jokes. But practical jokers are in fact horrid people— and there is menace in Amin's hearty laughter.

At one key moment in the film this country thug turned king unknowingly betrays a few seconds of actual fear. At least, I think he does. At the medical conference a long closeup fixes him looking strangely withdrawn, self-absorbed ... as though he is painfully aware of appearing stupid to the assembled doctors. He does genuinely respect their education, as though his grandiosity sometimes gives him moments of confusion. It is indeed a dilemma. One finds empathy for him: How in Heaven *did* he get where he is, and whose fault is it?

The *International Herald Tribune* described *Idi Amin Dada* as "the funniest show in Paris" when it opened there in 1974. The film has been to an extent similarly received here. Amin is crazy; the filmmaker has provided him the means with which to hang himself. Amin has shown himself to the world. The Orson Welles deliberately features the film back-to-back with a Bugs Bunny cartoon ridiculing Hitler. This is to put General Amin into "proper perspective," evidently.

I don't think Idi Amin is crazed. Quite the contrary, I believe he is frightfully sane. I believe that he is an aggrandized tribal chief, just as Francois Duvalier was a bloodthirsty Haitian witch doctor. That he is the ruler of modern Uganda is not really a reflection on Africa. That he is a ruthless, arbitrary tyrant and an undeniable butcher is not really a reflection on him. We in the West passed him the knife— the helicopters, the secret police, the bullet in the head in the cellar. Idi Amin is no more incomprehensible than the African kings who sold their people into slavery for Colt revolvers.

It would be lovely to see a film about Africa before the white man — the great forests and savannahs, the beasts, the naked dignity of the peoples whom Stanley pronounced "vicious." Two late, Dr. Livingstone. Too late.

Eckfeldt's very readable review achieves its interest from both a discussion of the film and an examination of its implications. He feels free to travel far afield.

So should you. The best critics are innovative as well as incisive. They are not the carrion crows of art but the keepers of the flame who insure that we stay ever alive to the wonders of human creativity.

A sage in motley

"Every genuine humorist is not only a poet," wrote playwright Luigi Pirandello, "he is a critic as well."

Humor is the hardest kind of feature writing to do, and it is the most valuable. The tragedian — notable in his most modern incarnation as anchorman on the nightly news— tells us life is a mess, there is death at the end of it and nothing to be done. Kings die, whole courts and kingdoms collapse: Hamlet is borne away in a funeral procession. The comedian similarly tells us life is a mess, but the whole situation is ridiculous rather than sorrowful, and the most appropriate response in the face of it is ribaldry. Classic comedies end in marriage ceremonies rather than funerary ones, and we are left with the hope of a new and better world at the end as a consequence. Comedy is a corrective, a criticism of life; it tells us there is some opportunity for optimism, man's indefatigable *ha!* hurled defiantly out at an adverse cosmos. "The world," observed Fred Allen, "is a grindstone, and life is your nose."

There is ever more thought in laughter than in tears.

Shakespeare often dressed his wise men in cap and bells, like Lear's fool. The jester, who seemed a rather frivolous fellow, in reality saw everything more clearly than his sober social betters and was less the minion of the royal court than its best counselor. Such are the many ploys and evasions in the activities of governments, sundry formal bodies and indeed all workaday members of the corporate world that there is something innately hilarious about the bald statement of truth.

You'll remember it wasn't until a child pointed a finger at a pompous old fraud and stated the obvious that everyone began to laugh at the emperor's nakedness. Well, the humorist is the perennially honest, inquiring innocent who informs us all that we are absolutely shell-pink starkers.

Mark Twain was a journalist who early discovered the risible power of the unabashed truth. Writing in the 1860s for the *Territorial Enterprise* in Virginia City, Nevada, and later for the *San Francisco Call,* Twain delivered himself of lines like these:

It could probably be shown by facts and figures that there is no distinctly American criminal class except Congress.

In the first place God made idiots. That was for practice. Then he made school boards.

Put all your eggs in one basket— and watch the basket.

Unassailable assessments.

Another noted journalist, who wrote for the *New York American* and the *Chicago Examiner* during the first two decades of this century, was an Oklahoma cowboy named Will Rogers. When he said, "All I know is what I read in the newspapers," he wasn't kidding; he used the news events of the day as material for his wry columns on the aberrations of so-called civilized man. Like Twain, his tool was the truth simply stated. It doesn't date:

> Young John D. Rockefeller says, "Love is the greatest thing in the world." You take a few words of affection and try to trade them for a few gallons of oil, and you will discover how great love is.

> I'll tell you about temperament. Temperament is liable to arrive with a little success, especially if you haven't been used to success. The best cure in the world for temperament is hunger. I have never seen a poor temperamental person.

> See by today's paper where Senator Borah made an appeal to the country to donate a dollar or more each to save the respect of the Republican Party. I just mailed $5 to make five Republicans respectable. Wish I could afford more, but this continued prosperity has just about got me broke.

Rogers looked like a hick— by design— but spoke like a sage.

Robert Benchley was a very funny man who found his material everywhere. He didn't have to search out the ridiculous —he found it constantly thrust upon him. Every situation in his immediate world was an excuse for copy. Frank Sullivan, in his introduction to *Chips Off the Old Benchley,* wrote of him:

> There are not many subjects he did not probe at one time or another. Often he dealt with the same common or garden variety of subject matter other writers tackled, but a subject was rarely the same after Mr. Benchley got through with it. "Well," the reader would think, "here he goes on Turkish baths; now, even Benchley could not think of anything new to say about Turkish baths." And then Benchley would say something new about Turkish baths.

Well, what was there to be said about a steam room? That it was hot? Yes—but in a fresh way. Benchley allowed himself to reflect on the cogitations of a man suffering through one of these experiences in perspiration. What if he died from it? How would the body be identified?

> The towel around your waist would do no good, as they are all alike. You regret that you were never tattooed with a ship flying your name and address from the masthead. The only way for them to tell who you were would be for them to wait until everybody else

had gone home and find the locker with your clothes in it. Then they would find those lavender drawers. . . .

Benchley satirizes our worst fears in the guise of being one of us. The broadsword of his wit is so sharp one never feels the slice of it; you just reach for your hat and suddenly find your head missing.

Vignettes and epigrams are funny— as Polonius pointed out, brevity is the soul of wit— but it is possible to be amusing at length on familiar matters of fact. All one need do is take any subject, stare at it suspiciously for a moment to allow the innate silliness of it to surface, then break it down into parts and deliver them deadpan. You of course never imply there is anything remotely hilarious at all in your approach; you simply move manfully through the material, and your seeming gravity makes matters seem more amusing. All good comics do this; Buster Keaton deified the method by never allowing himself even the vestige of a smile. The contrast of such dogged stylistic seriousness in setting forth an absurd subject makes us laugh because it is incongruous, like a stove pipe hat on a savage.

Jim Delay of the *Boston Herald American* is another very funny man. Watch him go to work on the unequal status of house pets and their subordinated human "masters":

> Behind so many closed front doors, where the cushions are cozy and the living is easy, there are all these cats. They are always smiling, yawning, and feeling mighty pleased about themselves. They are a smug and arrogant lot.
>
> One of the first things my friend Weinstein said to me after we were introduced was this: "Dogs are smart sometimes, and horses are smart sometimes, but cats are always stupid."
>
> At the time that Weinstein made this statement a certain gray and white cat was present, yawning up at Weinstein, smiling arrogantly. I know this certain cat well and know her to be a formidable adversary. But Weinstein did not know her. He was unconcerned that this cat heard the uncomplimentary remark. He ignored this cat, and the cat pretended to ignore Weinstein. But a little later, when Weinstein's back was turned, the cat knocked his cigarette lighter off a table and began pushing it across the carpet to a secret hole under a radiator.
>
> I picked up Weinstein's lighter just before it was pushed into the hole, and, as I picked it up, the cat made an irritable face and

attempted to bite my interfering hand.

I am sure of this: When the subject is cats, Weinstein does not know what he is talking about.

The truth is that cats are among the most brilliant of all creatures, and mysteriously so. Many people think that when the cleverest, pushiest and most self-centered humans die, they are reborn as cats.

I am one who believes this, and you should too. It may be that the reborn Cleopatra lives in your house snuggled into a cozy cushion, yawning, smiling. In other houses on your street may live the reincarnated Salome, Bonaparte, Aaron Burr, Bismarck, sisters Bronte, Eve, Adam, Caesar, General Franco, King Solomon, W.C. Fields, Warren G. Harding.

This is very mysterious, and yet it is only one thing to consider among all the mysteries that surround cats. Why are they always smiling? What is it that they know? How did they become so brilliant? There is much more. In fact, there are as many mysteries about cats as there are cats . . . and, Holy Smoke, there are all these cats. . . .

Think of it. In home after home all across America, all across North America, all across God knows where else, there are all these cats. Stretched in a line, ears to tails, they would reach from your street to Ursa Major. If they all purred at once the sound would rattle this planet to its core. Yet we have all these cats in our houses, and this is what they do for us:

Nothing.

They are mostly engaged in snoozing and are fussy about the places they choose to manufacture zzzzz's— atop clean clothes in a laundry basket; under the covers of your bed (where they make a small but recognizable lump); in your underwear drawer wrapped up in tee shirts, nightgowns, bras; exactly centered in the softest chair you own. This is not too dumb.

When they are not sleeping there are certain requirements all these cats have for the humans who live in their houses with them. Among these requirements are promptness and cooperation.

For example, when all these cats awake in the mornings they require food instantly. They have no interest in human preoccupations, like what time it is. These cats do not care whether the clock on the bedside table says 6 a.m. or 5:30 a.m. or any other a.m. They know what time it is. It is time they were fed. And all these cats become very annoyed with humans who are unaware of this way of measuring time. They have a requirement that food must be placed in the kitty bowl by dawn's early light. They are very insistent about this requirement. They will not take no for an answer. You can be sure that, one way or another, all these cats will force these humans to rise.

They will walk back and forth along the entire bodies of the sleeping humans. But that is only the beginning. They will do whatever they must.

If the humans appear to sleep on, the cats will walk up their human chests and stare into into their faces to see if these humans are putting them on. Then they will stick their mouths and noses into the ears of the sleeping humans and they will meow commandingly. Then they will walk across the faces of the sleeping humans with the heaviest steps they can manage. Then they will leap from the pillows of the sleeping humans to the night table where the humans' clocks stand with hands pointing to 6 a.m., or whatever. And the cats will push these clocks closer and closer to the edge of each night table. After every push these cats will look toward the face of each sleeping human to see if that human is ready to get up yet and open a little can of tuna and egg. If the human does not yet seem to be ready, the clock will be nosed over the edge and sent crashing to the floor.

If the human still pretends to be asleep each object atop his bureau will be pushed over the edge, one at a time— each penny, each nickel, each dollar bill, the jewelry box, the full ashtray— until the sleeping human goes berserk and leaps from bed, in a frenzy, to open the can of tuna and egg. And while the human calls the cat vile names and the human's face is distorted with anger, the cat will ignore the human and nibble away at the tuna. Then the cat will find a soft place to resume its sleeping.

And while all these cats sleep on, the human gets dressed and goes to work.

Yes, all these cats require that their humans work, and work sufficiently hard to bring home the tastier and more expensive kinds of food. Cats will not tolerate inferior products. They have all these humans who work for them.

As any properly humble individual who happens to room with a feline will tell you, Delay has merely offered up for evidence certain incontrovertible facts. Like the boy at the scene of the procession, Delay senses a jaybird somewhere. Then, so do we.

Sources for satire

I was best man at a Russian Orthodox wedding once, and just before that stunningly beautiful ceremony I remember witnessing the measured arrival of a sleek, mustachioed man of corpulent middle years obviously full of his own self-importance. There were rows of medals on his chest; his nut-brown cleanly-shaven scalp gleamed like the well-rubbed wooden knob on a newel post, and he sported a monocle through which he squinted about with evident disapproval. This great inflated foetus moved to the steps of the church like a slumming Cossack among serfs.

Suddenly, he stumbled.

Nearby, a scruffy little guy started to laugh. Then he drew himself up to his full five feet five and marched up to the steps in a perfect puffed pastiche of the big man's gravity, ending the procedure with a stiff nose-dive of a pratfall.

I roared, of course.

Because the little guy was a born satirist.

A satirist is a comedian who wants to restore order. He is a moral conservative who values three things: 1) common sense; 2) honesty; and 3) human kindness. Naturally, everywhere he looks he observes the opposite.

So he ridicules deviation from these values in an attempt to make society see how foolish it becomes when it misbehaves. His constant plea is for wisdom, humility and tact in a world not especially notable for those qualities.

He scoffs at excess by revealing its extremes. Like Hamlet's player, he "out-Herods Herod." Like my diminutive Russian acquaintance, he places vanity and hypocrisy in their properly grotesque context.

Obviously the opportunity for satire exists only in a free society. Because it is often directed toward the abuses of the powerful, it is a David of wit directed against a Goliath of potential repression, and dictators have read their history. They know better than to allow slings inside the organization.

The idea is to exaggerate a perceived misconduct, making it consequently silly. Here's how columnist Ellen Goodman did it for the *Washington Post,* mocking both the insecurity of a lot of people toward the sick and the infinite capacity of the ailing for self-pity:

> I woke up with the distinct feeling that it was a bad idea. To wake up, that is. It occurred to me that I must be hungover, except that cranapple juice doesn't usually affect me that way. On the other hand, it could be the flu. It had moved somewhere west of Dedham. Everybody said so.
>
> But there they were, all the symptoms— Chinese food syndrome around the eyes, a stomach that bore no relation to Newton's law, an abhorrence of standing up— all available and accountable.
>
> Yes, the flu. I was betrayed. This was the only case of flu on record (mine at least) overshadowed by a severe attack of embarrassment. Imagine, if you will, the utter humiliation of coming down with it after everyone else has recovered, contracting it after the health department has assured you the epidemic has peaked and you can all come out of your houses and sit across the table from each other again.
>
> Imagine being passe'. Even in sickness.
>
> I had always considered myself among the avant garde. I had a charter subscription of *Ms.* and an aversion to fuzzy tomatoes before we knew they were machine-made. I was the first on my block to fail at letting the hair on my legs grow. And even my Chevy Vega had been the first in its peer group to rust.
>
> Furthermore — and this is remarkable considering my background — I had been an imperfect mother before it was fashionable. It just came to me instinctively.
>
> Now, this wasn't fair. How could someone with a history like mine be among the last to get the flu? To add insult to injury to disease, the other problems that came with being at the tail end of the germ chain letter were manifold.
>
> For instance, sympathy. Lack thereof. When you are late, you get no sympathy. Those who managed to avoid the scourge themselves have used up their quotient of sympathy and can barely ask you how you're feeling. When you start to tell them that, on the whole, you'd rather be in Philadelphia, their response is, "Uh-

huh, uhhuh, that seems to be the general syndrome," and they go on talking about *Mary Hartman*. Syndrome! They talk about the syndrome when I'm dying. Mother, pin a rose on me, or at least a cold cloth. They are cruel.

The only peer group worse than those whom the angel of vengence passed over are those who have been through flu and survived. For some reason, people recently released from hospitals or from the grip of the grippe feel compelled to tell you about their recent brush with disease. (This is not, of course, a compulsion I share. This column is a literary exercise.)

It's a little bit like when you're pregnant and every woman from 93 down relates the gory story of her third birth, second miscarriage, or whatever. What happens is that these survivors use your current attack of the flu as a convenient lead-in to the recycled tale of their own battle with the bug.

To wit:

"How are you?"

"Terrible."

"Oh yes, well I felt like I was going to die. How much temperature did you have?"

"102."

"102? That's not so bad. I had 103 for two days, with aspirin. . . . Can you move your toes?"

"I'm not up to trying."

"Well, if you can move your toes, you have a mild case. Are you sleeping?"

"I was, but the phone rang."

"Oh, did I wake you up?"

"No, I had to get up to answer the phone."

"Oh, well if you can get up, you have a mild case. You're lucky. I was sick for six days. I was throwing up and couldn't eat and had such a headache I couldn't stand the light and was too sick to talk on the phone. You must have a mild case."

"Click."

Yes, the problem with being such a late-bloomer is that the other survivors have all rehearsed their tales of woe and can top yours with a single bound, or a metaphor. (I've got mine ready now: "You know how sick I was? I lost three pounds and didn't care. Now, that's sick!")

The other problem with being so tardy is that by the time you've got it, your boss has had it— I mean, had it with a sick staff, had it with doubling up and feeling sympathetic and filling out absentee sheets. If he's an editor he tends to say things like: "I need some copy around this place."

If you tell him you're too sick, he counters with: "Well, write about it." But of course I couldn't do that. It's passe'.

Goodman's satire is extremely good-humored because she directs most of the bite at herself. That's an effective method to earn the willing ear of an audience. If I call *you* foolish, you will quite fairly set about bringing your own guns to bear; if I call *myself* foolish, you may instead be prepared to identify with me.

Because down deep, in one way or another, we're *both* foolish, and we know it.

One accessible target— the self

The self is the safest— and most instructive— butt for a joke.

We're all a little at a loss in our lame progress through this life. We see ourselves each one as somehow peculiar, and in that we are the same. As humorist Jack Douglas put it:

When I was a child, it was the winter that I hated most. All the other children in our neighborhood had little red sleds. Mine was *beige*. That's when I first noticed the pains.

In the slow discovery that we are all in the same uncomfortable— and leaky — boat comes the confidence that permits open laughter. We recognize ourselves in the fretful quandaries of a Charlie Chaplin or a Woody Allen. We are all the little guy, sorely beset but game.

The idea of the little guy is a comic essential. Satire must be directed against large adversaries. If the adversary is more vulnerable than the jester, what results is cruelty rather than humor. Suppose the roles of my two Russians had been reversed; there would have been nothing genuinely amusing in the spectacle of a smug giant humiliating a smaller, less affluent guest. This is why jokes directed against deformity, poverty or human affliction come off so poorly, as do insult jokes directed against the inarticulate by flip fast talkers.

The largest adversary is after all the self. By poking fun at our own pretensions and ineptitudes, we poke fun at everyone's — and the audience stays to listen instead of refashioning our face. W.C. Fields commented on the symptoms of something very like a hangover once. His solution? "Right then I swore that I would never again poison my system with a maraschino cherry." It's a comment on the transparency of self-deception, and not alone Fields'.

Columnist Mike Royko wrote amusingly in the *Chicago Daily News* of applying for renewal of a driver's license. The lady behind the counter is more insistently perceptive than Royko would like her to be:

> "Color of hair?"
> "Brown."
> She glanced at my head. "Brown?" "Uh-huh. Brown. I've always had brown hair."
> She looked dubious and said: "I'd say it is, uh, gray."
> "Well, in this light, I suppose there's a little gray mixed in with the brown."
> She squinted her eyes, studied my head more intensely, and said: "No, it's mostly gray."
> "On the sides, yes. I'm probably getting a little gray along the sideburns."
> "Sir, you don't have much hair anywhere but on the sides."

All our collective frettings about growing old are implicit in the exchange.

Joan Beck of the *Chicago Tribune* kids her annual frustations over figuring out income tax. Prepare to empathize:

> This column is being written under direct orders from my psychiatrist. He says he only sees this strange combination of mania, depression, paranoia and melancholia in early April, when it is common. He assures me I'll experience a remission soon. But he warns me to expect periodic relapses every spring.
>
> As a part of my treatment, my psychiatrist says I must ventilate the anger I've been repressing, the resentments I've built up, the hostility I can't handle. I tell him it is too dangerous to put my dark and hateful feelings into words, that THEY will find out and punish me. My psychiatrist tells me I have no choice if I am to get well.
>
> I tell my psychiatrist that this newspaper deletes expletives. He replies that I can do what must be done without them. I do not

believe him. He tells me to get on with it. What else can I do? But I am frightened.

I hate the income tax. I hate the income tax because it takes my money — my money that I work so hard for, my money that I need, my money that I could use for a vacation, or something for the kids, or to pay the bills. I cannot afford the income tax.

I hate the income tax because I don't understand it. What does it mean, "Figure your tax on the amount on line 47 by using Tax Rate Schedule X, Y, or Z, or if applicable, the alternative tax from Schedule D, income averaging from Scedule G, or maximum tax from Form 4726?" Am I dumb? Am I crazy? It hurts my head.

I hate the income tax because it cheats me because I am married. My husband shakes his head and says, "If we were not married, if we were just living together, we would save $2,000 or $3,000 every year. Did you read about those couples who get divorced every December and remarried every January and save enough for great vacations?" It scares me, the income tax making my husband talk about divorce.

I hate the income tax because it snoops. I wouldn't tell my best friend all the personal stuff you have to give the internal revenue. Whatever happened to the right of privacy? And the right not to incriminate yourself?

I hate the income tax because it lets inflation push you into a higher tax bracket every year or two. You think, if you get a nice raise, that you can keep up. But you can't. It just makes your taxes worse.

I hate the income tax because I don't know how to cheat. Everyone else finds loopholes, gimmicks, tax dodges, and smart lawyers to set up cagey little trusts. Every time I even ask a question, the answer comes back costing me more than I thought possible.

I hate the income tax because it is not good for your health. It causes ulcers, insomnia and acid indigestion. It gives you high blood pressure, eyestrain and headaches. It makes you chew your fingernails, drink too much and grow old before your time.

I hate the income tax because I can't remember. "What's this check you wrote last August?" my husband yells. "Why don't you keep records?" he thunders. I tell him I do, but they always disappear by April. Income taxes are not good for a marital relationship.

I hate the income tax because the government wastes my money. It will use it to send 25 Congressmen to pick up a copy of the Magna Carta when there is one in the Library of Congress around the corner. It is taking my money to study pot and dirty movies, and to send a plane cross country with a general's forgotten golf shoes. I can do a better job of spending my money.

I hate the income tax because it makes me feel unAmerican. Why aren't we dumping the tax forms into Boston Harbor on top of the tea and waving flags at the IRS that say "Don't tread on me?" I don't want to have to join a tax rebellion, but the income tax keeps me from feeling free.

There, Doctor, I have tried the therapy you ordered. I have let all my hostilities hang out. But it hasn't helped. I still feel manic, depressed, persecuted and sad. Now, I think I'll try a primal scream.

She is kidding at once an institution, herself and a lot of folk like her who experience that signal symptom of our age — paranoia.

As Walt Kelly, the most perceptive of modern newspaper satirists, observed more than once: "We have met the enemy— and he is us."

"Cuckoo's Nest"— A Sane Comedy about Psychotics
by Vincent Canby

[Vincent Canby of the New York Times *offers this insightful perspective on a complex film. Note that he both applauds and demurs where appropriate, placing the work within a tradition and measuring it according to how well the director supplies the realism he purports to offer. As both analyst and illuminator, Canby demonstrates the critic's proper function as artistic umpire.]*

The
genre— In a certain kind of sentimental fiction, mental institutions are popular as metaphors for the world outside. The schizoids, the catatonics, the Napoleons and the Josephines are the sanes, while all of us outside who have tried to adjust to a world that accepts war, hunger, poverty and genocide are the real crazies. It's the appeal of this sappy idea, I suspect, that keeps Philippe De Broca's *King of Hearts* playing almost continually around the country. In that film, you remember, the Scots soldier (Alan Bates) seeks asylum among the certified lunatics while

World War I rages nuttily outside.

It's a comforting concept, and a little like believing in Santa Claus, to think that if we just give up, if we throw in life's towel and stop thinking rationally while letting our wildest fantasies take hold, that we'll attain some kind of peace. No fear. No pain. No panic. The world becomes a garden of eccentric delights.

Departure from the genre—

The thing that distinguishes *One Flew Over the Cuckoo's Nest*, Milos Forman's screen version of the 1962 Ken Kesey novel, is its resolute avoidance of such nonsense. Although the film is not without its simplicities and contradictions, its view of disconnected minds is completely unsentimental. I'm not at all sure that the terrifying events that Kesey describes so jauntily in his novel could take place, or would ever have taken place in any mental hospital 10 or 15 years ago, so one must accept the tale as a fictional nightmare of its time—the '60s. The mental hospital in *One Flew Over the Cuckoo's Nest* is, I suppose, a metaphor, but it is more important as the locale of one more epic battle between a free spirit and a society that cannot tolerate him.

There is always, of course, a certain sentimentality attached to this conflict, at least in our society. Twentieth-century Americans feel terrifically sentimental about— and envious of — non-conformists while knocking themselves out to look, sound, talk and think like everyone else. The only good non-conformist is the fictional non-conformist, or one who's safely dead. We apotheosize Yossarian while electing Presidents whose public images have been created in advertising agencies.

The plot in three graphs—

Randle Patrick McMurphy (Jack Nicholson), the fast-talking hero of *One Flew Over the Cuckoo's Nest*, more or less has this non-conformism thrust upon him, out of bravado and ignorance and the demands of this sort of fiction. All that we ever know about Randle before he turns up in the Oregon mental hospital, where we first meet him and which is the first scene of the film, is that he has been serving a six-month prison sentence for statutory rape. The girl was 15 though she told him she was 19, he says, probably lying. After two months on a prison farm, Randle has gotten himself transferred to the hospital for psychiatric observation, figuring that the loony bin would be a softer touch than picking peas.

Once Randle is in the hospital, however, the world shrinks to the size of his ward, which is the private domain of a singularly vicious character named Nurse Ratched (Louise Fletcher), a woman of uncertain age who is capable of understanding and sympathy only when they reinforce her authority.

The story of *One Flew Over the Cuckoo's Nest* is the duel between Randle and Nurse Ratched for the remnants of the minds of the other patients in the ward, a contest that starts out in the mood of a comedy on the order of *Mr. Roberts* and winds up, rather awkwardly, as tragedy.

One Flew Over the Cuckoo's Nest is indecently sentimental and simplistic if you take it as a serious statement on the American condition, which is much too complex to be represented by this mental ward. However, if you can avoid freighting it with these ulterior meanings — and Forman and his screenwriters have had the good sense not to bear down too heavily on them — *One Flew Over the Cuckoo's Nest* is a humane, loose-limbed sort of comedy containing the kind of fine performances that continually bring the film to explosive, very unsettling life.

Background— Forman, the Czech director of *Loves of a Blonde* and *Fireman's Ball,* has made one other American film, *Taking Off,* in which the eye through which we saw the world was clearly that of an amused, sympathetic, sometimes appalled visitor. Perhaps because the locale of *One Flew Over the Cuckoo's Nest* is more particular than the middle-class and hippie milieus of *Taking Off,* the new film betrays nothing except the director's concern for people who struggle to bring some order out of chaos. It's a struggle he finds supremely funny and sometimes noble, even when the odds are most bleak.

Insight— Jack Nicholson is something more than the star of *One Flew Over the Cuckoo's Nest.* He is its magnetic north. His is the performance that gives direction to those of everyone else in the cast. I can't believe that a non-professional like Dr. Dean Brooks, who is actually the superintendent of the Oregon State Hospital (where the film was shot), could have been so comically speculative in a key moment had not Nicholson been setting the tone of the scene. Nicholson's flamboyance as an actor here is of an especially productive sort. It doesn't submerge the other actors. It seems to illuminate them. This is most noticeably true of Louise Fletcher, whose Nurse Ratched is much more interestingly ambiguous than the character in Kesey's novel, as well as of Will Sampson, another non-pro, who plays Nicholson's deaf-mute Indian sidekick, and Brad Dourif as the ward's "kid" character.

Evaluation— There are some troublesome things in *One Flew Over the Cuckoo's Nest* that I'm not sure can be alibied by saying that it is, after all, a fiction and not a documentary. The ward that we see in the film is (most of the time) so spic and span that it seems to give the lie to horror stories we all know about the filth and overcrowding in so many mental hospitals. Also, can it be possible that shock treatments are (or were until recently) given out so arbitrarily as punishments, and could a single ward nurse ever have authorized a lobotomy without some second opinion?

These can be major factors in the way one responds to the film. But another is the extraordinary way that Forman has been able to create important, identifiable characters out of psychotics, people who are most often represented in films are misfit exotics, creatures as remote from our experience as members of a Stone Age tribe in the Amazon.

This Gourmand Is On the Loose, Ready Up the Bromo Seltzer
by Russell Baker

[To fully appreciate the following burlesque by Russell Baker, turn back to the end of chapter seven and read again Craig Claiborne's account of his $4,000 meal. A satirist might sense some excess in that and set about poking fun at it . . . màking himself of course the ostensible target. Nos compliments au chef.]

Satiric
source
identified— NEW YORK — As chance would have it, the very evening Craig Claiborne ate his historic $4,000 dinner for two with 31 dishes and nine wines in Paris, a Lucullan repast for one was prepared and consumed in New York by this correspondent, no slouch himself when it comes to titillating the palate.

Claiborne won his meal in a television fund-raising auction

and had it professionally prepared. Mine was created from
spur-of-the-moment inspiration, necessitated when I discovered a note on the stove saying, "Am eating out with Dora
and Imogene — MAKE DINNER FOR YOURSELF." It
was from the person who regularly does the cooking at my
house and, though disconcerted at first, I quickly rose to the
challenge.

The meal opened with a 1975 Diet Pepsi served in a dis-
posable bottle. Although its bouquet was negligible, its distinct
metallic taste evoked memories of tin cans one had licked ex-
perimentally in the first flush of childhood's curiosity.

To create the balance of tastes so cherished by the epicurean
palate, I followed with a *pate de fruits de nuts de Georgia,*
prepared according to my own recipe. A half-inch layer of
creamy-style peanut butter is troweled onto a graham cracker,
then half a banana is crudely diced and pressed firmly into the
peanut butter and cemented in place as it were by a second
graham cracker.

The accompanying drink was cold milk served in a wide-
brimmed jelly glass. This is essential to proper consumption of
the *pate* since the entire confection must be dipped into the
milk to soften it for eating. Making the presentation to the
mouth, one must beware lest the milk-soaked portion of the
sandwich fall onto the necktie. Thus, seasoned gourmandisers
follow the old maxim of the Breton chefs and "bring the mouth
to the jelly glass."

At this point in the meal, the stomach was ready for serious
eating, and I prepared beans with bacon grease, a dish I
perfected in 1937 while developing my *cuisine du depression.*

The dish is started by placing a pan over a very high flame
until it becomes dangerously hot. A can of Heinz's pork and
beans is then emptied into the pan and allowed to char until
they reach the consistency of hardening concrete. Three strips
of bacon are fried to crisps, and when the beans have formed
huge dense clots firmly welded to the pan, the bacon grease is
poured in and stirred vigorously with a large screw driver.

This not only adds flavor but also loosens some of the beans
from the side of the pan. Leaving the flame high, I stirred in a
three-day-old spaghetti sauce found in the refrigerator, added a

sprinkle of chili powder, a large dollop of Major Grey's chutney and a tablespoon of bicarbonate of soda to make the whole dish rise.

Beans with bacon grease is always eaten from the pan with a tablespoon while standing over the kitchen sink. The pan must be thrown away immediately. The correct drink with this dish is a straight shot of room-temperature gin. I had a Gilbey's 1975, which was superb.

For the meat course, I had fried bologna *a la Nutley, Nouveau Jersey.* Six slices of A&P bologna were placed in an ungreased frying pan over maximum heat and held down by a long fork until the entire house filled with smoke. The bologna was turned, fried the same length of time on the other side, then served on air-filled bread with thick lashings of mayonnaise.

The correct drink for fried bologna *a la Nutley, Nouveau Jersey* is a 1937 Nehi Cola, but since my cellar, alas, had none, I had to make do with a second shot of Gilbey's 1975.

Second service— The cheese course was deliciously simple — a single slice of Kraft's individually wrapped yellow sandwich cheese, which was flavored by vigorous rubbing over the bottom of the frying pan to soak up the rich bologna juices. Wine being absolutely *de rigeur* with cheese, I chose a 1974 Muscatel, flavored with a maraschino cherry, and afterwards cleared my palate with three pickled martini onions.

It was time for the fruit. I chose a Del Monte tinned pear which, regrettably, slipped from the spoon and fell on the floor, necessitating its being blotted with a paper towel to remove cat hairs. To compensate for the resulting loss of pear syrup, I dipped it lightly in hot-dog relish, which created a unique flavor.

With the pear I drank two shots of Gilbey's 1975 and one shot of Wolfschmidt vodka (nonvintage), the Gilbey's having been exhausted.

Third service— At last it was time for the dish the entire meal had been building toward — dessert. With a paring knife, I ripped into a fresh package of Oreos, produced a bowl of My-T-Fine chocolate pudding which had been coagulating in the refrigerator for days and, using a potato masher, crushed a dozen Oreos into the pudding. It was immense.

Irony— Between mouthfuls, I sipped a tall, bubbling tumbler of cool Bromo-Seltzer and finished with six ounces of Maalox. It couldn't have been better.

Appendix

The Deep Six Connection
by Howard Kohn and Clark Norton

[This carefully crafted story unites style and substance in two concurrent narrative movements. The first concerns one specific instance of modern piracy on the high seas. The second sets forth the facts and figures on the larger situation illustrated by the first. The units of each narrative movement, well ordered in themselves, do not interrupt but complement each other; one has action, the other information. Had Howard Kohn and Clark Norton restricted themselves to the first narrative, the piece would still have been a rattling good suspense yarn, but that's all it would have been. Had the writers stuck to the second, the essay format would not have enjoyed the wide readership of more dramatic material. What results is serious investigation that reads like sensational fiction, a rich articulation of the feature writer's art. See chapter five for a more thorough discussion of unity in "The Deep Six Connection."]

The three drifters had been hanging around Honolulu bars for several days, buying beers for thirsty sailors, easing into conversations about boats and the Pacific. They were of average size, in their mid-20s, wearing cut-off jeans, seasoned tans and hair scissored short enough to pass military inspection. Two had been discharged from the Marines: the other was a former Coast Guardsman.

Information flowed with the booze up the beach from Honolulu's high-class yacht clubs. Talk focused on the recent sailing marathon between Los Angeles and Oahu. Which boats, the drifters wanted to know, were really the top of the line? Which were really durable?

Someone mentioned the *Kamalii,* a 12-year veteran of the race but never a first-prize winner. She was too heavy — 75 tons of teakwood hull, double-plank mahogany decking and a hefty 300-horsepower diesel engine that kept her riding low in the water. But she was sturdy, well able to survive the anger of the sea.

The drifters added the *Kamalii* to their list. No one seemed suspicious about why they were interested only in boats capable of a long ocean journey. Nor did anyone pay attention when the two ex-Marines and the ex-Coast Guardsman moved down to the Ala Wai Yacht Harbor and set up surveillance. The Ala Wai offered a selection of more than 700 expensive pleasure boats moored a short walk from the Ilikai Hotel in the heart of the resort-beach skyline made famous by *Hawaii Five-O.* The drifters spent several more days studying the boats and talking to the crews.

The 73-foot *Kamalii* was definitely seaworthy. Her tanks held 800 gallons of fuel and another 800 gallons of potable water—and, in case the water turned sour, she was equipped with an automatic device that could desalinate the ocean at the rate of six gallons an hour. Plus she was stocked with a three-month larder: frozen turkey, legs of lamb, bacon slabs, canned spaghetti, corned beef. And the bar was loaded with a guzzling heaven of Seagram's, Beefeater and five cases of Budweiser.

The three drifters had carefully monitored this inventory as it was carried aboard the *Kamalii* during the first week of August 1971. The *Kamalii* owner, oil millionaire E.L. Doheny, was planning to send his boat back to his mainland quarters in Southern California. But by listening to harbor gossip-mongers, the drifters learned that Doheny had not yet set a departure date; it might be weeks away. In the meantime the *Kamalii's* daily affairs were, as usual, in the hands of her middle-aged crew: skipper Bob Waschkeit, 49; navigator Frank Power, 47; and cook John Freitas, 52.

Power's Tahitian wife was vacationing aboard. When she kissed Power goodbye and headed home to Tahiti, the drifters gathered their gear and lugged it down to the wharf.

Power was the only crew member still awake at 11 p.m. on August 6th when he spotted legs moving past his porthole and heard footsteps on the companionway. He tossed down his sailing magazine and clambered up the hatch to investigate. Probably some misplaced tourist, he figured.

"What can I do for you—?" He stopped and swallowed his words. The three drifters were dressed casually, except for the long machetes hanging from their belts, the bandoleers over their shoulders and the German-made P-38 automatics in their hands. At the top of the hatchway, one shoved a gun in Power's midsection. "Get below and keep your mouth shut."

Power backed slowly down the steps. Before he could shout a warning, he was pushed onto a garish blue settee; cotton was stuffed in his mouth and a red bandana cinched tightly around his lower jaw. His wrists were handcuffed behind his back. His ankles were lashed with rope, then drawn up and tied to his wrists.

Without another word the intruders grabbed a flashlight and slipped aft through the dark passageway. Waschkeit and Freitas, roused by the sudden shaft of light, spotted the guns and their bellies turned cold with fear.

They were also quickly gagged and bound. The hemp scraped harshly against Freitas's ankle, ulcerating a sore that had just begun to heal. Blood oozed down his foot and dripped onto the cabin floor, but he barely noticed the pain. He stared at the three strangers, trying futilely to gauge their motives.

Each crew member had a wallet bulging from paychecks cashed that afternoon. Freitas had immediately offered his money: "Take it, take everything I got." But the intruders ignored the cash. Instead they began rummaging about, jerking drawers open, ransacking closets. Their search yielded two rifles, 30-06s kept aboard for sharks— but no ammunition. "Okay, where's the ammo?" the two ex-Marines confronted the dog-eyed crew. "Dammit to hell, you better tell us!" The stuffing was jerked from Waschkeit's mouth. Then there was a cry of success from the ex-Coast Guardsman who brought forward two boxes of cartridges.

"Are there any more firearms aboard?" All three crew members shook their heads. "Okay," the crew was warned, "but we'll shoot your ass if you aren't telling the truth."

The rifles were stacked in the fo'c's'le alongside the intruders' duffel bags. There still was no hint of what they wanted. But the ex-Coast Guardsman was fumbling with the engine. Stubbornly it refused to respond. So Waschkeit's gag was removed again. "We need to know how this damn thing works and we need to know right now." Waschkeit, facing the machetes and the P-38s, quietly divulged the engine's peculiarities. The *Kamalii* careened backward out of the slip, its starboard side banging noisily against some pilings. Waschkeit, hoping for a chance to alert another yacht, pretended to lose his balance to create more disturbance. But the ex-Marines shoved the cotton back into his mouth and sat him down.

The *Kamalii* chugged out of the Ala Wai Yacht Harbor into the midnight darkness, passed by a string of boats that paid her no heed.

Frank Power watched the twinkling reflection of the harbor lights fade as the ex-Coast Guardsman pulled back the accelerator on the 300-horse Cummins Diesel. Above him on the ceiling Power noticed a telltale compass, an old-fashioned mariner's instrument used mostly for decoration on the *Kamalii*. The compass needle fidgeted briefly, then pointed to a course south-by-southwest on a bearing of 230 degrees. If the compass was accurate, the teakwood-and-mahogany ketch was being steered hundreds of miles south of the ocean's regular shipping lanes.

This was Friday. The *Kamalii* might not be missed until Monday or Tuesday, perhaps longer. By then no one in Honolulu would know where to begin looking. Only later would the FBI learn that the *Kamalii* was heading across the Pacific on an isolated course toward Thailand and a cargo of Asian heroin.

*

Between the spring of 1971 and the summer of 1974, 611 private pleasure boats similar to the *Kamalii* mysteriously vanished at sea, taking more than 2,000 persons with them. Although they departed ports scattered from Hawaii to the Bahamas, they all conformed in some part to a general profile: They were seaworthy and outfitted for long voyages; they were able to carry large cargoes; they departed their last ports of call unobserved; their owners had large sums of money or goods aboard; and the identity of at least one crew member or passenger was suspect.

Boats do get lost at sea, of course, but compared to preceding years, yachts and cabin cruisers seemed to be slipping away like soap in a bathtub. According to the Coast Guard, there were only one or two unexplained disappearances per month in 1970. By 1971, the monthly average had leaped to 12— and over the next three years it rose to nearly 17 per month. Some of the losses were recorded in the Caribbean's infamous Bermuda Triangle, a path of sea with disputed powers for making boats and planes disappear. But many others simply floated off to nowhere in the Gulf of Mexico and the previously docile Pacific. These were not fragile vessels easily overwhelmed by sudden storms. They were sizable, seagoing boats, often with large crews.

During the same period the Caribbean, Gulf and Pacific waters long favored by pleasure boat crews were invaded by an element that seemed a world apart: a tidal wave of drug smugglers. A decade-long shift in international drug trafficking had turned the French connection into the Asian and Latin American connections. Opium had emerged as a top cash crop of the Golden Triangle of Southeast Asia, funneled as heroin to the U.S. through laboratories in the Dominican Republic. Cocaine, newly chic, had become a prime export of Bolivia and Peru. Marijuana flourished thick and sweet in Colombia, Central America and the Caribbean. Colombia and Venezuela suddenly were bargaining centers for all kinds of drugs.

Amateurs entered into the smuggling business, once the domain of organized French and Corsican rings. A nickel-and-dime dope dealer who saved up, say, a stack of $25,000 could slip down to Colombia and shop freely. The only problem was transportation back to the U.S.

So the great American airlift began. Low-flying planes buzzed across the U.S. border, landing on isolated runways or ditching their cargoes from the air. A Florida Fish and Wildlife agent out searching for alligator poachers was almost drowned when smugglers mistook his lights for their rendezvous signal and dumped a load of marijuana near his boat.

But when the airways got too well monitored, enterprising drug runners switched from Cessnas to auxiliary-powered sailboats and, as business soared, to commercial fishing vessels and trawler yachts. Florida alone offered 1,350 miles of coastline conveniently pockmarked with sheltered bays and inlets. Neighboring states and California provided more of the same.

Many smugglers made pickups in small cigarette-shaped motorboats at Columbian and Venezuelan ports. Some headed for the East Coast after transferring their contraband to larger vessels at Caribbean islands like Martinique, Guadeloupe and Barbados. Others sailed to California after making similar transfers in Panama. A different smuggling route stretched from the poppy fields of Burma through

Polynesia to Hawaii and the West Coast.

In turn, the Drug Enforcement Administration (DEA) concocted some flashy responses labeled Operation Buccaneer, Operation Panhandle and Operation Dragnet. Piling into helicopters and high-speed interceptor boats, DEA agents mounted an antismuggling blitz that netted some impressive-sounding statistics for slick brochures: 16,-067 pounds of Jamaican grass seized in December 1973 from a shrimp boat off Gulf Beach, Alabama; 39,236 pounds of Colombian weed confiscated the next day aboard another shrimper in Overstreet, Florida.

But amid these highly publicized busts, the mystery of the missing 611 pleasure boats continued to grow— while suspicions mounted that drug smuggling contained a vital clue.

One of the few boats to be recovered, a $60,000 yacht named the *Imamou,* had been linked to the drug trafficking. Two longtime French drug smugglers were captured aboard the boat on the Caribbean island of Guadeloupe in January 1974.

The yacht had not been seen since May 1973 when it had disappeared en route to the Panama Canal from Colombia. At that time it was being skippered by its owner, a wealthy American, accompanied by a college student friend and two crewmen hired in Colombia. The two crewmen turned out to be French drug smugglers who claimed, when apprehended, that the American had generously given them the yacht. But when the two Americans could not be located, an uncle of the skipper hired a private investigator to look into the case. The investigator traveled to Central America where he found evidence that the *Imamou* had been hijacked and the Americans murdered by drug smugglers. Before he could complete his report, however, the investigator himself was murdered. The Americans were never found.

The *Imamou* case raised an alarming question: How many more of the missing pleasure boats had fallen victim to this deadly new technique of piracy on the high seas — yachtjacking — in which caches of drugs for booty had supplanted chests of gold?

Certainly, yachtjacking had great appeal to drug smugglers. Amateurs unable to afford a luxury yacht could simply help themselves (and when cash was aboard, even the dope could be financed). But most important, risk was minimal. Pleasure boats do not arouse suspicion when entering or leaving port (with over 200,000 registered boats in Florida alone, they all blend in), they often are not expected to report their whereabouts for long periods of time, there is no central registry to keep track of stolen boats and they are easily disposed of when no longer needed. After a few runs, they can be sunk or destroyed. "It's the perfect crime," says an investigator familiar with the method. "The beauty of it for the criminal is that he gets rid of all the evidence."

*

The *Kamalii* crew awoke the morning of August 7th, 1971, to a sky of everlasting sunshine and a sea as flat and empty as amnesia. The boat was still in the lee of the Hawaiian Islands but was moving briskly southwest. The ex-Coast Guardsman had opened the engine full throttle.

"Hey," shouted Waschkeit from his berth in the port stateroom. "She's gonna burn up if you don't slow her down." The ex-Coast Guardsman swore — "I'll burn you if you don't shut up" — but he checked the speed.

Waschkeit and the other two crew members had been allowed to spend the final hours of the night stretched out on their bunks, their mouths free of the cotton swabs. Their hands and feet remained bound, however, and their stateroom doors were locked. They had dozed only briefly. Freitas had begun to fret about his throbbing ankle. Power studied his porthole and wondered how close to Tahiti the *Kamalii* would pass. Waschkeit kept conjuring ruses to reach the boat's radio.

Waschkeit, a portly, affable seaman known for his generous sharing of seasoned jokes, had been skipper of the *Kamalii* since her christening in 1958. A year later he had recruited Freitas, an old high school buddy with flint black curls, a boxer's physique and an ability to set a delectable table undiminished by his culinary training in the military. Power, a slow-talking, chisel-featured navigator who once had shipped with Waschkeit in the merchant marine, joined the *Kamalii* in 1967. All three had spent their lives in and around the ocean. This was the first time they'd realized that pirates still existed.

At noon the hijackers untied Freitas and ordered him to fix sandwiches. He walked unsteadily to the galley, past the shimmering bronze bulkheads, and pulled a can opener from a drawer. As a young man he'd boxed in 46 professional fights; now he looked furtively about, sizing up the odds of attacking the ex-Marine assigned to guard him. Freitas was bigger and a head taller than the hijacker, who had holstered his pistol and stood smiling brashly at the graying cook, slapping the flat side of his machete against his palm.

Reluctantly, Freitas stabbed the opener into a can of Spam. He couldn't take the gamble, he decided, not as long as Waschkeit and Power remained helpless, easy targets for bullets from the other two hijackers. He spread mayonnaise onto slices of bread and then allowed the handcuffs to be slipped back on. The ex-Marine kept slapping the machete and acting overly polite. The Slapper, as his cohorts began calling him, seemed extremely nervous or extremely cool. Either way, Freitas figured, it was not an encouraging sign.

After lunch the hijackers conferred in the wheelhouse over a few cans of beer. Then, while the ex-Coast Guardsman stayed at the wheel, the ex-Marines began flinging the crew's gear overboard. The boat's lockers were cleaned out: wallets, letters, souvenirs, the green jackets emblazoned with a camel's face, the whimsical insignia the crew had adopted after a local newspaper referred to the boat as the *Kamal II.*

By late afternoon the crew's clothes and personal belongings had all been dumped. There would be no easy way for harbor police, say in Thailand, to know that Waschkeit, Freitas or Power had ever served on the *Kamalii.*

Next Waschkeit was untied and led on deck. The Slapper leaned against the mast, grinning madly, his rhythmic slaps growing more intense. The other ex-Marine aimed his P-38 at Waschkeit's ample stomach and spit out crisp orders.

"Okay, Skipper. I want you over the side right now."

Waschkeit felt his bowels go weak. He had expected the crew to at least be let off on some speck of land. His legs stayed riveted to the deck, unwilling to desert the only dry ground in uncountable miles of ocean.

"Hey, get your ass over the side!"

Waschkeit gingerly rubbed his hands and measured the distance to the P-38. "Listen," he pleaded, stalling for time. "How about giving us a break? Give us a life raft. We won't last five minutes without a raft. There are sharks all through these waters."

The ex-Marine paused, obviously irritated. The Slapper grew impatient and moved forward, machete flashing. Overhead the sun boiled unrelentingly. Waschkeit tensed himself to leap for the gun.

Then the gun-toting ex-Marine changed tactics. "Okay," he nodded. "Maybe you can have the raft. We'll talk it over." The two moved off to confer. Then the ex-Marine went below.

When he returned he was smiling as hysterically as the Slapper. He had Freitas and Power in tow. "Okay, boys, here's the deal." he announced to the three crewmen. "We're gonna flip a coin. Heads, you get the raft. Tails, you don't."

Both ex-Marines were clearly enjoying the crew's torment. They laughed coarsely, then whispered to each other.

"But first things first," the two hijackers decided. "First we want you in the water."

By now the crew realized the coin toss was a madman's gesture. There was no way to deter these pirates from playing out their ritual. The crew would, in effect, have to walk the plank.

When the Slapper moved this time, they went overboard, hanging briefly onto the guardrail, feet propped against the gunwale, and then splashed in. When they surfaced seconds later the *Kamalii* was speeding away.

Freitas had on a shirt and a pair of slacks. Waschkeit and Power were dressed only in shorts. It was two hours until sunset when the tepid waters would turn chill. They were nearly 150 miles from Hawaii and the westerly current was carrying them further away. These waters were usually traveled only by sharks and other fish. The men joined hands and formed a dark circle in the sunny blue.

*

The mystery of the disappearing boats began to unravel in November 1973 during a convention of narcotics officers in Nassau that dealt with changing patterns in drug smuggling. Some narcs mentioned that a few smugglers had been caught using stolen yachts.

Carl Perian, a blunt, tough-talking investigator familiar with the subtleties of dope, boats and politics decided to investigate. Perian had worked for 18 years as a congressional investigator and had uncovered, among other things, widespread corruption in the Panama government and investigated an alleged White House "Plumbers" plot to assassinate the Panamanian dictator, General Omar Torrijos.

Perian's first stop was the Coast Guard, where he learned the astonishing news that for three years an array of yachts had been vanishing under suspicious circumstances. But when Perian started asking questions, the Coast Guard seemed strangely short of answers, offering unconvincing explanations of tropical storms and a sudden swell of inexperienced sailors. So Perian took the mystery to his boss, Representative John M. Murphy of New York, chairman of the Coast Guard subcommittee. Murphy agreed that, at the next opportunity, Perian should pursue the matter.

In the spring of 1974 Perian returned to Nassau for a long talk with local smuggling experts. Then he flew to Puerto Rico and Miami, where he combed Coast Guard records, interviewed friends of missing crew members and talked with other law enforcement agencies.

After two months Perian had a file thick with cases of unmet itineraries, suspicious crewmen and scarred wreckage. Several had overtones of drug smuggling:

• An aging couple were sailing their boat *Como No* from Fort Lauderdale toward a retirement home in California in November 1972 when they disappeared somewhere beyond the Panama Canal. The last message received from the couple were daily letters written to their daughter, expressing growing distrust for the two boat boys hired in the Caribbean. An investigation requested by the daughter revealed that the boat boys were suspected drug smugglers who had used false identities when hired.

• Twelve persons were reported missing when the trawler *Puerto Limon* left Houston for Costa Rica in January 1973 and vanished into the Yucatan Channel. Although the boat was equipped with an automatic signal beacon, the Coast Guard failed to find it in a 100,000-square-mile search. Later it was learned that known drug dealers had been seen aboard at Houston.

• The trawler yacht *Saba Bank* was lost in March 1974 en route from the Bahamas to Florida. Suspected drug dealers were seen hanging around the yacht immediately before its departure.

In all these cases, Perian concluded, the missing sailors had been murdered and dumped overboard by drug-smuggling hijackers.

As his investigation continued Perian became increasingly convinced that the new breed of drug smugglers was resorting to the outlawry of the Barbary Coast. While in Miami he encountered reports of an execution-style slaying apparently related to a yachtjacking. A luxury cabin cruiser, the *Ardel,* was the focus of a grisly drama played out in July 1974 on an isolated beach near Key Largo, Florida.

Two Miami brothers and two New Jersey girls, fishing off a dock, had been shot in the head and left dead in the sand. Two days later the missing 28-foot *Ardel* was found nearby, apparently abandoned by drug smugglers who earlier had been seen aboard. According to a scenario put together by local police, the four had had the misfortune to witness the unloading of the *Ardel* on a smuggling run to the Florida coast. One of the smugglers, a local playboy who apparently had a falling out with his partners, was found dead ten days later, also shot in the head, bound with chains and wrapped in canvas.

Then in Puerto Rico, regarded as the hottest spot in world drug trafficking today, Perian found a pattern of violence that left him shaken. In 1974, 17 narcotics agents were murdered in Puerto Rico; one agent, lured out of his house by rocks thrown on the roof, had his head blown off in his driveway by an assassin with a shotgun.

The Puerto Rico marine patrol told Perian they had reports of a score of hijacked boats but had had difficulty convincing witnesses to testify in court. They had arrested Erick Marschner, a wild-eyed German with a long police record, for hijacking three yachts worth $100,000 each. But Marschner, armed with several pistols and an unnerving reputation for revenge, had kept all potential witnesses terrified.

Later, back in Washington, Perian received a letter from a young woman who told of a yachtjacking by an ex-Nazi. The woman had been one of seven college coeds to win international headlines in early 1971 when she'd crewed aboard the yacht *Ta-Aroa* on an around-the-world voyage. Afterward she had stayed in touch with the *Ta-Aroa's* captain and his girlfriend as they sailed around the Caribbean. In Costa Rica during September 1971, they met an ex-Nazi who allegedly tried to convince them to join a smuggling ring that handled both guns and drugs. Apparently the two refused. The ex-Nazi disappeared with the *Ta 'Aroa*. The girlfriend's body, with a bullet hole staring from her head, was fished out of the ocean. The captain's body was never found.

Perian investigated and confirmed that the woman's story, as far as could be determined, was true.

In August 1974 Perian reported to the Coast Guard subcommittee his conclusion that yachtjacking could prove a far more potent threat to sailors than most tropical storms. Altogether he had uncovered 50 suspected yacht hijackings, more than twice the number of airplane hijackings during the same period. In these 50 cases, more than 200 persons were missing—and likely murdered.

Perian found that a favorite yachtjacking tactic was for smugglers to hire on as crew members, capitalizing on a comradeship of the waves that long has made for easy and often impermanent relationships among captains and crews.

Other yachtjackers had duped their targets into traps at sea, issuing false distress signals, then commandeering the chivalrous vessels coming to their rescue. Still others, like those who hijacked the *Kamalii,* simply boarded unlocked and unguarded boats anchored in port.

*

When the abandoned crew first noticed the *Kamalii* circling back, there was a feeling of disbelief. From their angle in the water the crew could vaguely see the ex-Marines moving along the bow. *Jesus God, are they carrying the rifles? Are they going to shoot us? Pick us off like carp in a pond? That must be it! They want to finish the job!*

The *Kamalii* bore down on the bobbing heads, then slacked off. The ex-Marines seemed to be giggling. But they were holding aloft an Avon life raft. With a small struggle they heaved it over the side, pulling a cord that triggered a CO_2 bottle and inflated the synthetic tubing. The raft floated toward the beleaguered crew. "Hey," shouted the Slapper, flipping a coin into the orange and black craft. "Here's the dime that saved your lives." Both ex-Marines laughed again; the propellers threw spray and the *Kamalii* veered away.

Waschkeit, Freitas and Power climbed eagerly into the raft. They were safe.

But, they realized, this sudden deliverance could turn into a cruel ruse. They were drifting through a deserted margin of ocean. No fishing boats ventured this far from the islands. All commercial ships steered leagues north in the Kaiwi Channel. The nearest land in the drift of the current was Johnston Atoll, 1,000 miles away.

The raft contained no food, and more distressingly, no fishing tackle. The only provisions were nine pints of drinking water, enough for a couple days.

What hope they had rested with a transistorized radio beeper designed to attract passing planes, and six flares — three large parachute flares that could burst through an ocean night like Roman candles and three hand-held flares of the emergency roadside variety. There seemed little chance they would get to use them.

Freitas clutched his ankle and spit nauseously; he was weak and feverish. Power and Waschkeit slumped dejectedly, unable to sit comfortably. All three men were drained. One of them would have to take the first watch. Waschkeit held the dime in his fingers and managed a grin. "Should I flip it?"

By 7 p.m. the sun was fading into the ocean. Freitas and Power were nodding to sleep. Waschkeit, having volunteered for the watch, began counting stars as they appeared in the gathering darkness. Two and a half hours passed. Waschkeit's gaze grew fuzzy. Names of stars and sailboats caromed randomly through his head. He sensed that he was hallucinating. He was sailing in a race — he was winning — the finish line was reaching for him — there were lights dancing and people singing — there were lights ... *there were lights!*

"Land!" he shouted. "Land! There's land!" In his frenzy he grabbed and shook his sleeping companions.

Both could see immediately that the tiny raft was still lost in the vast wetness. But there *were* two lights, one green, one red, bouncing toward them — the range lights of a ship, mysteriously asteam 1,300 miles south of the summer shipping lanes.

In moments the ship would be moving past them and away. They couldn't delay. Waschkeit unwrapped one of the large parachute flares and set it arching skyward. The flare erupted and seemed to hover above the ship. But the ship did not pause. Again Waschkeit readied a parachute flare and set it off; it also flamed into the night. Still the green and red lights stayed on course.

Now there was anxious debate on the marooned raft. Only one large flare remained. To use it now would forfeit any future opportunities. Yet there might never be any. The ship was churning beyond them. They had to decide.

The conservative opinion prevailed. The final parachute flare stayed in its wrapper. Instead they reached for one of the hand-held flares. Because Power had the longest arms, he hoisted the flare above his head, stretching it toward the bright orange canopy that shaded the raft.

From the bridge of the *Benadir,* a banana freighter flying the Italian flag, the reflection of the flare against the canopy seemed like the glow of a boat afire. The deck officer, busy in the chart room, spotted the flare and yelled to the wheelhouse. "Change course. Hard to starboard." (He did not know then that two of his sailors had seen the parachute flares but, because the ship's watch was just changing, had not yet reported the sightings.)

As the hand-held flare fizzled toward Power's fingers, the green and red lights slowly turned and converged on the raft. Another flare was lit to provide a homing target for the freighter. Then suddenly it was alongside. A Jacob's ladder was flung from its rail. And the three incredulous refugees scrambled up.

The *Benadir's* captain explained that the ship, newly purchased from a German firm, had encountered engine trouble that his Italian engineers had been unable to fix. So the *Benadir* had strayed far off course, intending to stay near Honolulu in case of more engine trouble. A few hours before, however, the Italians had mastered the engines and the captain had set a course for Japan, a course that improbably carried them within a few paces of the black and orange raft.

From the *Benadir's* radio room a call was placed to the Coast Guard in Honolulu. In turn the Coast Guard phoned E.L. Doheny, the *Kamalii* owner, who thought the late-night message a bad joke and hung up. But, after a second call, he rushed out to join the Coast Guard in the hunt for the missing *Kamalii.*

Meanwhile, the hijackers, oblivious to the crew's dramatic rescue, were somewhere in the darkness, steering toward their smugglers' rendezvous in Thailand.

*

After Carl Perian's groundwork investigation, Representative John Murphy, New York Democrat and fishing enthusiast, launched a formal congressional probe into yachtjacking in August 1974. The picture his Coast Guard subcommittee found was not encouraging: a mishmash of bungling and inaction.

Though a Coast Guard officer recalled that "we began to have suspicions something untoward was in the wind by the spring of 1971," the Guard had taken no real action on yachtjacking until Perian started poking around. Then Captain M.K. Phillips, head of the Guard's operation center in Washington, drew up a warning to mariners about the yachtjacking threat. But, inexplicably, the warning was not released until four months later. While it languished in a Coast Guard public relations office, more boats disappeared. Phillips blamed a bureaucratic mixup for the delay but Murphy scoffed: "I had to send an investigator to Miami and Nassau to go through the files before this issue surfaced. How many killings does it take before you issue a warning?"

Murphy also accused the Coast Guard of trying to minimize the problem. Coast Guard officials at first claimed that, based essentially on cases with corpses and survivors, only five yachtjackings could be proved. (The *Kamalii* crew members were the only known survivors.) But, under Murphy's prodding, the Guard conceded there was strong circumstantial evidence in 30 more cases. Murphy contended, however, that his subcommittee investigation had uncovered at least 44 suspected yachtjackings. The debate in most individual cases rested on circumstantial evidence because, by the nature of the crime, no hard evidence remained.

Of the 611 pleasure boats that had mysteriously disappeared, 560 were unaccounted for. No specific evidence could be found to indicate the likelihood of yachtjacking in those cases. But Murphy argued that "a significant number of the 560 had to be hijacked — there isn't any other satisfactory explanation for that many missing boats."

Despite the Coast Guard's deserved reputation for vigilance in search-and-rescue missions, the subcommittee hearing revealed an agency that shied away from boat thefts and hijackings. Perian says he found the Guard piously indifferent to such matters: one admiral, he says, told him "the Coast Guard's concern isn't crime on the high seas." The Guard doesn't even compile a formal list of stolen boats that could be circulated to other agencies. But in formal testimony another admiral passed the buck: "If the case is identified as a hijacking . . . it becomes the responsibility of the DEA, Customs or the FBI."

This proved news to the FBI. "As an investigative agency we do nothing [about the yachtjackings]," explained an FBI public relations officer. The FBI, he protested, is a land-based agency that seldom bothers with stolen boats. Most cases are simply logged in its computer.

The Customs Bureau, for its part, was stripped of most investigative prerogatives when the DEA was formed in 1973.

But while the Coast Guard, FBI and Customs can all beg off the problem, the DEA has no alibi that drug hijackings are outside it's jurisdiction. So top DEA officials have tried powerfully to ignore the entire yachtjacking phenomenon, refusing to cooperate with Murphy's subcommittee or inquiring reporters. "The DEA doesn't want to talk about it because they're embarrassed about it," says Perian. "They can't admit it because they're supposed to be enforcing the law." One exception who did talk to Perian was Richard Thomas, then DEA acting special agent in charge of Puerto Rico. But after Thomas complained that DEA officialdom had not supplied him with enough men and equipment to stop smuggling, he found himself hurriedly transferred out of Puerto Rico.

The timing of the yachtjacking controversy has weighed in rudely at the DEA. For nearly two years the DEA had floated high on a reputation garnered almost exclusively from operations aimed at drug smugglers. Then in mid-1975 Senator Henry Jackson's permanent subcommittee on investigations issued a report on allegations the DEA had acted improperly in an investigation of Robert Vesco, the high-rolling fugitive financier who contributed lavishly to Richard Nixon's 1972 campaign. Jackson's subcommittee found that the DEA had ignored a promising lead allegedly linking Vesco to a million-dollar heroin smuggling scheme.

The findings in the Vesco case led Jackson's subcommittee to a full probe of the DEA. The subcommittee quickly received a memo from Assistant Customs Commissioner Robert Gaber, who ridiculed the DEA's supposed attack on drug smuggling as a sham. "The American people have been misled by the DEA," Gaber wrote, insisting that heroin in particular was pouring into the country as freely as ever. Instead of focusing on border operations to arrest smugglers, Gaber explained, the DEA was relying on ineffective buy-and-bust tactics, piling up low-level arrests "to justify high-level appropriations from Congress."

Even the DEA's proudly publicized antismuggling operations appeared, on closer inspection, to have had more flash than substance. The federal agents had zeroed in only on marijuana smugglers. Operation Buccaneer had seized 250,000 pounds of weed and defoliated acres of green grass in Jamaica. Operation Panhandle had confiscated 75,000 pounds of contraband and that too was virtually all marijuana. And Operation Dragnet, a blockade of South Florida that teamed 29 boats and 300 men who tracked 80 suspected vessels, managed a net haul of 50 undersized lobsters — and an ounce of grass taken from an off-duty cop partying aboard his boat.

By concentrating on marijuana, the DEA had in effect left yachtjackers free to specialize in the less bulky and far more profitable cargoes of heroin, cocaine and hashish. In all of fiscal 1974-75 DEA agents seized only a fraction of the heroin and cocaine that just one good-sized laboratory produces each year. Confronted with this criticism, DEA officials have retreated from their previous exclamations of an antiheroin victory and admitted something akin to failure.

Now Jackson's subcommittee has obtained evidence that serious corruption and mismanagement in the DEA extend to its top officials. The DEA head, John R. Bartels Jr., was forced to resign in the wake of these disclosures.

The DEA scandal has provided new ammunition for critics who suggest that menaces like yachtjacking are often the unintended offspring of an agency like the DEA — which is either powerless or disinclined to stop smuggling but which hassles smugglers just enough to turn them into pirates. If there were no restrictive drug laws for the DEA to enforce, these critics say, there would be no huge profiteering, no black markets, no drug running — and none of the brutal men and brutal methods that combination now breeds.

*

"Calling WJ-7256, come in WJ-7256. Calling the 'Kamalii,' Do you read me? This is the Coast Guard. You are ordered to reverse course."

Search planes had been dispatched to find the fugitive ketch. Just before nightfall on August 8th, two days after the yacht had been hijacked, a C-130 patrol plane had spotted the *Kamalii's* frosty green cabin top and polished mahogany decking. The hijackers also saw the plane and, ignoring the plane's radio call, tried to duck behind the gray cover of a low-flying rain squall.

The plane dogged the yacht, buzzing low and dropping a surrender order in a bottle off the *Kamalii's* bow. The fugitives stopped, retrieved the bottle, but then speeded up again and resumed heading for the squall.

The plane retreated and radioed the *Cape Corwin,* a Coast Guard cutter trailing in pursuit.

Through that night and the next day the hijackers, now on the run, roared for a getaway in Tahiti. But the *Cape Corwin's* bigger engine overtook the *Kamalii* by midnight of the second day. The *Corwin* pulled to within 350 yards, just out of rifle range, and hailed the yacht through a bullhorn.

"Fuck you," the hijackers shouted back, trying futilely to rev up the *Kamalii's* exhausted engine.

"You have a choice. Either you give up or we'll sink the boat. The *Kamalii's* owner is on board with us and he's given us permission to blow you out of the water." The *Corwin*'s crew unleased a tarp and uncovered a 50-caliber machine gun mounted on the deck.

There was no immediate reply. "You've got 60 seconds to surrender!" Abashedly the two ex-Marine and the ex-Coast Guardsman raised their hands.

Kerry D. (the Slapper) Bryant, 25, of Los Angeles, and Mark E. Maynard, 27, of Lewiston, Idaho, had served together in Vietnam where they'd first learned about the easy profitability of heroin smuggling. After their discharge they had hatched a plan to return to Southeast Asia with Michael R. Melton, 24, an ex-Coast Guardsman from Bakersfield, California.

Back in Honolulu, Melton confessed the entire scheme. He was let off on probation but Bryant and Maynard each received two five-year sentences for robbery on the high seas and interstate transportation of stolen property.

On August 28th, 1974, the same day the House Coast Guard sub-committee opened its hearings into yachtjacking, a luxury yacht named the *Sea Wind* departed with its crew from its home berth in Connecticut.

Three months later the Honolulu harbor patrol accosted the *Sea Wind* for a routine inspection. On board were a man and a woman, both with police records in narcotics trafficking. But the *Sea Wind*'s crew and their belongings were gone. The man and woman claimed the crew had jumped ship in the Bahamas and hired them to sail to Hawaii, a story that was quickly scuttled when police checked it out. So the pair was arrested and charged with interstate transportation of stolen goods. But the crew has never been found.

August 28th, 1974, was the same day the Coast Guard finally released its yachtjacking warning, advising mariners to stay on the lookout. "Yachtsmen planning to set out for a cruise in the waters of the Caribbean, the Gulf of Mexico, the waters along the Baja, California, coast and the western coasts of Central America should be aware that his yacht may become a target for a modern day pirate or hijacker. The principal motivation for such rash and drastic action is believed to be rooted in the flourishing amateur narcotics trade."

In a coincidence striking in its implications, the flood of missing boats that had continued unabated for three years abruptly came to a halt. Except for the *Sea Wind*, there have been no mysterious disappearances since the warning was issued— which is probably the most telling testimony of all that many of the 611 missing boats were lost to more than tropical storms.

The yachtjacking experience, though, has left a lingering fear in the once relaxed world of pleasure boating. Security is the new watchword. Crews are now closely scrutinized, with new recruits checked and rechecked. Boats are searched carefully for stowaways and itineraries are filed with authorities before departure.

*

The easy camaraderie of yacht clubs is gone. "Now when we sleep aboard a boat at night we always lock ourselves in," says Bob Waschkeit. "Everybody does. It's a shame. It used to be that nobody did— people used to leave the doors open and everything open, because no one bothered you. But no more. You can't do that anymore. Now everybody keeps guns on board, and everybody keeps them loaded. At all times."

About the Author

William Ruehlmann, author of *Saint With a Gun: The Unlawful American Private Eye,* holds a B.A. from American University in Washington, D.C., an M.A. from the University of Arizona in Tucson, and a Ph.D. from the University of Cincinnati. He has been platoon sergeant in an engineering company, high school teacher, summer stock actor, theater critic and journalism professor. He currently works as a reporter for the Scripps-Howard Washington bureau. He is 32.

Index

Books of Interest From Writer's Digest

The Beginnning Writer's Answer Book, edited by Kirk Polking, Jean Chimsky, and Rose Adkins. "What is a query letter?" "If I use a pen name, how can I cash the check?" These are among 567 questions most frequently asked by beginning writers — and expertly answered in this down-to-earth handbook. Cross-indexed. 270 pp. $7.95.

The Cartoonist's and Gag Writer's Handbook, by Jack Markow. Longtime cartoonist with thousands of sales reveals the secrets of successful cartooning — step by step. Richly illustrated. 157 pp. $7.95.

A Complete Guide to Marketing Magazine Articles, by Duane Newcomb. "Anyone who can write a clear sentence can learn to write and sell articles on a consistent basis," says Newcomb (who has published well over 3,000 articles). Here's how. 248 pp. $6.95.

The Confession Writer's Handbook, by Florence K. Palmer. A stylish and informative guide to getting started and getting ahead in the confessions. How to start a confession and carry it through. How to take a insignificant event and make it significant. 171 pp. $6.95.

The Craft of Interviewing, by John Brady. Everything you always wanted to know about asking questions, but were afraid to ask — from an experienced interviewer and editor of *Writer's Digest.* The most comprehensive guide to interviewing on the market. 244 pp. $9.95.

The Creative Writer, edited by Aron Mathieu. This book opens the door to the real world of publishing. Inspiration, techniques, and ideas, plus inside tips from Maugham, Caldwell, Purdy, others. 416 pp. $6.95.

The Greeting Card Writer's Handbook, by H. Joseph Chadwick. A former greeting card editor tells you what editors look for in inspirational verse . . . how to write humor . . . what to write about for conventional, studio and juvenile cards. Extra: a renewable list of greeting card markets. Will be greeted by any freelancer. 268 pp. $6.95.

A Guide to Writing History, by Doris Ricker Marston. How to track down Big Foot — or your family Civil War letters, or your hometown's last century — for publication and profit. A timely handbook for history buffs and writers. 258 pp. $8.50.

Handbook of Short Story Writing, edited by Frank A. Dickson and Sandra Smythe. You provide the pencil, paper, and sweat — and this book will provide the expert guidance. Features include James Hilton on creating a lovable character; R.V. Cassill on plotting a short story. 238 pp. $8.95.

How to be a Successful Outdoor Writer, by Jack Samson. Longtime editor of *Field & Stream* covers this market in depth. Illustrated. 288 pp. $9.95.

Law and the Writer, edited by Kirk Polking and Leonard S. Meranus. Don't let legal hassles slow down your progress as a writer. Now you can find good counsel on libel, invasion of privacy, fair use, plagiarism, taxes, contracts, social security, and more — all in one volume. 249 pp. $9.95.

Magazine Writing: The Inside Angle, by Art Spikol. Successful editor and writer reveals inside secrets of getting your mss. published. 288 pp. $9.95.

Magazine Writing Today, by Jerome E. Kelley. If you sometimes feel like a mouse in a maze of magazines, with a fat manuscript check at the end of the line, don't fret. Kelley tells you how to get a piece of the action. Covers ideas, research, interviewing organization, the writing process, and ways to get photos. Plus advice on getting started. 220 pp. $9.95.

The Mystery Writer's Handbook, by the Mystery Writers of America. A howtheydunit to the whodunit, newly written and revised by members of the Mystery Writers of America. Includes the four elements essential to the classic mystery. A comprehensive handbook that takes the mystery out of mystery writing. 273 pp. $8.95.

The Novel Approach: From Plot to Print, by Lawrence Block. Practical advice on how to write any kind of novel. 256 pp. $9.95.

1,001 Article Ideas, by Frank A. Dickson. A compendium of ideas plus formulas to generate more of your own! 256 pp. $9.95.

One Way to Write Your Novel, by Dick Perry. For Perry, a novel is 200 pages. Or, two pages a day for 100 days. You can start *and finish* your novel, with the help of this step-by-step guide taking you from blank sheet to polished page. 138 pp. $8.95.

Photographer's Market, edited by Melissa Milar and William Brohaugh. Contains what you need to know to be a successful freelance photographer. Names, addresses, photo requirements, and payment rates for 3,000 markets. 624 pp. $12.95.

The Poet and the Poem, by Judson Jerome. A rare journey into the night of the poem — the mechanics, the mystery, the craft and sullen art. Written by the most widely read authority on poetry in America, and a major contemporary poet in his own right. 482 pp. $7.95 ($4.95 paperback).

Songwriter's Market, edited by William Brohaugh. Lists 1,500 places where you can sell your songs. Included are the people and companies who work daily with songwriters and musicians. Features names and addresses, pay rates and other valuable information you need to sell your work. 384 pp. $9.95.

Stalking the Feature Story, by William Ruehlmann. Besides a nose for news, the newspaper feature writer needs an ear for dialog and an eye for detail. He must also be adept at handling off-the-record remarks, organization, grammar, and the investigative story. Here's the "scoop" on newspaper feature writing. 310 pp. $9.95.

A Treasury of Tips for Writers, edited by Marvin Weisbord. Everything from Vance Packard's system of organizing notes to tips on how to get research done free, by 86 magazine writers. 174 pp. $5.95.

Writer's Digest. The world's leading magazine for writers. Monthly issues include timely interviews, columns, tips to keep writers informed on where and how to sell their work. One year subscription, $15.

The Writer's Digest Diary. Plan your year in it, note appointments, log manuscript sales, be prepared for the IRS. With advice such as the reminder on March 21 to "plan your Christmas story today." It will become a permanent annual record of writing activity. Durable cloth cover. 144 pp. $8.95.

Writer's Market, edited by Bruce Joel Hillman. The freelancer's bible, containing 4,500 places to sell what you write. Includes the name, address and phone number of the buyer, a description of material wanted and rates of payment. 984 pp. $14.95.

The Writer's Resource Guide, edited by William Brohaugh. Over 2,000 research sources for information on anything you write about. 432 pp. $10.95.

Writer's Yearbook. This large annual magazine contains how-to articles, interviews and special features, along with analyses of 500 major markets for writers. $2.50.

Writing and Selling Non-Fiction, by Hayes B. Jacobs. Explores with style and know-how the book market, organization and research, finding new markets, interviewing, humor, agents, writer's fatigue and more. 317 pp. $9.95.

Writing and Selling Science Fiction, compiled by the Science Fiction Writers of America. A comprehensive handbook to an exciting but oft-misunderstood genre. Eleven articles by top-flight sf writers on markets, characters, dialog, "crazy" ideas, world-building, alien-building, money and more. 191 pp. $7.95.

Writing for Children and Teen-agers, by Lee Wyndham. Author of over 50 children's books shares her secrets for selling to this large, lucrative market. Features: the 12-point recipe for plotting, and the Ten Commandments for Writers. 253 pp. $8.95.

Writing Popular Fiction, by Dean R. Koontz. How to write mysteries, suspense thrillers, science fiction, Gothic romances, adult fantasy, Westerns and erotica. Here's an inside guide to lively fiction, by a lively novelist. 232 pp. $7.95.

(1-2 books, add $1.00 postage and handling; 3 or more, additional 25c each. Allow 30 days for delivery. Prices subject to change without notice.)

Writer's Digest Books, Dept. B, 9933 Alliance Road, Cincinnati, Ohio 45242